The Road of Inquiry

The Road of Inquiry

Charles Peirce's
Pragmatic Realism

Peter Skagestad

Columbia University Press
New York 1981

Library of Congress Cataloging in Publication Data

Skagestad, Peter, 1947–
    The road of inquiry, Charles Peirce's pragmatic
realism.

    Bibliography: p.
    Includes index.
    1. Peirce, Charles Santiago Sanders, 1839–1914.
2. Realism. 3. Methodology. I. Title.
B945.P44S5   191   80-25278
ISBN 0-231-05004-6

Columbia University Press
New York   Guildford, Surrey

To my wife
Elaine Ober Skagestad

Contents

Preface

THIS BOOK OFFERS an interpretation of certain prominent strands in the thought of the American philosopher Charles Peirce. Inside the philosophical profession it is no longer a secret that Peirce was one of the greatest philosophers this country has produced; indeed, Peirce scholarship has been a vigorous, thriving industry for almost half a century. With few exceptions, however, the numerous learned volumes written on Peirce's philosophy have reached only an audience composed chiefly of other Peirce scholars; thus there is a curious misproportion between the esteem accorded to Peirce by the profession and the degree to which his thought has become public property. Philosophers, like politicians, can properly be said to have arrived only when their public learns how to pronounce their names; Peirce (pronounced "Purse") is still largely denied this final accolade even within the community of professional philosophers. This state of affairs constitutes, to my mind, one reason for wanting to add to the already weighty body of literature on the subject.

There are several different types of book which might be written about a past philosopher, depending upon the author's motive for addressing his public. My motive lies less in purely historical curiosity than in an interest in philosophical problems which are alive and pressing today. Among these is the problem of the relation between science and non-scientific knowledge, a problem on which Peirce appears to me to have thrown considerable light. Others may want to tackle such philosophical problems directly, thinking it a waste of time and energy to make a detour through the history of past attempts at problem solution. My own conviction is that the better acquainted we are with the efforts made by the greatest minds of the past at solving problems similar to ours, the better equipped we will be for solving our own problems. In this way, to repeat an old but apt metaphor, those of us who are admittedly not giants can still benefit from standing on the shoulders of giants. Consequently, though this is a study in the history of philosophical ideas, it is written in the hope that current philosophical discussion may profit from improved acquaintance with those ideas. Wherever possible, therefore, I have tried to relate Peirce's ideas to present-day philosophical problems and concerns.

Though my original interest in Peirce lay in his ideas on the relation between science and non-scientific knowledge, I discovered early that these ideas cannot be properly understood in isolation from the rest of his thought. More specifically, practically everything he has to say on this subject requires a prior understanding of two key notions in his philosophy, labeled "pragmatism" and "scholastic realism." These two notions, whose meanings will be unravelled in detail in this book, have long appeared for various reasons to be mutually incompatible, and the problem of their interrelationship has therefore loomed large in earlier works on Peirce. In my perusal of the literature, however, while I found many valuable suggestions, I failed to find a fully satisfactory account of just how these two notions are related, and I found myself obliged, therefore, to address this question anew in some detail. Once I had hit upon the interpretation offered in this book, other pieces quickly fell into place, enabling me to see Peirce's theory of scientific inquiry, as well as its relationship to belief and action, in a new and interesting light.

This book is the fruit of three years of research and writing, financed by a generous grant from the Norwegian Research Council for Science and the Humanities (NAVF). The work was done in part at the Department of History of Ideas at the University of Oslo, in part at the Philosophy Department at Harvard University. I want to express my gratitude to my department chairman in Oslo, Professor Guttorm Flöistad, for encouragement and practical assistance in pursuing my research, and to Nils Roll-Hansen of the Norwegian Research Council, for numerous stimulating and illuminating discussions. At Harvard, I received invaluable assistance from Professors

Israel Scheffler and Hilary Putnam, both of whom gave generously of their time to read and discuss with me various drafts of this book. I am also indebted to Bruce Altshuler, both for valuable discussions, and for permission to make use of his unpublished doctoral dissertation. Finally, I am grateful to the Philosophy Department of Harvard University for permission to use the Peirce manuscripts in the Houghton Library.

Imperfect though it no doubt still is, the book has profited enormously from the editorial labors bestowed on it by Kathleen McCarthy of Columbia University Press. For her perceptive and careful attention to matters of substance as well as to details of style, I consider myself privileged. I am grateful also to Columbia's reviewer, Professor H. S. Thayer, for saving me from several embarrassing blunders.

Two more personal debts remain to be recorded. The first is to my old friend and college classmate Robert Brown, who first drew my attention to Peirce, and who guided me through the first difficult steps in finding my way around in the literature. The second debt is owed to my wife Elaine, not only for patiently putting up with the other love in my life, but also for providing expert editorial assistance at home, for being my most sympathetic and therefore most demanding critic, and for giving me a sense that what I am doing is worthwhile. As a small repayment of that debt I gratefully dedicate this book to her.

P. S.

Williamstown, Massachusetts
March 1980

Acknowledgments

For permissions to reprint copyrighted material the author is grateful to the following:

The Belknap Press of the Harvard University Press, for permission to quote from *The Collected Papers of Charles Sanders Peirce,* vols. 1–6, Charles Hartshorne and Paul Weiss, eds. (Cambridge, 1931–35); vols. 7, 8, Arthur Burks, ed. (Cambridge, 1958). References to the *Collected Papers* will follow the established convention of giving volume and paragraph number; thus "*CP,* 5.388" refers to volume 5, paragraph 388.

The Philosophy Department of Harvard University, for permission to quote from the Peirce Papers in the Houghton Library of Harvard University.

Universitetsforlaget, for permission to reprint, in English translation, chapters 3 and 4 of my *Vitenskap og menneskebilde: Charles Peirce og amerikansk pragmatisme* (Oslo, 1978).

The Review of Metaphysics, for permission to reprint, in expanded form, my article "Pragmatic Realism: The Peircean Argument Re-Examined" (March 1980) pp. 527–40.

The Road of Inquiry

Introduction

RECENT DECADES HAVE witnessed a growing interest in the thought of the American philosopher-scientist Charles Sanders Peirce (1839–1914), and, as is usually the case, the first fruit of increased scholarly interest has been disagreement. More and more philosophers seem to agree that Peirce is enormously important, while fewer and fewer seem to agree on why he is important, or what the precise significance of his contribution to philosophy is. Peirce is seen variously as a hard-headed empiricist, a speculative idealist, or a combination of the two; as a jealous watchdog of empirical science, or as a typical philosophers' philosopher; as the founder of an indigenous American tradition in philosophy, or as a brilliant disciple of Kant; as a forerunner of logical empiricism, or as a latter-day scholastic. Although such divergence of opinion is the natural concomitant of intellectual ferment, there are also several causes at work specific to Peirce. First, he was an exceptionally unsystematic writer. He began a great many philosophical treatises but never finished a single one; as a result his philosophical writings remain scattered and fragmentary. Second, Peirce was, or aspired to be, a highly systematic thinker. Consequently, his various fragmentary writings abound with cross-references, as well as with references to an overarching "architectonic" system, which is nowhere fully set forth. Third, in the course of his long and productive career Peirce repeatedly changed his mind; these changes are sometimes acknowledged, sometimes not. At times even the acknowledgements are retracted, so Peirce also changed his mind over whether or not he had changed his mind.

The interpreter of Peirce's thought is faced, therefore, with the classic problem of textual interpretation in an aggravated form. The systematic unity of any corpus of writings can be inferred only from its parts, which in their turn can be fully understood only from their place within the system. This is the familiar "hermeneutical circle," which can be squared by means of the "hermeneutical spiral staircase."[1] We begin by understanding a few of the fragments and forming a preliminary idea of the system. This preliminary system enables us to understand more of the fragments and perhaps improves our understanding of the original fragments from which we began. Through increased understanding of the fragments we are led to revise and improve our idea of the system, and so forth. It is an unending process, although not strictly speaking a circular one. In the case of Peirce's writings there is, however, a complicating factor: since Peirce repeatedly changed his mind on several issues we have no assurance that there is some one system within which his various statements are intended to be interpreted. Indeed, the provisional conclusion of Peirce scholarship to date seems to be that there is, in fact, no such system. Attempts have been made to interpret Peirce, in turn, as an empiricist (Buchler, Ayer), as an idealist (Feibleman), as a part-time empiricist and part-time idealist (Goudge), and as a synthesizer of the two (Gallie, Boler). For the time being the search for unity in Peirce's thought appears to have reached a dead end in and through the work of Murray G. Murphey, whose conclusion is that Peirce tried no less than four successive systems, none of which he ever completed.[2] This depressing conclusion, although not universally accepted among experts, is today probably the most influential interpretation of Peirce.

To forestall possible misunderstandings of my own approach, I want to stress at the outset that Murphey's pessimism may well be justified so far as it goes, that is, so far as it concerns the possibility of finding a comprehensive, unitary interpretation of Peirce's thought as a whole. I shall have to take exception to specific points in Murphey's interpretation, but I am not challenging his general conclusion. What I want to point out, however, is the oddity which would confront us if we were to accept Murphey's interpretation as the only legitimate one. If Peirce's various statements are intelligible only from their place within his system, and he has not got one, then it would follow that all his statements are literally unintelligible and that Peirce's thought is of interest only as a curious exhibit in the horror chamber of the museum of nineteenth-century thought. The fact is, though, that a number of intelligent people find many of Peirce's statements both intelligible and philosophically interesting and important. Granted that nobody knows for sure what Peirce's system is, and that many doubt whether he has one, the fact that he is found to be to some extent intelligible implies that at least a certain degree of understanding of at least some of his statements can be achieved without reference to his system as a whole. It does not follow that these statements are intelligible without any context at all. A plausible hypothesis is that certain of Peirce's doctrines form coherent subsystems within his thought, so that, on the background of these subsystems, we may interpret larger or smaller subsets of his statements, even though there may be no overarching total system within which we can interpret the whole body of his statements. So, even if we give up the search for a unitary system within which to interpret all of Peirce's thought, we may still search for the broadest possible coherent subsystem within which to interpret some part of his thought. This, in effect, is the approach taken in this book.

It follows from this choice of a method that several important areas of Peirce's thought will have to be left out of consideration; these omissions do not weigh heavily on my conscience, since comprehensive synopses and commentaries have long been readily available for the interested reader. What will be excluded from consideration here are Peirce's cosmology, doctrine of categories, classification of the sciences, and most of his work in formal logic, notably his system of logical graphs. The part of Peirce's philosophy on which this book will focus is his theory of scientific method—his theory of "inquiry," in Peirce's terminology. This part has lately come into the foreground of discussion as perhaps Peirce's most significant contribution to philosophy. It will be part of my argument that his contribution is of considerable interest for present-day discussions of scientific method. Nonetheless, Peirce's various utterances on this subject appear to be so teeming with discrepancies, tautologies, and contradictions as to defy all attempts to render an overall account of what his contribution consists in. These discrepancies form a set of problems which it is the task of any proposed interpretation to resolve.

The statements to be interpreted can be rendered intelligible only by being related to some coherent set of doctrines, and if the interpretation is to have any objective validity, such a coherent set of doctrines must be shown to *be* there, in the texts. While the measure of the validity of a proposed interpretation is its fidelity to the texts, as well as to the historical context, the measure of its interpretative success is the degree to which it resolves the *prima facie* discrepancies and inconsistencies found in the texts. It is appropriate for me therefore to preface my interpretation of Peirce with a preliminary statement of some of the most important discrepancies which need to be accounted for.

In the first place, Peirce held that the entire meaning of any abstract term—such as a theoretical term in science—consists in the possible experimental consequences of the statements in which it occurs; that is, he seems to have championed an "operationalist" or "verificationist" criterion of meaning. At the same time, he defended the doctrine of "scholastic realism," i.e., the doctrine that there are real universals, to which some abstract terms refer. These two doctrines are commonly held to be incompatible. In the second place, and similarly, Peirce held that experimental testability is required of any hypothesis provisionally admitted as scientific, while at the same time he held speculative hypotheses, involving unobservable entities, to be preferable to purely empirical hypotheses. In the third place, he maintained that science is concerned only with that which has a possible bearing on action, while denying that practical application is the goal of science or ought to be the goal of any scientist. In the fourth place, his theory of induction has been taken by some as an inductive and hence circular justification of induction, and by others as an aprioristic and even analytical justification of induction, despite Peirce's repeated condemnations of "*a priori* dicta."

Of these *prima facie* discrepancies I take the first one, the discrepancy between verificationism and realism, to be by far the most important; this topic, therefore, will loom large in what follows. Once this discrepancy has been resolved, however, its solution will turn out to hold a good part of the solution to the other discrepancies. Put briefly, the solution will hinge on an interpretation of Peirce's realism as a "pragmatic realism," i.e., as a realism which functions as an empirical hypothesis explaining the contribution of scientific inquiry to the success of our total activity. In this sense, pragmatic realism seems to be a species of what Hilary Putnam has recently called "empirical realism."[3] I prefer to use the term 'pragmatic,' both to preserve Peirce's terminology and to connote the implicit reference which the realist hypothesis bears to human actions and objectives. In this interpretation of Peirce as a pragmatic realist, his verificationism too will turn out to be an empirical hypothesis, rather than a criterion of meaning. The verificationism accounts for the scientist's understanding of scientific terms within the context of his own research activity, while the realism explains our understanding of why this activity is successful in dealing with the world, to the extent that it is successful. The working scientist, in this view, can fully understand the abstract terms he employs merely by referring them to their experimental consequences, but he cannot rationally pursue scientific activity with any hope of success unless he believes that the terms refer to real entities; nor can we understand the practical success of his activity without sharing that belief—although we may understand every word he says without either believing in theoretical entities or imputing any such belief to him. Thus verificationism refers to the semantics, realism to the pragmatics of scientific discourse. While this interpretation admittedly does not resolve all the discrepancies in Peirce's writings on meaning and reality, my argument will be that it does resolve the most important ones.

Although verificationism and realism may be thus reconciled, it is still a puzzling question why Peirce should have wished to maintain two such apparently opposed commitments and impose upon himself the laborious task of reconciling them. My argument will be that both commitments flow from Peirce's persistent rejection of all attempts to draw *a priori* boundaries around the domain of inquiry. The thread that runs through all of his writings on scientific method is summed up in his motto: "Do not block the way of inquiry!" Peirce's rejection of all apriorisms is frequently expressed in his demand that all scientific statements must be susceptible to experimental testing, and that their very meaning consists in their testable consequences. At the same time, he recognized the dangerous apriorism inherent in attempts to restrict scientific inquiry to that which is currently testable. So his constant demand for experimental consequences was accompanied by an equally constant warning against prejudging the question of what is or is not testable.

These philosophical commitments of Peirce's are in turn rooted in what Maurice Mandelbaum has recently called a set of "primary beliefs," specifically, in an extra-philosophical concern for reconciling the conflicting claims of science and non-scientific beliefs, including religious beliefs. This not uncommon nineteenth-century concern, which was intensified by the Darwinian controversy in mid-century, sheds considerable light on Peirce's view of the relation between science and action and on his view of induction as "self-correcting." Roughly, Peirce's position was that science and science alone has a method which will lead us towards the truth in the long run. Science must therefore be left free to follow its own path of development, unhampered by the intrusion of extra-scientific considerations—of politics, ethics, theology, or whatever. But science can reach its long-term goal only by employing indirect strategies, which in the short run may often lead us farther away from the goal. For purposes of practical action, what we want is short-run reliability, not the hope of long-run self-correction. In the short run, and until the task of science is complete, the conclusions of science carry no special reliability and hence have no claim to superiority over the conclusions of religion where the two conflict.

This is so far only the barest preliminary statement of the interpretation which will be advanced, with no suggestion of argument as yet. All the issues indicated are presumably of interest to devoted Peirce scholars. It has not, however, been my intention to address this book exclusively to those already interested in Peirce scholarship. Especially at a time when interest in Peirce's philosophy appears to be on the increase, it is desirable that a new book on this subject should address itself to as wide an audience as is compatible with the comparative difficulty of the issues to be discussed. Any discussion of specific issues presupposes a certain amount of background knowledge of Peirce's philosophy; I have therefore chosen to begin by

presenting a general outline of Peirce's theory of inquiry, as I understand it, thereafter proceeding to a more detailed discussion. In
chapter 1, I shall be less concerned with arguing my interpretation
than with presenting it. To that extent, chapter 1 is somewhat in the
nature of an IOU, which I hope the rest of the book will redeem.

While the book itself constitutes the only possible defense of my
interpretation of Peirce's thought, a few words need to be said at the
outset about my general approach to the history of ideas. What I
have proposed is to single out a part of Peirce's thought in order to
look for a subsystem of doctrines which is both coherent and of current philosophical interest. This project may invite several objections;
and, when an author knowingly chooses a debatable point of departure for his work, a decent respect for the opinions of possible
opponents requires him to state the reasons which impel him to do
so. This can best be done by considering some of the most readily
foreseeable objections.

One objection which can be easily answered is that by isolating
parts of Peirce's thought, I may deceive myself into attaching a false
and one-sided significance to statements which can be properly
understood only in the light of Peirce's thought as a whole. The
answer is that the risk is indeed there, and that there is no way of
avoiding it. The scholarly labors carried out by men such as Goudge
and Murphey have convinced me that we cannot hope to be able to
relate Peirce's various doctrines to his thought as a whole. The only
avenue left open is the more modest attempt at partial interpretation.

Some more potent objections can be raised to my attempt to find
both coherence and current philosophical interest in Peirce's thought.
In a way, this attempt is little more than an application of a time-
honored maxim of textual interpretation known today as the "principle of charity." What this maxim says is that the interpreter of
texts should adopt at the outset the working hypothesis that the statements to be interpreted are both meaningful and true, and that he
should abandon this hypothesis only after it has proved impossible,
despite his best efforts, to reconcile it with the textual evidence. This
principle, which can be traced back at least as far as Luther's
catechism, is not today fashionable among historians of ideas. There
are good reasons for this; charity, as we all know from everyday life,

may be profoundly misguided. To the historian of ideas, it presents at least two pitfalls: arrogance and anachronism.

The temptation towards arrogance is warned against by Murphey in a recent article. If we try to assess the philosophical significance of a past thinker, it is all too easy to judge him in terms of what we find significant now.[4] The result, though Murphey does not put it in precisely these terms, is that we may succumb to the temptation of treating the intellectual giants of the past as if they were our students, to whom we give good or bad grades for their answers to our exam questions. To take this attitude towards a thinker of Peirce's stature would surely be unbecoming. There are, however, more ways than one to patronize a dead thinker. The college professor is at least obliged to listen to his student before passing judgment. It would be infinitely more patronizing were the historian to cast himself in the role of a museum curator, exhibiting Peirce as an interesting specimen. A more respectful attitude than either of these is evinced by Nicholas Rescher in his recent book on Peirce: "I look on him not as a thinker of bygone days, but as a colleague and co-worker of abiding interest."[5] This quote would echo my own sentiments, had Rescher said: "not only . . . , but also . . . ." Peirce is a thinker of bygone days, and this fact needs to be acknowledged. It gives the interpreter an advantage over Peirce: the interpreter is alive, while Peirce is dead and cannot talk back. This difference should not be ignored, but its ill effects should be deliberately counteracted by the historian. For this purpose, the proper attitude to take is neither that of a professor towards a student nor that of a curator towards a museum exhibit, but rather that of one colleague towards another older and more distinguished colleague.

There remains the risk of anachronism. What seems a coherent philosophical position today did not necessarily seem so a hundred years ago. In searching for a coherent set of doctrines in a past thinker, it is all too easy to find currently fashionable doctrines in his thought and to impute to him problems and concerns peculiar to our own age. Historians of philosophy have received repeated warnings against this tendency towards anachronism, most recently from Murphey and Maurice Mandelbaum. Mandelbaum has issued a special warning against the tendency to interpret past philosophers as responding to what we in retrospect recognize as a philosophical tradition (such as "British Empiricism"), instead of interpreting them as trying to solve problems arising from their own "primary beliefs," that is, their extra-philosophical beliefs about science, religion, morality, politics, or art.[6] Murphey has similarly called for a historiography which takes account of the "flesh and blood" of past philosophers, and he has more especially deplored what he calls "presentism," that is, the tendency of historians of philosophy to write only the history of those philosophers whom we today find interesting and important; against this presentism he opposes "historicism," that is, the presentation of the past as it was in itself.[7] Both Mandelbaum and Murphey emphasize that while philosophers may be entitled to use the philosophical past for the purpose of shedding light on present-day problems, historians of philosophy are not entitled to indulge in such practices. A historian looking at the past from the vantage point of present-day concerns and interests necessarily distorts the past by presenting it otherwise than it appeared to the historical agents, the philosophers of the past.[8]

I agree with so much of what Mandelbaum and Murphey have said that it is difficult for me to defend my own approach without leaving a misleading impression of disagreement where no disagreement exists. I should not have been able to make sense of Peirce (to the extent that I have) if I did not know a fair amount about his extra-philosophical beliefs or about the historical problem situation in which those beliefs had a point or purpose. I do believe that both Mandelbaum and Murphey draw an arbitrary and gratuitous distinction between philosophy and the history of philosophy. If the interpretation of past philosophers in the light of present-day problems necessitates distortion, then this would be as vicious in philosophy as in the history of philosophy. The most obvious truism inherent in Mandelbaum's and Murphey's argument was originally stated forty years ago by R. G. Collingwood as a criticism of contemporary philosophers, not of historians of philosophy. This obvious truism is that the philosophers of the past were confronted with problems different from ours, that even their language reflects ideas peculiar to their age and alien to ours, and that the historian of philosophy may ignore these differences only at the penalty of forfeiting his credentials as a historian. But the philosopher who distorts the past will be equally remiss; far from shedding light on present problems, he will succeed only in engendering confusion. This was brought out very clearly by Collingwood, who chastised his colleagues for discussing Plato and Aristotle as though they were twentieth-century Oxford philosophers.[9] By discussing the ancient Greeks' use of the verb δεῖ as though it meant the same thing as the verb 'ought,' these philosophers evoked the nightmare of people who believed that the word τριήρης meant 'steamboat,' and who, when it was pointed out to them that the ancient descriptions of triremes did not sound like descriptions of steamboats, triumphantly replied that this just went to show that the ancient Greeks had thoroughly confused ideas about steamboats.

What is the correct moral to draw from Collingwood's nightmare? If asked whether a trireme is a steamboat, I believe Collingwood would have had to answer that no, it is a boat with three banks of oars and fitted with sails. Whether we say that a trireme is a steamboat or that it is a rowboat with sails, either way we are translating the ancient Greek word into modern terms. Indeed, our ability to recognize 'steamboat' as mistranslation of 'trireme' essentially depends on our having a more appropriate translation available; hence, the example shows the rather important difference between translation and mistranslation. Peirce has fallen victim to travesties similar to those depicted by Collingwood. For instance, it has been assumed that his "pragmatic maxim" was an attempt to formulate the verifiability criterion later proposed by the logical empiricists, and Peirce has even been criticized for formulating this criterion with less precision than Carnap (see chapter 3, note 11, below). This obviously is a mistranslation, amounting to anachronism; there is, however, no anachronism in explaining how the maxim resembles and how it differs from Carnap's criterion. There seems to me to be a profound confusion in Murphey's dichotomy between "presentism" and its antonym "historicism," between history as it appears to us and as it was in itself. The task of any historian is to make history "as it was in itself" apparent to the present-day reader. Likewise, Mandelbaum gives the whole game away in his remark: "When older problems are seen in a contemporary light they reflect what has transpired in the intervening years, and the original meaning that they had is translated into modern terms."[10] But of course it is! It is precisely the task of a historian of ideas to translate old and inaccessible thoughts into terms intelligible to his reader. For this purpose he is obliged to take into account that historical experience which colors the reader's outlook, but which was lacking to the original author. No historian—of ideas or of anything else—can choose whether to relate his subject to its original context or to the context of his readers; to perform his task he must make points of contact with both contexts. In this respect, the historian is in the same predicament as a translator in the literal sense: In translating from Norwegian to English I may choose to emphasize either literal fidelity to the original text or readability in English. I cannot, however, choose between the Norwegian or the English language, not if I want to make the text intelligible to readers unfamiliar with Norwegian. Similarly, a historian has considerable leeway in his choice of emphasis, and my emphasis is different from Murphey's; but the dichotomy implied by Mandelbaum, and made explicit by Murphey, is thoroughly unreal. The historian of ideas has no real choice between presentism and historicism; history as it actually was is the matter which he has to deal with, and he had better try to render it intelligible to the present age.

A final note of caution is in order. It will be part of my interpretation that Peirce was a matter of fact "ahead of his times" and did indeed anticipate views which have later come to the fore in philosophical discussion. Because claims such as these can almost always be made with a show of plausibility, they are nowadays met with a healthy suspicion by historians of ideas. Among historians of science, "precursitis" has long been diagnosed as a professional disease. Still, there is surely no *a priori* reason why anticipations should not, as a matter of historical fact, take place. But they must be shown to be historical facts; conjecture, however plausible, must be candidly admitted. I have taken pains, therefore, to make it clear where I imagine myself to be on solid textual ground, and where I am indulging in flights of speculation—in itself not a useless activity.

With Peirce, I firmly believe that "one of the main purposes of studying history ought to be to free us from the tyranny of preconceived notions." If this is to be effected, historical testimony must be mediated to the present; historical thought must be brought into dialogue with present-day prejudices and preconceptions. Such mediation is the chief purpose of this book.

Chapter One
Outline of Peirce's Theory
of Inquiry

a. Life and work

CHARLES SANDERS PEIRCE (1839–1914) was born and raised
in Cambridge, Massachusetts. He was the son of Benjamin Peirce
(1808–80), a professor at Harvard and one of America's foremost
mathematicians of his time. From childhood on, Charles received a
thorough education in mathematics, physics, chemistry, and philosophy. At the age of twelve he built his own chemistry laboratory,
and in his teens he read and reread Kant's *Critique of Pure Reason*
until he knew it almost by heart. His father coached him in his
philosophy studies as well as in his own field, mathematics. In 1862
Charles received his M.A. from Harvard, and in 1863 he received
Harvard's first B.Sc. *summa cum laude* in chemistry. By this time, he
was already embarked on what seemed fated to be a singularly successful career as a scientist.

Although posterity has remembered Charles Peirce primarily as
a philosopher, his contemporaries knew him chiefly as a mathematician and astronomer. From 1861 to 1891 he was attached to the
U.S. Coast and Geodetic Survey, originally assisting his father with
computations, later with astronomical observations, and eventually
doing experimental research in his own right.[1] In 1867 Benjamin
Peirce, then Superintendent of the Coast Survey, assigned Charles as
an assistant to the Harvard Observatory, which was affiliated with
the Coast Survey. In 1870 Charles accompanied his father on an
expedition to Sicily to observe that year's solar eclipse. From 1872 to
1878 he was engaged in original experimental research in the two

fields of gravity research and photometry. His pathbreaking pendulum experiments created new standards of accuracy for measuring the force of gravity; his research in photometry resulted in the establishment of an independent standard for the meter by the use of a wavelength of light and in the book *Photometric Researches* (1878), the only book Peirce ever published. These scientific pursuits were not unrelated to Peirce's contributions to philosophy. As an astronomer, Peirce was forced to reflect on the theory of measurement and especially on the role of probable error; as we shall see later (especially in chapters 5 and 6) his work on induction and probability is to a large extent influenced by these preoccupations.

At the same time, Peirce seemed already well on the way to establishing himself as a philosopher or, perhaps more exactly, as a logician. In 1866–67 he gave the Lowell Institute Lectures, "The Logic of Science and Induction," and in 1869 and 1870 he delivered the University Lectures at Harvard, both times lecturing on logic. From 1872 to 1874 Peirce was the center of an informal group of young philosophers, scientists, and lawyers calling themselves "The Metaphysical Club." This club, which has won fame as the birthplace of pragmatism, numbered among its members some of the most distinguished intellects in Cambridge of that day, including the psychologist William James, the mathematician Chauncey Wright, the philosopher Francis Ellingwood Abbot, and the lawyers Nicholas St. John Green and Oliver Wendell Holmes, Jr. The club had no publication and kept no records; to ensure the club a tangible memory, Peirce wrote out a paper he had read to the club and published it as part of a series of articles entitled "Illustrations of the Logic of Science" in *Popular Science Monthly* in 1877–78. These articles have become Peirce's most widely read writings. In 1879 Peirce received his first—and only—academic appointment, when he was engaged as an instructor of logic at the newly established Johns Hopkins University in Baltimore.

Benjamin Peirce died in 1880, and it is around this time that Charles' personal and professional fortunes begin to decline. In 1883 his appointment at Johns Hopkins was terminated, for reasons as yet unknown; despite repeated efforts by William James on his behalf he was unable to obtain a position at Harvard. In 1876 he was deserted by his wife, the Cambridge-born Harriet Fay; in 1883 he divorced her, and shortly thereafter married the Frenchwoman Juliette Froisy. In 1891 Peirce was asked to resign from the Coast Survey; after using his capital to purchase a house in Milford, Pennsylvania, he spent the last twenty-five years of his life in poverty and obscurity, making a meagre living partly by writing book reviews and dictionary entries, partly by giving occasional lectures through engagements secured for him by his old friend William James. So, for instance, he lectured in the home of Mrs. Ole Bull in Cambridge in 1898 and at Harvard in 1903, and in the latter year he again lectured at the Lowell Institute.

The reasons for Peirce's professorial failure are matters for speculation; there are too many possible reasons for us to be able to pinpoint the real reason. While Benjamin was alive, he treated Charles as a child prodigy and apparently was in the habit of telling colleagues that his son was a genius. There is evidence that, as a consequence, Charles grew insufferably arrogant, which could largely account for his failure to get ahead in the academic world once he was no longer under his father's protection. Then again, the first Mrs. Peirce came from an old, distinguished New England family; by divorcing her to marry a mysterious Frenchwoman, Peirce may well have made himself *persona non grata* in Cambridge. Finally, it may be too easy to blame Peirce's failure on the pettiness and mental narrowness of his contemporaries; we have no right to assume that such a man would necessarily be a success in today's academic world. Although an incredibly prolific writer, Peirce never published a philosophical book. This was due partly to his erratic work habits, which led him time and again to start ambitious projects which he never finished. Partly, also, it was due to his refusal to "descend" to the level of his readers, which must have been to some degree responsible for his failure to find a publisher for the works which he did write, such as the *Grand Logic* (1893). Peirce knew how to popularize; we know that from his articles in *Popular Science Monthly, The Nation,* and other periodicals. But these were *intended* as popular writings. In his philosophical writings, he does not seem to have realized any need to popularize *vis-à-vis* academic colleagues; hence, these writings passed virtually unnoticed in his lifetime even when they did appear in print, in journals such as *The Monist* or *The Journal of Speculative Philosophy*. When other philosophers complained of Peirce's lack of intelligibility—as his highly sympathetic reader William James habitually did—Peirce simply answered by blaming the lack of understanding on his readers.[2]

Peirce was, as I have just mentioned, a highly prolific writer. The corpus of his philosophical writings is made up in part by articles published in journals and dictionaries during his lifetime, in part by a wealth of more or less unfinished manuscripts left unpublished at the time of his death. The manuscripts were sold to Harvard after Peirce's death, and a bulky selection of them were edited and published (along with selections from his published work) in an eight-volume *Collected Papers* in the years 1931–1958. These papers cover most of the areas of philosophy, with an emphasis on logic, semantics, and scientific method. Many of the manuscripts, now lodged in the manuscript collection in the Houghton Library at Harvard, remain unpublished, and editions of previously unpublished writings keep appearing on the market.[3] We are still in the process of discovering Peirce, as more and more hitherto unnoticed aspects of his thought come to the attention of the philosophical public. This fact may to some extent account for the striking variety of interpretations noted in the Introduction.

Peirce at times labelled himself a logician, at times an experimentalist. To him, these were not two distinct vocations; logic, to Peirce, meant the study of methods, above all the study of the methods of experimental science. He was also, however, a logician in a narrower sense, as some of his most pathbreaking work is found in the area of formal logic. He ranks among the founders of the logic of relations, and he discovered quantification independently of Frege. Our concern, however, is not with Peirce's technical contributions to logic, but rather with his contributions to philosophy proper. Even within these confines, as was noted in the Introduction, we will limit our attention to one of Peirce's central contributions to philosophy, namely his theory of scientific inquiry. In this chapter we shall approach our subject by first sketching the theory of knowledge which Peirce set forth in a series of articles in 1868, and then move on to outline the theory of inquiry which he set forth in a second series of articles ten years later.

b. The rejection of the 'foundation' metaphor

Although the immediate frame of reference for Peirce's theory of knowledge is the state of American thought following the impact of Darwin, a more general frame of reference is found in the development of modern European philosophy from Descartes to Kant, a story which I shall assume to be sufficiently familiar to the reader for the purposes of this exposition. Suffice it here to call to mind the linguistic formulation which the problem of knowledge was given in the Cartesian tradition. The problem was conceived of as that of finding secure 'foundations' on which to 'build' the entire 'structure' of human knowledge. Were these foundations to fail, the entire 'edifice' of human knowledge would collapse. This formulation is taken from the idiom of the construction trade, and the Cartesian tradition is nowadays not infrequently referred to as the "foundationalist" tradition. Within this tradition and this idiom the problem of knowledge turned out to be insoluble; what Berkeley and Hume definitively showed was that if human knowledge is a building, then it is a building erected on sand and ready to collapse at any moment. Peirce followed in the footsteps of Kant, who accepted the validity of Berkeley's and Hume's arguments, but rejected both their premises and their skeptical conclusions. (Hume, of course, also shrank from absolute skepticism—as a gut reaction against conclusions which he was logically unable to escape.) Peirce's point of departure is that we do in fact have knowledge, and that the philosophical problem consists in explaining how this knowledge is possible. An "explanation" which leads to the conclusion that knowledge is not possible simply fails as an explanation and immediately arouses suspicion of an erroneous point of departure. And the point of departure for Humean skepticism is no other than Descartes's foundationalism, i.e., the conception of knowledge as an edifice requiring secure foundations.

Peirce's antagonist, then, is Descartes, and his theory of knowledge is formulated largely as a number of critical objections to Descartes. Before we take a look at these objections, let us pause for a moment and consider the general drift of Peirce's attack on Cartesianism. This subject has been admirably presented by Israel Scheffler in his book *Four Pragmatists*,[4] and my account in this section will closely follow Scheffler's. It is no exaggeration to say that Peirce revolutionized the theory of knowledge by rejecting foundationalism and introducing a new idiom and thereby a new approach to the problem of knowledge. To Peirce, knowledge is no longer regarded statically as a body of propositions resembling a more or less finished building, but dynamically as a process of inquiry. Peirce at times described this process as a march forward towards truth as an infinitely distant goal. During this march we never have firm rock beneath our feet; we are walking on a bog, and we can be certain only that the bog is sufficiently firm to carry us *for the time being*. Not only is this all the certainty that we can achieve, it is also all the certainty that we can rationally wish for, since it is precisely the tenuousness of the ground that constantly prods us forward, ever closer to our goal. Only doubt and uncertainty can provide a motive for seeking new knowledge. In Peirce's metaphor, as long as we have relatively firm ground beneath our feet we are tempted to halt and rest until the ground begins to give way and we are once again forced onward in an endless search for firm ground. Science "is not standing upon the bedrock of facts. It is walking upon a bog, and can only say, this ground seems to hold for the present. Here I will stay till it begins to give way" (*CP*, 5.589).

The notion of gradual scientific progress was something of a commonplace in the nineteenth century, and even the notion of infinite progress was not original with Peirce; nonetheless I believe the credit belongs to him for carrying this notion into epistemology, explicitly rejecting the foundation metaphor and replacing it with a new metaphor and thereby a new angle of attack on the problem of knowledge. One is struck, however, by the large number of thinkers in our century who, apparently independently of Peirce, have formulated the problem of knowledge in similar terms. This phenomenon is vividly illustrated by Scheffler, who has found echoes of Peirce in the writings of Bertrand Russell, Ludwig Wittgenstein, Karl Popper, and Otto von Neurath.[5] Especially striking is Neurath's famous simile: scientists are like sailors who have to rebuild their ship in high sea, without being able to seek port. Each plank in the hull may be jettisoned in the process, but it is not feasible to jettison all the planks at the same time.[6] The moral of this simile is the same as the one Peirce formulated in rejecting the notion of a "bedrock of facts": we canot step outside the confines of our actual knowledge to some sort of Archimedean point from which to evaluate and justify our entire body of knowledge. The only vantage point we have available is the vantage point of our actual knowledge, with all its uncertainty and (as Wittgenstein has it)[7] will all the "friction" of unforeseen and recalcitrant experience. The problem of knowledge, like all other problems, can be tackled only from this vantage point. Among the best known present-day spokesmen for this approach is Willard V. O. Quine, who is in this respect directly influenced by both Peirce and Neurath.[8]

The rejection of the foundation metaphor is a revolutionary turning point in epistemology in two respects, both of which must be emphasized. On the one hand, we must give up Descartes's hope of finding some sort of absolute guarantee for the reliability of our knowledge. No such guarantee can be found. On the other hand, we need not land in Hume's skepticism: if we have no independent vantage point from which to *justify* our body of knowledge as a whole, neither do we have an independent vantage point from which to *reject* our knowledge as a whole.[9] The only vantage point available is the one provided by the knowledge which we in fact have. Within the framework of this knowledge we may criticize and reject each one of our beliefs individually, but we cannot step outside this framework and reject all our beliefs collectively. Total skepticism is as impossible as absolute certainty. As an alternative to both, Peirce proposes an undogmatic and experimental attitude which he calls "fallibilism" or "critical common-sensism." What this attitude involves will be made clear after we have looked at his anti-Cartesian articles in some detail.

c. Peirce's anti-Cartesianism

Peirce's objections to Descartes are found chiefly in two articles published in the *Journal of Speculative Philosophy* in 1868 with the titles "Questions Concerning Certain Faculties Claimed For Man" and "Some Consequences of Four Incapacities." The titles call to mind medieval disputations, and the articles are in fact cast in the form of such disputations, opening with a list of disputed questions, proceeding with arguments *pro et con,* objections to objections, etc., and concluding with the author's reasoned answer to each question. This form of exposition was not an elaborate joke on Peirce's part; rather, it reflects his genuine admiration for the scholastic style of philosophizing. As we shall see in chapter 2, he was also sympathetic to certain scholastic doctrines in philosophy.

In the first of the two articles Peirce enumerates seven mental faculties which the Cartesian philosophy has attributed to man. He then questions each one of these faculties, weighs arguments for and against, and concludes in each case that the faculty in question has not been shown to exist and need not be assumed to exist. In the second article, he focuses on four of these non-existent faculties—four "incapacities"—and draws certain further philosophical conclusions. We shall here confine our attention to these four incapacities, which Peirce lists as follows:

1. We have no power of Introspection, but all knowledge of the internal world is derived by hypothetical reasoning from our knowledge of external facts.

2. We have no power of Intuition, but every cognition is determined logically by previous cognitions.

3. We have no power of thinking without signs.

4. We have no conception of the absolutely incognizable. (*CP*, 5.265)

In these four anti-Cartesian theses we find Peirce's theory of knowledge in a nutshell.

The first thesis states that there is no special source of private cognition of the internal, mental world. What Peirce is here attacking is the status of Descartes's intuition, *Cogito*—"I think"—as an original and fundamental point of departure for reaching knowledge about the world. He is not denying that we have self-knowledge, or even that we have a relatively certain self-knowledge. But this knowledge is neither direct nor fundamental. A child learns the word 'I' only after he has acquired considerable linguistic skill and has learned the names of numerous external objects. And the child is aware of both will and emotion long before he is aware of a self, in which these attributes inhere. A table standing in his way is perceived as something which wants moving; only later does the child realize that he himself wants to move the table. This self-awareness comes about through the disappointment of expectations. The child believes, for instance, that a certain stove is cold; he reaches out and touches it, and becomes aware for the first time of error and ignorance. But the error is not a property of the stove, which is quite simply hot; thus the child is driven to infer the existence of a self which has committed the error. The next step is the realization that any expectation may be disappointed, with unpleasant consequences, and that all knowledge of external facts bears witness to the existence of a thinking and feeling self: "To the developed mind of man, his own existence is supported by *every other fact*, and is, therefore, incomparably more certain than any one of these facts" (*CP*, 5.237). Our self-knowledge, then, is neither fundamental nor absolutely certain; it is an inference from our knowledge of the external world and is therefore no more certain than our knowledge of the external world. But nothing *can* be more certain than our knowledge of the external world, since "there is no doubt perceptible in either case" (*ibid.*), i.e., either in the case of the external world or in the case of the internal world. Our self-knowledge is on a par with our knowledge of the external world: neither is absolutely certain, but both are as certain as anyone could rationally wish. The denial of the faculty of introspection is not, therefore, an argument for skepticism.

Peirce's second thesis is undoubtedly the most difficult one of the four. When he says that every cognition is logically determined by previous cognitions, this should be taken to mean that every cognition—that is, every item of knowledge—is the conclusion of an inference from previous cognitions. What is here denied is Descartes's doctrine that all inferred and derivative knowledge must be justified by a logical deduction from a set of first premises which are themselves known through "intuition," i.e., through direct and indubitable knowledge. What Peirce is claiming is that we have no faculty of intuition, and that there are therefore no first premises. This may seem a strange claim, and Peirce's argument for it will probably seem even stranger. The doctrine of the need for first premises was originally set forth by Aristotle on the seemingly compelling ground that no conclusion can be reached through an infinitely long chain of inferences, since no infinite series can be traversed in a finite time. First premises must exist, so the argument goes, because without them we should never. have obtained those later premises which eventually lead to our conclusion.[10] Put differently, any process of reasoning now going on must have been set going at some point. Peirce's answer is that although any reasoning process is finite in length and hence has had a beginning, still when we analyse the process as a chain of inferences, we will find it infinitely divisible into steps of inference. All knowledge has its starting point in perceptions received by the senses. But perceptions do not in and of themselves constitute knowledge, and they cannot serve as premises for inferring knowledge. What we perceive are sensible qualities, such as 'red.' But what we know or cognize are perceptual *facts*, such as "this thing is red." Now Peirce's claim is that time is continuous in the sense that any finite interval, no matter how short, can be divided into shorter intervals which in turn can be divided, etc., without any indivisible interval ever being reached. So, between each perception and the cognition to which it gives rise, there takes place a thought process which is indeed of finite duration, and usually of very brief duration, but which is nonetheless infinitely divisible. If we try to trace the steps of inference by which a given cognition has been reached from a given perception, we shall have to traverse an infinite series of inferences, which is impossible. For each premise we uncover, we shall always be able to find a prior premise from which it is inferred, without ever reaching a first premise. I should add that this argument does not prove that first premises do not exist; the argument is designed to show only that we do not need the hypothesis of first premises in order to account for any known facts and that these facts do not therefore serve as evidence for the existence of first premises. For Peirce, these are sufficient grounds for rejecting the existence of first premises, at least until someone comes up with some *other* evidence for their existence.

While this thesis may at first blush seem strange, and Peirce's arguments for it are highly abstract, his reasons for holding this thesis are not difficult to grasp. On the one hand, Peirce is concerned with avoiding the dogmatism of holding that certain beliefs are in principle immune to discussion and criticism. A first premise is, by definition, a statement for which no reason can be given, and over which there can consequently be no discussion; such a statement can only serve as dogma which blocks the road of inquiry in that particular direction. On the other hand, as Peirce is concerned to explain the possibility of knowledge, he is also concerned with avoiding skepticism. One of the cardinal errors of Cartesianism was that it laid itself wide open to skeptical attacks by postulating a need for something which is not to be had, namely secure foundations of knowledge. This error, which Peirce lays at the door of Descartes, is shared also by Descartes's empiricist critics for whom the "first premises" were not rational intuitions, but immediate sense perceptions. Against both these varieties of foundationalism Peirce tries to show that the postulate of first premises is unwarranted and that it is unneeded, since knowledge can do as well without first premises.

Peirce's third thesis claims that we have no ability to think except by means of signs. Peirce's concept of "sign" is rather broader than the usual concept of linguistic term; for Peirce, everything is a sign to the extent that it is significant, that is, to the extent that it is capable of being interpreted as meaningful. The sign function of diagrams, for instance, was of special interest to him. For the purposes of considering the present argument, however, we may confine our attention to linguistic signs. There are several arguments for the thesis. One is that there can be no conceivable evidence against it. In order to refute the thesis an opponent would have to produce at least one thought which does not have the form of a sign, but to do so he should have to state the thought, that is, put it into words. All the thoughts that can be identified confirm the thesis, and we can identify no thought which would serve as a counterexample (*CP*, 5.251). Another argument is that a sign, in order to be a sign, must be interpretable, and signs can be interpreted only by other signs, so if we try to get at the meaning of any sign, we shall find only some other sign. Hence, if we think by means of signs at all—which we evidently do—we can never get outside the realm of signs (*CP*, 5.284).

This may be the place to mention Peirce's belief that a conclusion should not be based on a single deductive chain, which would be no stronger than its weakest link, but rather on a series of parallel chains forming, as it were, a cable of intertwined fibers of argumentation, each perhaps weak and inconclusive, but all of them mutually reinforcing each other and lending their cumulative strength to the conclusion (*CP*, 5.265). We see here an example of how Peirce practiced what he preached. The third thesis evidently ties in with the first two theses and reinforces them. It supports the first thesis, to the effect that there is no purely private source of knowledge. Any language—indeed, any use of signs—presupposes a community of subjects capable of using and understanding the same signs. A sign is not a sign unless it is intersubjectively interpretable. Hence, if every thought is in the form of signs, there can be no such thing as purely private and inward knowledge which is in principle immune to confirmation or correction by the community. The third thesis also gives added support to the second thesis, to the effect that every cognition is an inference from previous cognitions. This thesis implicitly presupposes that all thinking has the form of chains of inferences, and hence of signs. (This, I should add, was made explicit in a third article, which will not here be discussed; see *CP*, 5.318–57.) On both counts the third thesis provides a further argument in favor of the indirectness of knowledge: knowledge of objects is mediated by signs which represent the objects. So, once again, what is denied is the existence of some rock bottom of immediate and infallible knowledge which might serve as a foundation for all other knowledge. We may note, in passing, the parallel, by now perhaps obvious, between Peirce's first and third theses and Wittgenstein's later philosophy, where the possibility of a "private language" is strenuously denied—although Wittgenstein was not directly influenced by Peirce.[11]

According to Peirce's fourth thesis, we can have no conception of something absolutely incognizable. Here it is Kant's concept of the "thing-in-itself" that is under attack. Peirce's argument is that our conception of anything is our conception of it as a possible object of knowledge, so that the concept of something incognizable would be self-contradictory. It might be objected, Peirce notes, that we do have the concept 'not' and the concept 'cognizable' and that we can form the concept 'incognizable' simple by joining together these two concepts. His reply is that the concept 'not' is synonymous with 'what is other than'; hence it gives a partial characterization of its object, whereby that object is partially known. It is known, at least, as being other than something else. 'Not cognizable,' therefore, is a contradiction in terms (*CP*, 5.257).

Another argument more directly reveals the connection of the fourth thesis with the three others. Our concept of the 'real' essentially involves the notion of a public process of inquiry carried out by a community of investigators. We need the concept of the real only in order to distinguish between true cognitions and illusion. The hallmark of an illusion is the fact that it is purely private and will not be confirmed by other observers. As Peirce was to put it years later, "One man's experience is nothing if it stands alone. If he sees what others cannot, we call it hallucination" (*CP*, 5.402n). The concept of the real, then, serves only the purpose of distinguishing between purely private, idiosyncratic cognitions and cognitions which will stand up to public scrutiny; in the 1868 articles Peirce put this point as follows:

> The real, then, is that which, sooner or later, information and reasoning would finally result in, and which is therefore independent of the vagaries of me and you. Thus, the very origin of the conception of reality shows that this conception essentially involves the notion of a COMMUNITY, without definite limits, and capable of a definite increase of knowledge. (*CP*, 5.311)

Since the 'real' is defined in this way as the object of the belief which inquiry would finally result in—that is, as the object of a particular species of knowledge—it follows, once again, that the concept of something real which is not a possible object of cognition contains a self-contradiction.

Once again, Peirce's dual purpose is clear. That which we cannot possibly know is by definition unreal, so skepticism has all its teeth pulled out. At the same time, the thesis has an equally clear message for dogmatists: the assertion that something is essentially beyond the reach of cognition has long been a favorite excuse for dogmatism and mysticism, as well as for pretentious but empty philosophical systems. To avoid both skepticism and dogmatism we must presuppose that any assertion can be questioned, and that any question which has a clear meaning also has a possible answer, though it may require the combined efforts of an indefinite number of generations to arrive at the answer.

Even if Peirce has shown the concept of the 'incognizable' to be self-contradictory, it remains an open question whether the concept of the 'cognizable' is sufficiently clear for his philosophical purposes. The cognizable is not simply that which is known, it is that which it is *possible* to know, and the concept of the 'possible' is rather slippery. We clearly cannot equate the conceivable with that which it is within our practical possibility to know, since any future scientific progress would then be inconceivable. If, on the other hand, we take the word 'possible' in the sense of 'possible in principle,' it becomes so flexible that its content is no longer clear. We shall leave this problem for consideration in chapter 2, and now turn our attention to some of the consequences which Peirce derives from his four incapacities.

d. Fallibilism and critical common-sensism

The labels "fallibilism" and "critical common-sensism" were introduced later in Peirce's career, although the doctrines denoted by these labels appeared in the 1868 articles. Before concluding our exposition of these early articles, it may be helpful to glance at some of the later, more explicit formulations of these two doctrines.

In a manuscript from about 1897 Peirce sums up his fallibilism in this pithy formulation: "There are three things to which we can never hope to attain by reasoning, namely, absolute certainty, absolute exactitude, absolute universality" (*CP*, 1.141). In a manuscript from about 1910 he reiterates: "I will not, therefore, admit that we know anything whatever with *absolute certainty*" (*CP*, 7.108). To the apparent counterexample 'twice two equals four,' Peirce replies that, although it would be folly seriously to doubt this proposition, it would be a still greater folly to assert that we know it with absolute certainty. We do make errors of addition; we may even err in adding two and two, and what may happen once may happen again. Two and two have been added together only a finite number of times, and we have no guarantee that we have not made a mistake every time. One might think that this addition has been repeated often enough with identical result to produce certainty. This, however, implies that there is some number N which is the smallest number of repetitions sufficient to produce certainty; then, after N–1 repetitions we should not be absolutely certain, yet one more repetition would be enough to produce absolute certainty, which is absurd.

Yet Peirce admits that he has not the slightest doubt that twice two equals four. Is this not inconsistent? It would be, Peirce grants, if we could simply doubt and believe at will. Doubt, however, is a somewhat coarse feeling, which is only imperfectly under conscious control. To achieve just the right degree of doubt commensurate with the uncertainty of the proposition 'twice two equals four' would involve a prodigious waste of mental energy which is better spent on more serious matters, specifically, on resolving those doubts which are forced upon us willy-nilly (*CP*, 7.109).

This presentation of fallibilism hints at the doctrine of critical common-sensism. I have not found an equally brief, epigrammatic formulation of the latter doctrine, unless it be the slogan "Dismiss make-believes" (*CP*, 5.416) from the article "What Pragmatism Is;" published in *The Monist* in 1905. In "Six Characters of Critical Common-sensism" from the same series of articles in *The Monist*, Peirce characterizes critical common-sensism by citing the following tenets, among others: There are indubitable propositions; these are original and acritical beliefs; they may change over time, but do so very slowly; they are believed instinctively, not rationally; and they are essentially vague beliefs (*CP*, 5.438–52). Yet, Peirce added in the manuscript "Consequences of Critical Common-sensism," probably from the same year: "A third mark of the Critical Common-sensist is that he has a high esteem for doubt. He may almost be said to have a *sacra fames* for it. Only, his hunger is not to be appeased with paper doubt: he must have the heavy and noble metal, or else belief'' (*CP*, 5.514).

These two doctrines are embryonically present in the 1868 articles, in the consequences which Peirce drew from his rejection of Cartesianism. One consequence of Peirce's four theses is that philosophy cannot begin from complete and universal doubt, as Descartes recommended. We can never reach new knowledge without presupposing some prior knowledge which we do not doubt. But, since there are no first premises or direct intuitions, it follows that no knowledge is in principle beyond possible doubt; so if we were to reject every belief which could possibly be doubted, we should have to reject all our beliefs and we should end in total skepticism, with no hope of ever attaining any knowledge. Hence, the Cartesian universal doubt is logically unjustifiable as a point of departure for acquiring knowledge. Luckily such doubt is also psychologically impossible: we come to philosophy with a network of preconceived opinions which it never occurs to us to doubt, because we are not aware that they can be doubted, or even that they are there. If we imagine that we doubt everything that can be doubted, we simply deceive ourselves and give our prejudices free play in determining our future beliefs:

> We cannot begin with complete doubt. We must begin with all the prejudices which we actually have when we enter upon the study of philosophy. These prejudices are not to be dispelled by a maxim, for they are things which it does not occur to us *can* be questioned. Hence this initial skepticism will be a mere self-deception, and not real doubt; and no one who follows the Cartesian method will ever be satisfied until he has formally recovered all those beliefs which in form he has given up. . . . Let us not pretend to doubt in philosophy what we do not doubt in our hearts. (*CP*, 5.265)

Another consequence is that what concerns the theory of knowledge is not knowledge as individual, subjective certainty, but knowledge as the objective validity of beliefs. The real is that which remains confirmed by all investigators in the long run, that which forms the object of the final opinion that will be reached through the indefinite prolongation of inquiry. Knowledge does not, therefore, consist in the subjective feeling of certainty of any individual, but in that final and unshakeable consensus which the community of investigators reaches when nobody any longer doubts a particular belief. From this perspective, certainty becomes irrelevant: so long as anyone doubts a particular belief, the final consensus has not been reached, and the certainty of those who do not doubt is no substitute for consensus. As soon, however, as no one actually doubts the belief anymore, the question of its certainty will not arise, since no one will bother to raise it. Beliefs are not, therefore, to be judged on the basis of their capacity to inspire subjective feelings of certainty, but only on the basis of their capacity to withstand public criticism:

> In sciences in which men come to agreement, when a theory has been broached it is considered to be on probation until this agreement is reached. After it is reached, the question of certainty becomes an idle one, because there is no one left who doubts it. We individually cannot reasonably hope to attain the ultimate philosophy which we pursue; we can only seek it, therefore, for the *community* of philosophers. (*CP*, 5.265)

This perspective, we may note, has recently been vigorously advocated by Karl Popper in his epistemology of "objective knowledge."[12] Popper has also made explicit the Darwinian theme which seems to lurk just below the surface in passages such as the one just quoted above; in Popper's view, science progresses through a sort of "survival of the fittest" among theories.[13] When we turn in the next section to Peirce's theory of inquiry, we shall see that he, too, toyed with this idea—without quite being able to swallow it.

Let me close this section by recapitulating its central ideas. Cartesian doubt is not a possible starting point for philosophy, partly because it is psychologically impossible, partly because there are no Cartesian intuitions or first premises which we would be left with after undergoing such doubt, even were it possible to do so. Peirce's "common-sensism" entails that we should not pretend to doubt what we do not in fact doubt, since this can lead us only into a blind alley of insoluble philosophical problems, from which there is no escape other than total skepticism. But Peirce does not advocate a naive and uncritical faith in common sense. He is a "fallibilist" who believes

that any opinion may turn out to be false; as a consequence his common-sensism is "critical." This entails that any habitual belief may
be criticized, and should be criticized as soon as we find reason to
doubt it. The ability to doubt is, in fact, the motive power which
propels inquiry towards the truth. But this can be effected only by a
real and living doubt, not by a mere "paper doubt." A naive faith in
our habitual beliefs would block the road of inquiry, since it would
conceal genuine problems of scientific interest. But so would the
pretense at universal doubt, since such doubt would deprive us only
of our consciously articulated beliefs and leave us at the mercy of our
unconscious, and hence indubitable, prejudices. In addition to the
slogan already quoted, "Dismiss make-believes," we find here the
substance of another slogan which Peirce was later to articulate: "Do
not block the way of inquiry!" (*CP*, 1.135).

e. Inquiry as adaptation

Among Peirce's best-known writings is the thumbnail sketch of his
theory of inquiry in the article "The Fixation of Belief," published in
Popular Science Monthly in 1877 as the first installment of his
"Illustrations of the Logic of Science." In this preliminary outline it
will be profitable to approach Peirce's theory of inquiry by first
considering this relatively early article and then looking at some later
writings. I should state at the outset that my reading of this article
owes a great deal both to Scheffler's book and to Murray G. Murphey's article "Kant's Children: The Cambridge Pragmatists,"[14]
although my interpretation departs somewhat from both.

In the Introduction I suggested that Peirce's theory of inquiry is
largely intelligible as an attempt to reconcile the conflicting claims of
religion and natural science, specifically as these claims were seen to
clash in the Darwinian controversy. This perspective is, I think,
fruitful for interpreting "The Fixation of Belief," where Peirce
explicitly refers to the Darwinian controversy when setting the stage
for his discussion (*CP*, 5.364). In this article Peirce initially adopts
the Darwinian image of man as simply a member of the animal
kingdom; human actions, in this image, are presented as physio-

logical operations directed towards optimal organic adaptation to the environment. Scientific inquiry is a species of human activity; as such, it too is to be understood as a form of adaptation. Inquiry, Peirce says initially, is simply the struggle to end *doubt* and attain *belief* (*CP*, 5.374). We may imagine that what inquiry aims at is *true* belief, but this is a redundancy. The fact is that as soon as we have attained belief, we *ipso facto* believe that our belief is true; this is what is meant by the phrase "attaining belief." Hence with the attainment of belief inquiry comes to an end (*CP*, 5.375). The process of inquiry, therefore, can be understood under the psychological categories of doubt and belief; these can in turn be defined as physiological states of the brain and central nervous system. Belief is the state in which we are when our actions are governed by stable habits, "such a condition that we shall behave in some certain way, when the occasion arises" (*CP*, 5.373). Doubt is an uneasy and irritating state which signifies the disruption of habits and paralyzes practical action, but which at the same time stimulates us to the kind of action which will bring the irritation to an end, as when the irritation of a nerve stimulates a reflex action to remove that irritation.

I must pause here to note a controversy over interpretation. In "The Fixation of Belief," which originated as part of a paper on pragmatism read to the Metaphysical Club, there is no mention of the Scottish psychologist Alexander Bain. Yet, in 1906, reminiscing on the Metaphysical Club, Peirce was to recall discussions of Bain's definition of belief as "that upon which a man is prepared to act," from which "pragmatism is scarce more than a corollary" (*CP*, 5.12). Clearly, it is Bain's definition of belief which is employed in the above. The distinguished Peirce scholar Max Fisch has argued, on this ground, that Bain's psychology is the intended frame of reference in "The Fixation of Belief," and that the explicit reference to Darwin is relatively unimportant: ". . . certainly in Peirce's mind to the end of his life the Bain connection was so much the more important that he seldom remembered the Darwinian one at all."[15]

It must be granted that the exaggerated attention often given to Darwin has slanted our perceptions of nineteenth-century intellectual history; Fisch deserves every credit for having discovered the long-forgotten role of Bain in the genealogy of American pragmatism.

Nonetheless, as has been pointed out by Philip Wiener, the Metaphysical Club included not only the Bainian Nicholas St. John Green, but also the Darwinists Chauncey Wright and John Fiske.[16] In 1906, Peirce still remembered disagreements with Wright over the compatibility of Darwinism and empiricism (*CP*, 5.12), and as late as 1909, he upbraided William James for still being under Wright's pernicious influence.[17] The biographical facts, then, cut both ways. More importantly, though, the dichotomy Bain *or* Darwin is a fallacious one; as has been recently emphasized by Altshuler[18] and Kuklick,[19] it was precisely Bain's definition of belief which enabled Peirce to treat beliefs in a Darwinian manner: it is only when beliefs are regarded as dispositions to action that they can be seen as interacting with the environment, thereby becoming subject to natural selection. Everything considered, it is fair to conclude that Peirce in 1877 was preoccupied with Bain *and* Darwin; and it is not far-fetched to interpret "The Fixation of Belief" as in part a quasi-Darwinian rebuttal of Wright's Darwinian empiricism.

This conclusion anticipates to some extent an interpretation which I have not yet given; before I do so I must proceed with the exposition. Peirce's article has the following plan: Peirce begins by raising the question of how best to attain stable belief, proceeds to consider three pre-scientific methods and rejects them all. He then presents the scientific method and concludes by proclaiming its superiority over the three others. It is clear that on the basis of the conception of inquiry as a process of organic adaptation the various methods can be evaluated only on the score of their actual effectiveness in dispelling doubt and establishing belief. The best method, from this perspective, can only be the 'fittest' method, i.e., the one which, in competition with the others, will in the long run survive the test of adapting the inquirer to his environment. An evaluation of whether any one of these methods will lead to true beliefs is in this perspective not immediately relevant. Recognizing this (*CP*, 5.375, 377), Peirce explicitly sets out to show the superiority of the scientific method in establishing stable belief, without immediate regard to the truth or falsity of beliefs.

The first pre-scientific method which Peirce considers is "the method of tenacity." Since the goal of inquiry is stable belief, and not necessarily true belief, it may seem simplest and most economical just to decide to go on believing everything which one already believes, come what may. This method is of course irrational, but Peirce rightly remarks that this is no real objection, since we have no right to assume at the outset that a rational method will necessarily be more effective than an irrational one. More to the point is the objection that the method of tenacity cannot in fact survive in the long run. Since we constantly associate with other individuals we are confronted with beliefs contrary to our own, and this confrontation creates a social pressure which tenacity is not capable of resisting:

> The social impulse is against it. The man who adopts it will find that other men think differently from him, and it will be apt to occur to him, in some saner moment, that their opinions are quite as good as his own, and this will shake his confidence in his belief. . . . Unless we make ourselves hermits, we shall necessarily influence each other's opinions; so that the problem becomes how to fix belief, not in the individual merely, but in the community. (*CP*, 5.378)

Before proceeding, I must pause to comment on the force of the clause "in some saner moment." It is man's rationality which makes him abandon the method of tenacity, but we have already seen that Peirce does not want to criticize this method on the ground that a rational method is *a priori* preferable to an irrational one. The point is, rather, that thorough irrationality is *a posteriori* known to be impracticable because the irrationality of one individual will not as a matter of fact have the strength to resist the force of contrary social pressures. This idea that there are non-rational social forces which impel us to rationality was a central idea in the social philosophy of the Scottish moralists of the eighteenth century, above all of Hume and Smith.[20] The epistemological application of this idea, which I believe was first made by Peirce, has lately been much emphasized by Popper and Donald Campbell.[21] But this is an aside.

The second method, "the method of authority," takes the social impulse into account. This method consists in letting the state legislate all beliefs, conduct systematic indoctrination, keep the population in ignorance of everything which may create doubt, and punish all those who profess divergent beliefs. This is a far more effective method; it has been employed with a great deal of success, in ancient Egypt and in medieval Europe, for example; and it will probably remain the best method as far as the mass of mankind is concerned: "If it is their highest impulse to be intellectual slaves, then slaves they ought to remain" (*CP*, 5.380). But there are two reasons why this method, too, will fail in the long run. In the first place, no institution can possibly legislate public opinion on *all* questions; on a number of questions individuals will have to form their own opinions, and they will necessarily have to do this by some other method, which will in some cases come to compete with the official one. In the second place, as different communities come into contact with one another, some of their inhabitants will discover that one and the same method leads to one opinion at home and the opposite opinion abroad, and this too will create doubts about the method (*CP*, 5.381). Some individuals will thereby come to feel the need for a method which not only determines *how* belief is to be settled, but also determines the *content* of what is to be believed (*CP*, 5.382).

A possible criticism of Peirce on this point might accuse him of nineteenth-century parochialism. In his age, it might be objected, authoritarian mind control may have seemed a thing of the past, discarded by the forward march of history; but we, who are raised on *1984* and *Brave New World* and who are acquainted with the spectacle of real-life modern totalitarianism, know better. We may abhor totalitarianism, but ineffectiveness is the last thing we will accuse it of. Now Peirce, as we have seen, did not dismiss the method of authority as totally ineffective. He believed, like Lincoln, that you *can* fool some of the people all of the time and all of the people some of the time, but you cannot fool all of the people all of the time. And this has not been disproved by the realities of twentieth-century totalitarianism, as distinct from the literary images evoked by Orwell and Huxley. It may even be argued that the course of Soviet history brilliantly bears out Peirce's judgment; for instance, it is instructive to note that the two foremost Soviet dissidents of our time are the creator of the hydrogen bomb and the leading official novelist of the de-Stalinization epoch. No totalitarian regime can get along without a scientific intelligentsia to provide technical know-how and a literary intelligentsia to legitimate the regime vis-à-vis the public. In order to fulfill their roles, the Sakharovs and the Solzhenitsyns have to know what they are doing; *they* must be permitted to form their own opinions by their own methods, and eventually they will constitute a threat to the regime.[22] To that extent, the example of the Soviet Union provides an unforeseen verification of Peirce's analysis.

To recapitulate: the failure of the second method brought with it the realization that an effective method for fixing belief must not only specify a procedure for forming opinion, but must also determine the content of opinion. This is partly effected by the third method, "the *a priori* method," which consists in believing whatever is agreeable to reason. He who follows the *a priori* method chooses to believe that which is plausible and reasonable, but does not consult experience to see whether his beliefs agree with the facts. This, according to Peirce, is the method which most philosophers have followed down through the ages, and it has resulted in some of the most impressive creations of the human mind. In terms of establishing stable belief, however, its record has been less impressive. Instead of creating a lasting agreement, the *a priori* method has produced only a succession of changing intellectual fashions. Belief has been fixed for certain periods, only to be disrupted by the next change of fashions (*CP*, 5.383). All three pre-scientific methods, then, are ineffective in fixing belief for any long term, and hence in producing adaptive habits in the human organism.

f. Inquiry and truth

So far, but no farther, the article follows the original plan. Towards the end of the article, when Peirce introduces the scientific method, he tacitly drops the naturalistic, or psycho-biological, perspective adopted at the outset. From that perspective what he was obliged to show was that the scientific method is more effective than the three others in settling belief, and that it would therefore be naturally selected in a competition with the three others. Instead, what he in fact does is rest its claim to superiority on the assertion that it is the only method which will lead to true belief. One shortcoming of the first three methods is that they do not let beliefs be determined by the

facts themselves, but by our ephemeral individual or collective prejudices. For a belief to be stable it must be determined by something
stable, namely by an external reality: "It is necessary that a method
should be found by which our beliefs may be determined by nothing
human, but by some external permanency—by something upon
which our thinking has no effect" (*CP*, 5.384). Such a method, Peirce
claims, is the scientific method, which he goes on to characterize as
follows:

> Its fundamental hypothesis . . . is this: There are Real things, whose
> characters are entirely independent of our opinions about them; those
> Reals affect our senses according to regular laws, and, though our
> sensations are as different as are our relations to the objects, yet, by
> taking advantage of the laws of perception, we can ascertain by rea-
> soning how things really and truly are; and any man, if he have suffi-
> cient experience and he reason enough about it, will be led to the one
> True conclusion. (*CP*, 5.384)

Will this method be effective in settling belief? Strangely
enough, Peirce does not raise this question, but argues instead that
this method, unlike the three others, will correct all erroneous conclusions to which it may at first lead us; in the long run, therefore, it
will gradually lead us towards the truth. This is the chief superiority
of the scientific method over the three pre-scientific methods:

> A man should consider well of them [i.e. the first three methods]; and
> then he should consider that, after all, he wishes his opinions to coin-
> cide with the fact, and that there is no reason why the results of those
> three first methods should do so. To bring about this effect is the pre-
> rogative of the method of science. (*CP*, 5.387)

The oddity of this conclusion has been nicely pin-pointed by
Scheffler, in the following passage:[23]

> In defending the method of science, [Peirce] does not even mention its
> superior effectiveness, but calls in a variety of new considerations,
> some metaphysical (relating to the supposition of real things), some
> methodological (relating to self-correctiveness), some epistemological
> (relating to the need for opinions to aspire to coincide with fact), and
> some even moral . . .

Not only does Peirce in fact fail to argue for the superior effectiveness of science, but, as Scheffler goes on to point out, Peirce cannot make such an argument with any show of plausibility. While science in its mature stages achieves relative stability for numerous beliefs, it achieves this result by initially casting doubt on our habitual beliefs; hence science is a far more unsettling method of forming opinion than any of the three others mentioned by Peirce.[24] We should note here that what Peirce means by 'truth' is a belief which will remain unshaken in the long run; hence, for him there is no difference between a method which will lead towards the truth and a method which in the long run will be successful in settling belief. What makes his introduction of the notion of truth problematic in the doubt-belief context is its dependence on the notion of "the long run." Peirce is assuming, I think, that the only evidence we can have that a method will lead us towards truth is its short-run effectiveness in settling belief. But such short-run effectiveness is not equated with truth-productiveness. The method of authority is credited with a high degree of effectiveness in the short run, yet there is not the slightest reason to believe that this method will lead us to true beliefs more often than not. Conversely, a method which will eventually lead to a lasting settlement of belief (i.e. to truth) may wreak havoc with our beliefs in the short run. The superior effectiveness of the method of science in settling belief was surely not evident to the theological opponents of Galileo or Darwin. It becomes evident only when the long-run task of the method has been completed, and when we no longer need a method for settling belief. In the meantime, we may infer the long-run effectiveness of the scientific method from the evidence of its effectiveness to date. This inference is simply the extrapolation of a trend; it is not logically compelling, but it is capable of being inductively tested. In the process of establishing this trend, however, we must take account also of the short-run failures of the method; hence, the two notions of truth and effectiveness to date are logically distinct and often mutually at odds. Here we may also note the second oddity, that on this point Peirce is in perfect agreement with Scheffler. At the outset of the article, when he argued that considerations of truth are irrelevant for evaluating methods of inquiry, Peirce made precisely the same point: we can only seek truth, he wrote then, by rejecting any belief which has not been formed by a truth-producing method, that is to say, "by creating a doubt in the place of that belief" (*CP*, 5.375). These oddities in Peirce's argument have also been noted by Murphey, who has concluded that the natural-scientific approach adopted at the outset of the article is not to be taken too seriously: "The apparent empiricism of the *Popular Science Monthly* series is a mask: Peirce's goal was the rebuilding of the world view in terms which were theological and metaphysical in the extreme."[25]

It must be granted that Peirce's introduction of considerations of truth, i.e., of correspondence with facts, breaks with the biological perspective originally presupposed. So long as we regard belief as a physiological state—specifically, the state of being governed by stable habits—it makes no difference whether a belief is true or false, as long as it is stable. The truth of a belief may, to be sure, be a contingent cause of its stability, insofar as true beliefs about the immediate environment will be less easily upset than untrue ones, and hence may contribute to an animal's degree of adaptedness. But there is here no invariant correlation which permits us to substitute truth for stability as a criterion by which to evaluate methods of inquiry. The two criteria will frequently yield opposite results, especially with regard to beliefs which go beyond the immediate environment. The erroneous belief that all gray animals are wolves would contribute to stable and adaptive habits in a lamb situated in an environment where wolves are the only gray animals it ever sees. The true belief that only a tiny minority of all gray animals are wolves would be useless, if not directly dangerous, to that lamb. If the lamb were to venture out into a wider environment with a richer fauna, the correct belief would come in handy; but it could not be acquired beforehand except at the expense of a habit-governed life. Nor is this a contrived example. People living in secluded communities will usually generalize from their immediate physical surroundings to form an entire world view in that image; they would hardly do so if it were not on the whole advantageous. To a greater or lesser extent, all human communities may be somewhat secluded. For instance, the belief that the sun everywhere on earth rises every morning and sets every evening is probably still held by most people living between the Arctic and Antarctic Circles, i.e., by the majority of mankind; and I dare say this erroneous belief serves them well in their day-to-day affairs. At least when a belief has this kind of generality, there may in most cases be an inverse correlation between truth and adaptive value—something which Peirce, by the way, fully recognized (see *CP*, 5.366, 5.445, 5.511, 6.50).

Once this is granted, I do not, however, think we are forced to conclude that Peirce is either inconsistent (Scheffler) or disingenuous (Murphey). What is fair to conclude is that Peirce is less than clear as to what sort of argument he wishes to propose. "The Fixation of Belief" contains a causal, evolutionary story about the rise and fall of the three pre-scientific methods, and a normative story about the superiority of the scientific method. The normative story is not part of the causal story, and the causal story is left unfinished; my suggestion is that the point of the total story is that the causal story *must* be incomplete. From Peirce's other writings it is fairly clear that although he was for a while excited by the Darwinian revolution he never accepted Darwin's theory as a complete account of the evolution of man as a cognitive being. Thinking, in Peirce's view, is an activity which is essentially subject to normative evaluation. This activity is essentially governed by the notion of truth as an ideal goal, and our thinking is good or bad, right or wrong, according to whether or not it conforms to norms which will lead us towards that goal. No cognitive activity, such as scientific inquiry, can be even adequately described, let alone explained, by an account which does not employ normative concepts, such as 'truth' or 'validity.' "In reasoning," Peirce was to write in 1902, "we have the singular phenomenon of a physiological function which is open to approval and disapproval" (*CP*, 2.152). A complete account of reasoning must therefore include an account of its normative aspect, namely, its capacity for being true or false, valid or invalid.

When Peirce, then, purports to adopt the Darwinian image of man as the frame of reference for his theory of scientific inquiry, what he actually does is adopt this image as a tentative working hypothesis, which in the end proves insufficient to account for all the facts. It is a fact that the scientific method has arisen, and this fact cannot be accounted for in purely causal terms—though the demise of the rival methods can be so accounted for. So understood, the argument of the article may be restated somewhat as follows: As a biological organism, man is driven to seek to dispel doubt and attain stable beliefs, that is, stable habits of action. However, so long as man seeks to fix belief by methods which give immediate satisfaction, he will inevitably be disappointed in the long run. Long-run stability of belief is something which can be reached only by a method which lets the beliefs be determined by external facts. Such a method requires willingness to adopt the search for truth as one's only aim, and to surrender any belief which conflicts with the facts of experience. In the short run, therefore, one must give up any hope of stable belief and be ready to accept any amount of doubt and uncertainty as means towards long-run stability. What this amounts to is that one must select a method by which beliefs are chosen not by the criterion of instant satisfaction, but by the criterion of conformity to general norms which are such that they will lead in the end to lasting, long-run satisfaction. So the process of scientific inquiry is fully intelligible only as an activity which is motivated by the search for truth and guided by the notion of truth as a norm-giving ideal.

This, though a somewhat free rendering of Peirce's article, happens to be close to the interpretation which Peirce himself offered in 1908, when he commented on his article of 1877: "The first part of the essay . . . is occupied with showing that, if Truth consists in satisfaction, it cannot be any *actual* satisfaction, but must be the satisfaction which *would* ultimately be found if inquiry were pushed to its ultimate and indefeasible issue" (*CP*, 6.485).

The Darwinian interpretation of the evolution of the pre-scientific methods of fixing belief is also confirmed in Peirce's later writings. So, around 1902 Peirce wrote, concerning the sentiment that an opinion is something to be chosen because one likes it and thereafter to be defended by fire and sword: "As civilization and enlightenment advance, however, this style of thought tends to weaken. Natural selection is against it; and it breaks down" (*CP*, 2.149).

Peirce might not agree in every respect with my interpretation. For the sake of accuracy it should be added that, around 1906, Peirce apparently thought that he had incorporated his normative story of scientific inquiry into the causal story of pre-scientific inquiry. In a manuscript from about 1906, we find this comment: "My paper of November 1877, setting out from the proposition that the agitation of a question ceases when satisfaction is attained with the settlement of belief, and then only, goes on to consider how the conception of truth gradually develops from that principle under the action of experience . . ." (*CP*, 5.564).

The problem of "how to get there from here," of how adaptations which have only long-term benefits can arise from an evolutionary mechanism which selects adaptations only for their short-term benefits, is a problem that still vexes evolutionary biologists; Peirce cannot fairly claim to have solved it.[26] If Peirce in 1906 was right about his own intentions in 1877, if his intention was to tell a causal story about the gradual emergence of the concept of truth as a normative ideal, then he failed, and Scheffler's criticism would to that extent be justified. Where I believe he succeeded was in pushing the causal story as far as it could be pushed—farther than most present-day biologists would be prepared to push it—and then showing convincingly that the story could not be completed without the introduction of normative concepts. However this may be, it is clear that Peirce did think of man's pre-scientific mental evolution in terms of his causal doubt-belief model, and that this model—though not, in my view, the whole story—is an essential part of his story, not a mere mask to conceal sinister metaphysical intentions.

g. Scientific method: Progress and fallibility

"The Fixation of Belief" says very little about what the scientific method actually is, although the article presupposes certain definitive views on such matters as the nature of scientific progress and the relationship of science to practical action. Some of these views are made explicit in later articles in the same series in *Popular Science Monthly*; since these articles are in fact fairly technical, I wish to postpone discussion of them until later chapters. For good general statements of Peirce's views on scientific method we must go to his later writings. In concluding this chapter I shall attempt to spell out these views as they are expressed in various places in Peirce's body of writings.

Peirce, as we know, was himself an experimental scientist and proud of it. However, although he was highly ambitious on behalf of science as such, he was not overawed by the science of his own day—perhaps precisely because he knew it too well from the inside. Like most of his contemporaries, he firmly believed in the inevitable march of science towards Truth as a foreordained goal. Unlike materialists or positivists, he could make room for philosophy and even religion alongside science, because he was ambitious only on behalf of the method of science, not on behalf of any of the conclusions so far reached by that method. Confident that science was on the path towards truth, he harbored no illusion that science already possessed the truth. As we have seen, Peirce regarded the scientific method as a method which would inevitably lead towards truth in the long run, and this reference to "the long run" is the salient point. In the short run the scientific method will lead us astray at least as often as it will lead us aright; but the unique merit of this method is that its further application will in the long run tend to correct those errors which in the short run it has led us into. This, of course, is no comfort at all in the short run, that is, in the world in which we have to live and act. Here we have to go upon the best knowledge available, and there is no particular reason why the conclusions of science to date should be preferable to the conclusions reached by any other method. We have every reason to rely on the method of science, but we have no particular reason to rely on any given conclusion reached by this method. Such conclusions, therefore, carry no special authority when they conflict with religious creeds or with inherited moral convictions.

This dichotomy between method and conclusions may seem a bit odd on two counts. First, once we have chosen the scientific method, we follow only that method; we do not mix it with tenacity, authority, or *a priori* reasoning. Hence all the conclusions which we will actually reach will be the conclusions of science, and so the conflict between the conclusions of science and those of other methods should not arise for the person who has chosen to rely on the scientific method. The answer to this objection would be, I presume, that we do not begin applying *any* method of fixing belief until we have in an unsystematic manner amassed a number of beliefs, some of which we have begun to doubt. Whenever we are faced with a choice between two conflicting beliefs we presumably doubt them both, and the only rational way of choosing between them, that is, of allaying our doubt about one of them, is to follow the scientific method. This, however, will take time. If I have to choose now which one to act upon, it is rational to choose the one which seems less doubtful, and there is no special reason why this should be the one which accords with the conclusions of science to date.

Second, according to a time-honored conception, the empirical sciences follow an "inductive method"; the scientist observes facts and proceeds to infer laws and make predictions by induction from his observations. When we call this method reliable we mean that we can rely on the predictions inferred from the observations, and it would make little sense to say that one relies on the method if one is not willing at the same time to rely on the conclusions reached by the method. Now Peirce frequently refers to "the inductive method," but it is evident that what he means by "induction" is the subsequent testing of predictions derived from hypotheses. As Peirce conceives it, the scientific method is what we would today call "the hypothetico-deductive method."[27] In this view, scientific laws are preconceived guesses, or hypotheses; they may be intelligently arrived at, but they are always under-determined by the available observations. When we have formed a hypothesis, we deduce predictions from it and test these by observation or experiment. If the predictions are falsified, we know at least that the hypothesis is false; this is a positive advance in knowledge, and a step towards truth through error-elimination. So long as the predictions are confirmed, we keep the hypothesis on probation; but we can never prove it to be true, since it is always possible that the next prediction may turn out to be false. Paradoxically, then, we learn more from refutations than from confirmations; it is precisely by forming *erroneous* opinions and subjecting them to the test of experience that we get gradually nearer to the truth:

[The active scientist] entertains hypotheses which are almost wildly incredible, and treats them with respect for the time being. Why does he do this? Simply because any scientific proposition whatever is always liable to be refuted and dropped at short notice. . . . The best hypothesis, in the sense of the one most recommending itself to the inquirer, is the one which can be the most readily refuted if it is false. This far outweighs the trifling merit of being likely. (*CP*, 1.120)

Peirce's scientific optimism consists only in the conviction that every erroneous hypothesis will sooner or later be refuted, if subjected to sufficiently thorough testing: "It is true that agreement [i.e. with observation] does not show the guess is right; but if it is wrong it must ultimately get found out" (*CP*, 1.121). This optimism goes hand in glove with a critical attitude to those results at which science has arrived to date. From the viewpoint of the hypothetico-deductive model, these two attitudes are mutually consistent and complementary: it is precisely by suspending belief vis-à-vis his hypotheses that the scientist is motivated to continue the process of experimental testing and thus bring science nearer to the truth.

The experimental testing of predictions drawn from hypotheses is what Peirce calls induction, and he often appeals to the "self-correcting" tendency of induction as its rational justification:

Nor must we lose sight of the constant tendency of the inductive process to correct itself. This is of its essence. This is the marvel of it. The probability of its conclusion only consists in the fact that if the true value of the ratio sought has not been reached, an extension of the inductive process will lead to a closer approximation. (*CP*, 2.729)

This claim is easily misunderstood, because the term 'induction' is commonly reserved for the confirmation of hypotheses and the consequent ascription of degrees of trustworthiness to their predictions, while Peirce uses the word simply for the testing of hypotheses, whether the testing results in confirmation or refutation. A self-corrective justification of induction in the former sense would have to show that induction corrects itself by leading to increasingly reliable predictions. And for this purpose, as has been noted, e.g., by Edward Madden,[28] Peirce's justification is useless, since it shows at best that induction will tend to correct our predictions only when they are no longer predictions—when they have already been tested and refuted. This, I think, is all that Peirce ever wanted to show. He had no stake in the reliability of scientific predictions as a basis for action, only in the reliability of the scientific method as a road to truth.

It has become fashionable in recent years to claim that the hypothetico-deductive method is intimately allied to an interest in technical control over physical phenomena, and pragmatism has frequently been accused of being a philosophical apology for modern technology, or even for industrial capitalism. It is interesting to note, therefore, that Peirce advocates a sharp separation of scientific research from practical or technical action—precisely on the grounds of his understanding of the scientific method. Scientific inquiry, to be sure, is a type of activity, but it is an activity which is directed towards a particular end, namely the discovery of truth; if it is turned towards some practical end, both the scientific activity itself and that practical end will suffer. The reason is that the type of action which enters into scientific inquiry is experimental action, which requires that nothing be staked on a particular outcome of the experiment. The experimenter must be ready to accept whatever outcome presents itself; the proper attitude for him to take is one of doubt towards his hypothesis. But this detached and experimental attitude is quite inappropriate for purposes of practical action, where matters of life and death may depend not only upon the truth of a particular hypothesis but even upon the agent's firm belief in that hypothesis:

> Nothing is *vital* for science; nothing can be. Its accepted propositions, therefore, are but opinions at most; and the whole list is provisional. The scientific man is not in the least wedded to his conclusions. He risks nothing upon them. He stands ready to abandon one or all as soon as experience opposes them. . . . There is thus no proposition at all in science which answers to the conception of belief. But in vital matters, it is quite otherwise. We must act in such matters; and the principle upon which we are willing to act is a *belief. (CP,* 1.635-36)

Ideally, a scientific hypothesis is a wildly improbable guess, which may or may not turn out to be true. Such a guess is an appropriate candidate for experimental testing, but it is not an appropriate candidate for belief, to the extent that a belief is that upon which a man is prepared to act. Peirce does not deny that one *may* believe in a well-confirmed hypothesis, or even that it is often quite sensible to do so, say, if one is a physician or an engineer. But in such a case one adopts an extra-scientific attitude towards the hypothesis in question; this attitude is not sanctioned by science, nor does science take any responsibility for it. For all that, it may well be a rational attitude to take, especially if one has to act in a sphere to which no pre-scientific beliefs apply. Often it is not a rational attitude, as when people try to adjust their religious beliefs and practices to the latest results of critical-historical scholarship. Peirce did hold that religious beliefs can lay claim to truth only to the extent that they are continually subjected to the test of experience; only, the believer ought not to be in a hurry to adjust his condŭct of life to the provisional results of such testing, results which further testing might annul. What is never sensible is the attempt to carry the concern for practical results, with its concomitant attitude of belief, into the scientific enterprise itself. This attempt can serve only to deflect the investigator from the path of scientific progress,a path which often leads away from the prospect of immediate applicability, and which often involves the examination of hypotheses which defy each and every attempt at belief:

> The point of view of utility is always a narrow point of view. How much more we should know of chemistry today if the most practically important bodies had not received excessive attention; and how much *less* we should know, if the rare elements and the compounds which only exist at low temperatures had received only the *share* of attention to which their *utility* entitled them. (*CP*, 1.641)

By drawing a sharp line of demarcation between pure science and practical application, Peirce is making two points. On the one hand, he wants to uphold the freedom of inquiry to follow the path of its own internal development, unhampered by social, political, or religious constraints. As soon as science is looked upon as a means towards practical ends, it is tempting for religious and political authorities to regard it as a tool for their particular ends. Peirce saw clearly that this would threaten the freedom, and hence the progress, of science; he therefore strenuously opposed the British statistician and social reformer Karl Pearson, who claimed that science exists to strengthen the welfare and stability of society.[29] On the other hand, he was concerned to defend religion and morality—and, in fact, historical scholarship—against scientistic imperialism. So, for instance, his writings on probability and statistics contain frequent polemical asides against those German historians who employed probabilistic reasoning to attack the veracity of the Gospels and the records of ancient history. As we shall see later, Peirce held their probabilistic reasoning to be fallacious. But he also held that science has no right to legislate religious belief: science progresses by means of bold and highly uncertain guesses, while faith and morality concern vital questions, where we require a degree of certainty and reliability which we are more likely to find in traditional or instinctive beliefs than in science. This does not mean that Peirce wants to make religion permanently safe from science. That would be blocking the road of inquiry. No question is in principle immune to being answered by the scientific method; however, we cannot now foresee the ultimate result of the application of that method. In the long run religion will either be replaced by science or vindicated scientifically; we cannot now say which. In the meantime, we have to act on the most reliable beliefs available, not on the most promising or interesting conjectures of science.

Chapter Two
Peirce's Early Realism

a. Peirce's experimental outlook

IN THE PRECEDING chapter, Peirce's theory of inquiry was presented in general outline. Nothing has yet been said about the problem of meaning; and, although the problematic character of Peirce's conception of reality was noted in passing, the problem has not been taken up for explicit discussion. Since the conceptions of meaning and reality are at the heart of Peirce's theory of inquiry, they will occupy us at length. This chapter and the two following will be devoted to Peirce's early statements of realism, his pragmatic theory of meaning, and his later synthesis of the two under the label "pragmaticism."

Readers who are not steeped in the literature of modern philosophy of science may wonder why the conceptions of meaning and reality need occupy any position, let alone a central one, in a theory of scientific inquiry. The first thing we may note in reply is that these two conceptions are closely related; if we need one we also need the other. Philosophers concerned with the nature of reality have long been in the habit of approaching their subject through an analysis of language. We have no direct access to reality itself; it is not the sort of thing which we can place under a microscope, in a test tube, or on a dissecting table. However, there is an indirect approach open to us. When we make statements we normally intend to say something true; that is, we normally intend to talk about something real. An anlysis of the meaning of our statements may therefore reveal at least what we, the members of our language community, hold to be real. Accordingly, modern philosophers, starting with Berkeley, have attempted to stake out the boundaries of reality by examining what sort of entities our language commits us to. If, for instance, statements about 'minds' and 'thoughts' are really indirect ways of talking about the behavior of material bodies, then only material bodies (and possibly their behavior) need be assumed to be real. If, conversely, statements about material bodies are indirect ways of talking about mental ideas or sense impressions, then only ideas or sense impressions need count as real. In this way, it has long been thought, the debate between materialists and idealists can be settled through an analysis of meaning.

Unfortunately, this gambit may also be played in reverse: when we make statements we normally want to talk about something real, so if we already have a definite conception of the nature of reality, we can therefrom infer the meaning of statements. If we are idealists we already know that only ideas are real; hence we can infer that statements apparently about material bodies are actually disguised statements about ideas; this is their meaning. Conversely, if we are materialists we can infer that statements apparently about minds or thoughts really are statements about the behavior of material bodies. So, the concept of meaning is usually thought to involve a concept of reality, and vice versa. Lest the reader conclude that philosophy is necessarily circular, let me hasten to add that language has several dimensions; as we shall see in chapter 4, an analysis of language need not be an analysis of meaning. In the mainstream of modern philosophy, however, this is what it has been.

In the philosophy of science, questions about the nature of reality have frequently raised questions about meaning, and vice versa. There are several reasons why these kinds of question need arise at all. At least since the time of Galileo, natural science has increasingly been concerned with descriptions of idealized states of affairs which are never encountered in "real life" outside the laboratory; and, at least since the time of Newton, these descriptions have taken an increasingly abstract mathematical form, in physics usually the form of differential equations. Science, then, has become a set of highly abstract and to most people unintelligible statements about states of affairs never actually encountered; still, nobody seriously doubts that these statements have some connection wih the world in which we live and breathe. This connection has been thought of in various ways. Some have thought that the statements of science describe a deeper level of reality, underlying the world of experience, and acting as a cause of the phenomena which we experience. Others have thought that these statements describe only the experienced phenomena, and that their abstract and idealized form is a kind of mental shorthand, adopted either for reasons of intellectual economy or for reasons of aesthetic pleasure. Still others have thought that the statements of science describe nothing at all, but are only instruments or calculating devices for predicting and controlling phenomena. These different views seem to embody incompatible conceptions both of the nature of reality and of the meaning of scientific statements. Which view one chooses has a practical importance at least for popularization purposes, perhaps especially for the purpose of popularizing the most advanced science of the day vis-à-vis less advanced sciences which may profit from incorporating more advanced methods and results.

The need for an explicit theory of meaning may also arise within one particular science. The various technical terms of a science are interconnected by way of definitions; hence a technical term may lose its meaning through the redefinition of other terms. If such terms continue to be used, their use is apt to generate pseudo-problems which may impede the progress of science. For instance, the term 'essence' was a perfectly meaningful technical term in Aristotelian physics; it is not given a meaning in modern physics; yet questions about the essence of gravity or of heat kept vexing scientists until well into the nineteenth century.

This little preamble is not intended to be either exhaustive or very precise; I hope, however, that it will have served to explain why Peirce, in developing his theory of inquiry, had a need to address himself to the related questions of the nature of meaning and the nature of reality. This chapter will be devoted mainly to a consideration of Peirce's early statements of his "scholastic realism," embodying his conception of reality. Discussion of his theory of meaning—his "pragmatism"—will be postponed to the next chapter; it will, however, be helpful to approach his realism through a preliminary look at his pragmatic theory of meaning, since the latter gives the clearest expression to Peirce's experimental outlook, which is fundamental to his theory of inquiry.

Peirce's scholastic realism is expressed in a number of publications and manuscripts from the years 1868 through 1873. Statements of his pragmatism did not appear in print until 1878, in the *Popular Science Monthly* series, but a theory of pragmatism was presented to the Metaphysical Club in 1873, and was originally formulated, so Peirce tells us (*CP*, 6.482), in 1871. For twenty years Peirce did not write another word about pragmatism; then, in 1898, William James revived both the theory and its name, while giving the theory a somewhat different twist from what Peirce had intended. Peirce now was obliged to distinguish his own pragmatism from James', and from 1898 until at least 1905 he wrote extensively on pragmatism and its relationship to scholastic realism, specifically in his Harvard lectures in 1903 and in a series of articles in *The Monist* in 1905. These writings include frequent reminiscences about what he had originally meant to express in his pragmatic theory of meaning, and how he had been led to hold this theory. So, for instance, in his articles in *The Monist,* Peirce claimed to "have inhabited a laboratory from the age of six until long past maturity," and he added that "having all his life associated mostly with experimentalists, it has always been with a confident sense of understanding them and of being understood by them" (*CP*, 5.411). We do not have to take Peirce's word for this; we know that this claim is not far from the truth. Peirce was speaking from first-hand experience when he proceeded to give the following characterization of the "typical experimentalist":

> But when you have found, or ideally constructed upon a basis of experience, the typical experimentalist, you will find that whatever assertion you may make to him, he will either understand as meaning that if a given prescription for an experiment ever can be and ever is carried out in act, an experience of a given description will result, or else he will see no sense at all in what you say. (*CP*, 5.411)

On the basis of this observation, Peirce then tells us, he early in life formulated a theory of meaning which he labelled "pragmatism," after Kant's *pragmatisch,* expressing a relation to some definite human purpose (originally from the Greek *pragma*: act, deed, affair). This theory is now restated as follows:

> That a *conception,* that is, the rational purport of a word or expression, lies exclusively in its conceivable bearing upon the conduct of life; so that, since obviously nothing that might not result from experiment can have any direct bearing on conduct, if one can define accurately all the conceivable experimental phenomena which the affirmation or denial of a concept could imply, one will have therein a complete definition of the concept, and *there is absolutely nothing more in it.* (*CP*, 5.412)

We shall shortly see that the emphasis in this statement is on the word "conceivable"; Peirce is not proposing to reduce concepts to actual experimental phenomena. At this point, however, some historical observations are in order, lest the reader be left with the anachronistic impression that Peirce is here generalizing wildly from the limited experience of a highly specialized profession, that of the experimental scientist. Peirce no doubt was, among other things, an experimental scientist in the modern sense, but we miss a great deal if we think that the word 'experimentalist' meant to him what we mean by 'experimental scientist.' Peirce reached intellectual maturity in the 1860s. To put ourselves into the frame of mind of his generation we need to recognize that both today's academic specialization and the vocabulary which reflects that specialization are creations of a later date—roughly of the period 1890–1914—when Peirce's fundamental outlook had long been formed, and by which time he was no longer affiliated with any academic institution. Peirce's generation, we may note, had no equivalent of the word 'scientist' with its modern connotations. The *OED* lists the first occurrence of this word as 1840; it only gradually gained wide use, and until late in the century it was used in a much broader sense than it is today.[1] The word 'science' is of older vintage, but throughout the better part of the nineteenth century, this word denoted any methodical, systematic branch of learning, as the German word *Wissenschaft* does to this day. For the more theoretical and exact branches of learning, the word 'philosophy' was used interchangeably with 'science.' Newton had been a 'natural philosopher'; John Herschel's introduction to scientific method, entitled *Preliminary Discourse on the Study of Natural Philosophy*, appeared in 1831 (second edition 1851); and as late as 1864, in his *System of Logic*, J. S. Mill included a book "On the Logic of the Moral Sciences." The word 'science' (unlike the word 'scientist') was widely used to lend prestige and authority to a variety of intellectual productions; but it denoted neither a particular part of an academic curriculum nor a particular current of intellectual life. At the same time, there were of course people whom *we* identify as 'scientists'; in their own eyes and in the eyes of their contemporaries, the Maxwells, Faradays, and Helmholtzes were 'experimentalists.'

The word 'experimentalist' is considerably older than 'scientist'; according to the *OED*, it first appeared in 1762. By the mid-nineteenth century, 'experimentalism' (the word was introduced by Coleridge in 1834) had become an intellectual movement with a momentum which today may be hard to imagine. Physics had been self-consciously experimental since the sixteenth century, as is evident from the writings of Galileo and Bacon; but it was not until the latter half of the eighteenth century that Lavoisier established chemistry as an experimental science. From this time on, the idea that man can understand only that which he can produce in the laboratory rapidly gained a hold on men's imaginations until, in 1818, it found its unsurpassable popular expression in Dr. Frankenstein's insane urge to create a living being for no other purpose than that of proving to himself that he had understood the mystery of life. In the 1840s and '50s, biology was placed on an experimental footing through the parallel, if discordant, labors of Claude Bernard and Louis Pasteur, and the experimentalist creed found probably its most eloquent statement in Bernard's *Introduction to the Study of Experimental Medicine*, published in 1865. Likewise, in the 1850s Gustav Fechner did his pioneering work in experimental psychology, work which was carried on in Germany by Wilhelm Wundt and, in the United States, by William James, G. Stanley Hall, and Charles Peirce.

In the 1870s, as we noted in chapter 1, Peirce did original, indeed pioneering, experiments in photometry and gravity research. At the same time, he made significant contributions to experimental psychology, especially by devising and performing tests of various of

Fechner's theories. Fechner's perhaps best-known contribution to psychology is his "psycho-physical law," which states that a sensation varies in strength proportionally with the logarithm of its stimulus, or, in simpler terms, that the strength of a sensation increases arithmetically as the force of its stimulus increases geometrically.[2] While engaged in his photometric research at the Harvard Observatory, Peirce found occasion to test this law by comparing the observed brightness of stars with their intensity of light as measured by spectral analysis; in 1878 he reported that he had found Fechner's law approximately correct.[3] Later, at Johns Hopkins, he tested another of Fechner's theories, the theory of the *Differenzschwelle,* that is, the threshold beneath which the senses cannot discriminate between small differences in the degree of stimulus. Together with his student Joseph Jastrow, Peirce carried out a series of experiments on the sense of touch, so designed that the threshold effect, if it did exist, would show up. In their joint paper "On Small Differences of Sensation," published in 1884, Peirce and Jastrow reported that they had found no evidence of any *Differenzschwelle.* To Peirce this was, in fact, the expected result, since it confirmed the applicability to the theory of measurement of the method of least squares, a method which depends on treating errors of observation as continuously measurable quantities (*CP,* 7.21–35).

We see, then, that when Peirce identified himself as an experimentalist and advocated the experimentalist outlook, he was not speaking from the point of view of the specialized laboratory worker. The "pendulum swingers," he remarked self-ironically in 1882, are undoubtedly useful to science; but a man who spends all his time in the laboratory of one particular science "is in danger of profiting but little more from his work than if he were an apprentice in a machine shop" (*CP,* 7.65–66). An experimentalist, in Peirce's time, was a practitioner of laboratory research, yes; but he was also a member of a self-conscious, ambitious, and so far highly successful movement which, in the course of less than a century, had given birth to the sciences of chemistry, biology, and psychology. Peirce, as we shall see, reserved for himself the right to interpret this movement; he did not subscribe to its orthodox creed as it was formulated, for instance, by Bernard. Nonetheless, he shared the fundamental experimental outlook. For someone who shared that outlook and had contributed to the success of the experimentalist movement, it was not unreasonable to believe that the experimental method was capable of indefinite further extension. It was not unreasonable to believe, for instance, that any meaningful statement whatever can sooner or later be put to some experimental test, and hence that a statement can have no other meaning aside from the prescription it provides for a conceivable experiment, together with a prediction of an expected experimental outcome. This is the crux of Peirce's pragmatic theory of meaning, formulated in the early 1870s during his busiest years of experimental research.

b. The problem of universals

Given an intimate relationship between concepts of meaning and concepts of reality, one would expect the pragmatic theory of meaning to have quite definite implications for Peirce's view of reality. One might expect, for instance, that only experimental phenomena and their observed antecedent conditions are real, since all that can be meant by a meaningful statement is a prescription for an experiment together with a prediction of its outcome. Such a view was to be explicitly advocated by John Dewey, who considered himself in this respect a faithful follower of Peirce. In Dewey's view, scientific terms in general do not refer to some "fixed and antecedent reality";[4] these terms are simply tools by which man interacts with, and transforms, his environment. It is part of this view that reality does not contain what we call 'universals'—such as 'man' or 'animal,' as distinct from individual men and individual animals. The general terms employed by science do not, according to Dewey, refer to some real entities called 'universals'; general terms are simply labor-saving devices, "hand-made by man in pursuit of the realization of a particular interest—that of the maximum convertibility of every object of thought into any and every other."[5] The language of science is like a conventionally adopted currency; the only real value supporting the currency lies in those concrete, particular experiences which we can reproduce through experimental action. Dewey at times referred to this view as merely an extended application of what Peirce had called "the laboratory habit of mind,"[6] something which would *prima facie* seem to be borne out by Peirce's 1905 article, briefly quoted in the last section. What is noteworthy, though, is that the next thing Peirce does in his article is disassociate himself explicitly from the pragmatisms of Dewey, James, and F. C. S. Schiller by renaming his own doctrine "pragmaticism"—"which is ugly enough to be safe from kidnappers" (*CP*, 5.414).

Part of what is at issue beween Peirce and his fellow pragmatists is indicated later in the article, where he compares and contrasts his own doctrine with "positivism." Pragmaticism, he holds, will show that "almost every proposition of ontological metaphysics is either meaningless gibberish . . . or else is downright absurd" (*CP*, 5.423). To that extent, pragmaticism may be regarded as a species of positivism, or "prope-positivism." However: "What distinguishes it from other species is, first, its retention of a purefied philosophy; secondly, its full acceptance of the main body of our instinctive beliefs; and thirdly, its strenuous insistence upon the truth of scholastic realism" (*CP*, 5.423).

What is of particular interest for our discussion is Peirce's insistence on the truth of scholastic realism, namely, the doctrine that some universals are in some sense real. To Peirce, the most important of these universals are what we call 'modalities,' such as necessity, possibility, and probability. This point is elaborated in the second of Peirce's articles in *The Monist*. After arguing that critical commonsensism is a consequence of pragmaticism, he goes on to say: "Another doctrine which is involved in Pragmaticism as an essential consequence of it, but which the writer defended before he had formulated, even in his own mind, the principle of pragmaticism, is the scholastic doctrine of realism. . . . Indeed, it is the reality of some possibilities that pragmaticism is most concerned to insist upon" (*CP*, 5.453). Peirce then proceeds to argue for the reality of objective modalities, that of possibility in particular. I shall return to this argument in chapter 3. At this point, a few words must be said about the problem of universals and the solution offered by the scholastic realists.

The medieval problem of universals was briefly this: The scholastic doctors of the thirteenth century shared Aristotle's belief that the individual things which we perceive with our senses are real; at the same time, they were fully aware that we know these individual things only through general concepts. The problem, then, was that of avoiding two opposite but equally skeptical conclusions: Either things are really universal and our perception of them as individual is simply a delusion of the senses (Platonism, or extreme realism), or else things are really individual and our discursive knowledge of them imposes the illusion of universality (nominalism). According to extreme realism, universals exist antecedently to things (*universalia ante res*); according to nominalism, individual things exist first and we subsequently create the universals, which then exist either as mental concepts or as mere words (*universalia post res*). The one position entails that we are deceived by our senses, the other that we are deceived by our reason. To resolve this dilemma the scholastics developed a third position, namely that universals are real, but that their reality consists only in the existence of individual things (*universalia in rebus*). The best-known version of this view, called moderate realism or scholastic realism, is probably that of Thomas Aquinas. Aquinas's solution of the dilemma depends on the Aristotelian distinction between form and matter; the form or essence of things is universal, while things are individuated through their numerically different matters or substances. This solution was rejected by Duns Scotus on the ground that the unique matter of each individual thing is itself an individual thing which can, nonetheless, be discursively grasped only through a general concept—the concept 'matter'—so we are back where we started.

To get at Scotus's own solution we must formulate the problem in terms of two scholastic distinctions: logical distinctions and distinctions *in re*. The nominalist position was that the distinction between a thing's individual existence and its universal essence is a logical distinction, i.e., a distinction in the mind alone. The extreme realist position was that it is a distinction *in re*, or a "real distinction," i.e., a distinction in the thing itself. Scotus avoided this dichotomy by introducing a third type of distinction, the "formal distinction," which is a distinction in the mind, yet with a sort of factual basis. As E. C. Moore puts it, "What Scotus held was that it was possible to make a distinction in the mind which had a basis in fact, but which was still not a real distinction."[7] For instance, a thought process cannot in fact take place in separation from the content of thought; but we are able to separate them in the mind just because they are in fact different, even though not separate. This distinction enabled Scotus to hold both that the distinction between universals and particulars is a purely mental separation, and that this separation is nonetheless possible only by virtue of a real difference between universals and particulars, so that universals are in some sense real. Peirce was to remark that Scotus's realism is separated from nominalism by a hair's breadth (*CP*, 8.12); the same thing, as we shall see, may fairly be said of Peirce's own realism.

This thumbnail sketch of scholastic realism renders apparent certain problems concerning the relationship between realism and pragmatism in Peirce's thought. To start with, although the pragmatic theory of meaning in the intuitively plausible interpretation adopted by Dewey seems to accord well with positivism, it is difficult to see how the metaphysical doctrine of scholastic realism can be reconciled with any species of positivism, which is usually thought of as the denial of the possibility of all metaphysics. Moreover, it is not immediately clear how scholastic realism can be reconciled with the pragmatic theory of meaning in any plausible interpretation. Scholastic realism holds that certain abstract entities are real (although their reality depends on the existence of concrete, particular objects), and that it is to such entities that abstract terms refer. But if the meaning of an abstract term lies exclusively in the conceived experimental consequences of affirming or denying that term of an individual subject, then it would seem superfluous to postulate, in addition, an abstract entity as its reference. Hence, apparently, the reality of abstract entities cannot be a consequence— let alone an essential consequence—of pragmatism. Worse yet, it is not clear that any experimental consequences follow from the affirmation or denial of the realist doctrine itself, and so that doctrine would seem to be "meaningless gibberish" from the point of view of the pragmatic theory of meaning.

In stating these problems I do not wish to imply that they cannot be solved, only that they need to be faced. I should point out that the problem of reconciling Peirce's pragmatism with his realism is a rather central one in Peirce scholarship, and one which has already been discussed by practically everyone who has written at length about Peirce.[8]

My own interpretation will be that there are at least two different and incompatible strands in Peirce's pragmatism. At times, his pragmatism is presented as a criterion of meaning with the avowed purpose of eliminating metaphysics. In this version pragmatism is, I believe, incompatible with realism, as well as untenable in itself. More often, however, pragmatism seems to be advocated as an empirical hypothesis about meaning; as such, it is itself modifiable by experience and cannot, therefore, function as a criterion of meaning, in any strong sense of the word 'criterion.' In this version, pragmatism not only is compatible with realism, it also serves as a premise from which realism may indeed be derived as a consequence. The argument by which Peirce derives his scholastic realism from pragmatism is, I believe, close to the following: Scientists can fully understand the abstract terms of science in terms of conceived experimental consequences and their conditions. But they will have no success in employing abstract terms so understood, unless those terms actually refer to something. Hence we can explain the success of science (when it succeeds) only by assuming the reality, in some sense, of abstract entities; and hence, also, scientists can employ abstract terms with a rational hope of success only if they believe that these terms actually refer to abstract entities. Underlying this argument is Peirce's fundamental and frequently expressed conviction that, although there can be no reality which is incapable of being signified, yet a sign can be analyzed in terms other than those of its meaning. To function as a sign, a sign not only must mean something, it must also stand for something; what this something is cannot be inferred from the meaning of the sign, but must be ascertained empirically. Scholastic realism, which asserts that some signs refer to abstract entities, is therefore itself an empirical proposition, testable by the degree in which the employment of abstract terms contributes essentially to the progress of science.

For instance, the meaning of the word 'force' in classical mechanics can be fully explained in terms of correlations of changes in the velocities of material bodies. To say that a body is acted upon by a particular force is to say that, if a particular acceleration takes place in the system of bodies to which it belongs, a different, specifiable acceleration will follow. To use one of Peirce's examples, that the inkstand on my desk is acted upon by the force of gravity means, among other things, that if the desk were removed the inkstand would fall to the floor with a computable velocity. Still, the force of gravity does not consist in these correlated motions—the acceleration of the inkstand following upon the removal of the desk. The inkstand remains subject to the force of gravity even if the desk is never removed. Thus, that to which the word 'force' refers is different from the *meaning* of the word 'force.' This difference is not easy to express in words, because the meaning and the reference of a word cannot be distinguished within one and the same language. By the word 'force' I refer to force; if pressed further, I can do no more than try to identify the reference by telling my listener what I *mean* by 'force.' In the case of words referring to ordinary physical objects the difference is nonetheless clear enough on an intuitive level. Suppose that by the word 'chair' I mean 'piece of furniture with one seat and a back.' In a conversation with someone who does not know that this is what I mean by 'chair' and who does not himself attach any meaning to the word, I may still succeed in referring to a particular chair by stepping outside the language and pointing at the chair. Obviously, this stratagem is not open to us for identifying abstract entities like forces, which we cannot simply point to. There is, however, an analogous stratagem available; we may step outside the language of physics and use English as a meta-language in which we may talk about physics. In this meta-language we may distinguish between that which physicists mean by 'force' (e.g., 'acceleration') and that to which the word refers, i.e., that feature of the world which permits physicists to predict accelerations with a high degree of accuracy. In the meta-language, then, the statement that there is something to which the physicist's term 'force' refers is an empirically testable statement. Within the meta-language, of course, 'force' has a different and broader meaning, which includes within it the meaning which the word has in physics; and, within the meta-language, the meaning and the reference are, once again, indistinguishable.

In certain respects, my interpretation of Peirce will resemble that advanced by Thomas A. Goudge,[9] since it will entail that there are throughout Peirce's development two opposed and ultimately irreconcilable Peirces. But I do not propose to slice up Peirce's thought in exactly the same place as does Goudge, nor do I want to make quite as deep a cut. This difference may be due to the fact that Goudge dealt with Peirce's thought as a whole, while I have chosen to limit my attention to his theory of inquiry. At any rate, Goudge's interpretation poses an unbridgeable chasm between Peirce's "naturalism" and his "transcendentalism." Without denying that both elements are there, I intend to argue that some of the elements of Peirce's thought which seem transcendental are in fact to be taken empirically, and that some of the elements which seem naturalistic can only be taken as *a priori* dicta. My bisection, then, is between an empirical, or pragmatic, Peirce, who shunned all apriorisms, including aprioristic empiricism, and an empiricist Peirce, whose very empiricism functioned as an *a priori* dogma. Although these two attitudes are opposed to each other, there is nevertheless a fine line of division between them. Peirce's naturalism involves a commitment to proceed empirically and avoid blocking the road of inquiry; but when that commitment is itself set forth as a doctrine it occasionally ossifies into an *a priori* dogma, thus defeating its own purpose. The image of the "two Peirces" is a simple and striking one and will be employed for the sake of convenience; but perhaps a more accurate one is the image of Peirce walking along a brink and sometimes stepping over the edge.

This interpretation will be developed and documented chiefly in chapters 3 and 4. The present chapter will merely make a beginning, by presenting Peirce's early formulations of his realist position.

c. Scholastic realism: Early statements

So far, we have taken a brief look at scholastic realism, but we have not yet attended to the meaning of the term 'realism' in general. This term is notorious for its use in a variety of senses, and Peirce was not a realist in all the senses of the word. We may conveniently distinguish three realisms, with their respective antitheses:

1. *Scholastic* (or moderate) *realism,* which holds that general terms, such as the theoretical terms of science, are not mere linguistic fictions but refer to something real—something which nonetheless exists only by virtue of its particular manifestations. It is opposed both to *nominalism* and to *Platonism* (or extreme realism).

2. *Scientific realism,* which holds that the abstract and idealized theories of science are intended as descriptions of a deeper level of reality, underlying the realm of observable phenomena.[10] Insofar as it is acknowledged that no scientific knowledge reached to date is final or infallible, scientific realism is frequently expressed as the thesis that science progresses by long-run convergence towards truth as an ideal limit. Its chief opponents are *phenomenalism,* which holds that scientific theories are shorthand expressions describing actual, observed phenomena, and *instrumentalism,* which holds that scientific theories are not meant to describe anything but are instruments for predicting individual events.

3. *Representative realism,* which holds that our knowledge is made up of images or ideas which are caused to arise through the action of real, external objects. The real objects are the causes of our knowledge, but we have no direct knowledge of these objects themselves, only of the effects which represent them. This theory, which found its classic expression in the works of Descartes and Locke, is opposed to both *subjective* and *objective idealism.* Both these idealisms hold that only that which can be known is real; but whereas subjective idealism holds the objects of knowledge to be the ideas in the mind of the knower, objective idealism holds the objects to be external to the individual mind.

The catalogue could be lengthened, but the picture is already sufficiently confusing. We may note a certain kinship among nominalism, phenomenalism, instrumentalism, and subjective idealism: all deny the objective reality of universals, and all were lumped together by Peirce under the label 'nominalism.' We may also note a less frequently observed kinship between scholastic and scientific realism: it is at least arguable that a scientific realist, in the above sense, must be committed to the reality of laws and causes, that is, of at least some universals.[11] It is less obvious what the relations of representative realism and objective idealism to the other doctrines are. At this point it is sufficient to note that while Peirce was a scholastic and a scientific realist (he rarely bothered to distinguish between the two), he rejected representative realism in favor of objective idealism. One thing which Peirce emphatically and consistently rejected was the conception of the 'real' as something inaccessible to human knowledge. There can be no *Ding-an-sich*; the admission of such a reality would mean blocking the road of inquiry. As an objective idealist Peirce held that the reality of things depends on their cognizability, while it does not in the least depend on our actual cognition of them. Truth and reality are external to any human mind and to any number of minds; still, nothing which is in principle beyond the reach of inquiry can be recognized as real (*CP*, 5.311).

In Peirce's 1868 article "Some Consequences of Four Incapacities," his argument is chiefly designed to show that scholastic realism is compatible with objective idealism and opposed to representative realism. Having delivered his famous attack on Descartes in 1868, Peirce next developed an argument to the effect that Berkeley's nominalism is the logical consequence of Descartes's representative realism, and that the latter is therefore implicitly a species of nominalism. This argument was published in his review of Frazer's edition of *The Works of George Berkeley* in the *North American Review* for October 1871, and enlarged upon in the manuscript "Logic of 1873," parts of which have been published in the *Collected Papers*. These are the three chief sources for Peirce's early scholastic realism. The "Logic of 1873" contains among other things what appear to be alternate drafts of the 1877–78 articles which were to present pragmatism to the world, in substance if not in name. Later, after 1898, Peirce was to become aware of a certain tension between pragmatism and realism, a tension which he thought he had resolved by 1905. In these early papers, however, there is no awareness of any tension; the two doctrines are presented as two sides of one and the same coin.

The argument of "Some Consequences of Four Incapacities" was briefly considered in chapter 1; it is time now to spell it out in greater detail. Peirce attacks his problem by asking, first, for what purpose do we *need* the concept 'real'? What facts need to be accounted for by the distinction between the real and the unreal? His answer is that the only fact which calls for this distinction is the fact of the experience of having corrected oneself. The real is the object of the correct opinion, as opposed to the one which stood in need of correction. If there were no difference between a true and a false opinion, we should have no reason for exchanging one opinion for another. Given that we often have reason to do this, there is such a difference and this difference is what we express by saying that the one opinion corresponds to something real, while the other does not. This does not mean, however, that the real is simply the object of our present opinion, as opposed to our old opinion. Our present opinion may itself in time come to be replaced by a third opinion, etc., so it would not be rational to abandon the old opinion merely in order to attain the present one. It is an experienced fact that we do not exchange one opinion for another without thinking that we have a reason to do so; explaining this fact means exhibiting the reason, that is, exhibiting that for the sake of which we do change our opinions. And the only good reason for exchanging one opinion for another which we may eventually have to discard is the hope that we may in this way ultimately reach an opinion which we shall have no reason ever to abandon. So the presumed fact of experience that we do have reasons for changing our opinions can be accounted for only by the notion of an opinion which in the long run would withstand all attempts at correction or refutation. The real is the object of that opinion:

> Now the distinction for which alone this fact [i.e., error-elimination] logically called, was between an *ens* relative to private inward determination, and an *ens* such as would stand in the long run. The real, then, is that which, sooner or later, information and reasoning would finally result in, and which is therefore independent of the vagaries of me and you. Thus, the very origin of the conception of reality shows that this conception essentially involves the notion of a COMMUNITY, without definite limits, and capable of a definite increase of knowledge. And so those two series of cognitions—the real and the unreal—consist of those which, at a time sufficiently future, the community will always continue to re-affirm; and of those which, under the same conditions, will ever after be denied. (*CP,* 5.311)

The next step in the argument is to claim that since cognitions need to be formulated in general terms and since the real is simply the object of a particular type of cognition—a cognition which will hold in the long run—it follows that there must be something real corresponding to some general terms: "But it follows that since no cognition of ours is absolutely determinate, generals must have a real existence" (*CP* 5.312).

To amplify, the point is not simply that true cognitions must contain general terms, but that these terms, in order to fulfill their role as signs, must remain essentially *vague*. A sign can function as a sign only so long as it is capable of being interpreted, and interpretation must always be in the form of other signs (*CP*, 5.287). So the generality of a general term can never be exhausted by the enumeration of particular objects, since an exhaustive enumeration would preclude the possibility of further interpretation and hence nullify the sign-character of the term. Vagueness—that is, indefinite capability for further interpretation—is essential to signification; hence, if general terms are to function as signs, their generality cannot be reduced to their particular instances. Since their generality is thus irreducible, and since some general terms are true of something, some generals—that is, universals—must be real.[12]

The philosophical import of this doctrine is then immediately made clear: Peirce does not want to countenance universals as shadowy, occult entities subsisting beyond the bounds of cognition; on the contrary, what he wishes to do is to exorcize that shadowy and occult character which, in his view, nominalism attributes to all real objects. If general concepts are *universalia post res*, needed because they are our only way of grasping the particular things which alone are real, it will then turn out that all real objects are things essentially beyond cognition—an absurd proposition from Peirce's point of view:

> Now this scholastic realism is usually set down as a belief in metaphysical fictions. But, in fact, a realist is simply one who knows no more recondite reality than that which is represented in a true representation. Since, therefore, the word "man" is true of something, that which "man" means is real. (*CP*, 5.312)

Peirce then proceeds to guard himself against the possible charge of Platonism by invoking Duns Scotus's logical distinctions:

> The great argument for nominalism is that there is no man unless there is some particular man. That, however, does not affect the realism of Scotus; for although there is no man of whom all further determination can be denied, yet there is a man, abstraction being made of all further determination. (*CP*, 5.312)

As has been shown by John F. Boler and others,[13] Peirce was thoroughly familiar with medieval philosophy, and it is no accident that he invokes the name of the "Subtle Doctor" Duns Scotus, rather than the names of better known scholastics, such as Abelard or Aquinas. We have already seen Scotus's solution to the problem of universals; for Peirce's version of Scotism we have to turn to an earlier article, published in the *Proceedings of the American Academy of Arts and Sciences* in 1867.

The article entitled "On a New List of Categories" is frequently used as a point of departure for presenting Peirce's early philosophy. It is, however, highly compressed and does not lend itself easily to exposition; I have chosen instead to depend on the article "Some Consequences of Four Incapacities" which presents many of the central themes of the earlier article, though in a more digestible form—by which I do not mean to suggest that either article is to be recommended as bedside reading. What need to be said in general about the 1867 article is that it introduces both Peirce's theory of signs and the list of categories derived from it; the former will be discussed in chapter 4, the latter falls largely outside the scope of this book. Having come to philosophy through reading Kant's *Critique of Pure Reason,* Peirce became convinced that metaphysics needs to be founded on logic. Better acquainted than Kant with formal logic, he came to regard Kant's twelve categories as special cases of three more general categories: *quality, relation,* and *representation.* These are founded on the three references of every sign, the reference to a *ground,* the reference to a *correlate,* and the reference to an *interpretant* (*CP*, 1.555). I shall not at this moment enter into the details of the theory of signs. Suffice it to note here that, for Peirce, all cognition has the form of signs, and that the distinction between the real and the apparent (the "noumenal" and the "phenomenal") can be drawn within the realm of signs, so that we have no need of Kant's *Ding-an-sich* in order to reduce the manifold of perception to unity.

While the article "On a New List of Categories" is best known for Peirce's revision of Kant, it also contains his version of Scotus' "formal distinction." In this article (esp. in *CP*, 1.549) Peirce distinguishes among discrimination, dissociation, and prescission, also called "abstraction." Discrimination is simply a distinction between signs with different meanings; it corresponds to the logical distinction of the scholastics. Dissociation is a separation of those percepts which are not conjoined by constant association. It plays a role similar to that of the real distinction of the scholastics. Prescission is somehow intermediate between the two and is distinguished from both in that it does not involve a symmetrical relation. To illustrate: I may discriminate space from color, and also color from space; that is, each concept can be held in mind independently of the other. I cannot dissociate space from color, or color from space; I cannot perceive either a colorless space or a non-spatial color. I may, however, dissociate red from blue, and also blue from red. These relations, then, are symmetrical. But I may "prescind" space from color—I can conceive of space separated from color—at the same time as I cannot prescind color from space—I cannot conceive of color separated from space. A colorless space is conceivable, a non-spatial color is not. This relation of prescission, then, is asymmetrical; in this respect it differs from both a separation among signs and a separation among percepts, both of which involve symmetrical relations. This means that I have the ability to make a distinction which is not purely logical, yet which does not presuppose that the distinct percepts are in fact separable. So, without supposing that a percept's individual existence and its universal nature are in fact separate entities, I can still make a distinction between them which is something more than just a logical fiction. Without, therefore, holding that universals are separately existing entities, Peirce can still maintain that they are real, in the sense that the mental operation by which we distinguish them is non-arbitrary, being subject to the objective constraint of asymmetry.

As applied to the universal 'man,' I take the implications to be these: I can conceive of man without conceiving of any individual man, although I cannot conceive of a universal man who is separate from all individual men. Universals are not, then, Platonic Ideas subsisting in a realm of their own. Since prescission is asymmetrical, the implication is also that I cannot prescind any individual man from the universal. That is to say, I cannot conceive of an individual man without conceiving of him as an instance of the universal 'man.' Universal concepts, then, necessarily enter into singular judgments, as well as into universal ones.

It is time to note one complication in Peirce's realism. While he emphatically affirmed the truth of realism and denied the truth of nominalism, he did not use the word 'real' in quite the sense in which it has been used by most nominalists. Nominalists have usually wanted to deny that universals actually *exist* somewhere "out there"; and this Peirce, too, denies. To Peirce, only individual things exist; this follows trivially from the meaning of the word 'existence,' namely, that mode of being which belongs to individuals. His argument is directed, not against avowed nominalists only, but against all those who would use the word 'real' as synonymous with 'existing.' This includes some self-styled realists, namely those espousing some sort of representative realism. The drift of the argument is explicit in his 1871 review of *The Works of George Berkeley,* where Peirce outlines two conceptions of reality, one nominalistic, the other realistic. Initially, Peirce adopts the definition of the 'real' as "that which is not whatever we happen to think it is, but is unaffected by what we may think of it" (*CP*, 8.12). This recalls his 1868 formulation: "that which is independent of the vagaries of me and you." This conception may, however, be further elucidated in two different ways. The nominalistic one is formulated as follows within his argument against representative realism:

> We have . . . nothing immediately present to us but thoughts. These thoughts, however, have been caused by sensations, and those sensations are constrained by something out of the mind. This thing out of the mind, which directly influences sensation, and through sensation thought, because it *is* out of the mind, is independent of how we think it, and is, in short, the real. (*CP*, 8.12)

In this view, Peirce continues, universals cannot be regarded as real. It may be admitted, in a sense, that one man is like another, but this cannot mean that two men, considered as external realities, really have anything in common. We do not know these external realities, we know only their sensible effects upon the mind. We may say that two sensations caused by two different objects are capable of being represented indifferently by one and the same sign 'man,' but we cannot therefore attribute any common nature to the two external objects causing these sensations.

So far, Peirce is clearly siding with Berkeley against Descartes and Locke. More immediately, as Bruce Kuklick has pointed out,[14] he is polemicizing against the Scottish "common-sense realist" William Hamilton, as well as against his American disciple Francis Bowen, Alford Professor of Natural Religion, Moral Philosophy, and Civil Polity at Harvard during Peirce's student days and for several decades after. Having thus taken Berkeley as an ally in rejecting the realism predominant in his own day, Peirce then turns against Berkeley's nominalism. The real, that which is independent of how we think about it, need not be an external *cause* of our thoughts, it may be thought of, rather, as the *goal* towards which all human thought is universally tending through the gradual elmination of everything one-sided, accidental, and arbitrary in the thought of any individual:

> There is . . . to every question a true answer, a final conclusion, to which the opinion of every man is constantly gravitating. . . . The arbitrary will or other individual peculiarities of a sufficiently large number of minds may postpone the general agreement in that opinion indefinitely; but it cannot affect what the character of that opinion shall be when it is reached. This final opinion, then, is independent, not indeed of thought in general, but of all that is arbitrary and individual in thought; is quite independent of how you, or I, or any number of men think. Everything, therefore, which will be thought to exist in the final opinion is real, and nothing else. (*CP*, 8.12)

This conception of reality, Peirce concludes, is realistic, "because general conceptions enter into all judgments, and therefore into true opinions. Consequently a thing in the general is as real as in the concrete" (*CP*, 8.14). This, of course, is the 1868 argument over again.

The question must now be raised, does Peirce disagree with Berkeley *only* over the meaning of the word 'real'? Does he agree that there are no real objects actually existing outside the mind and acting upon our senses? Is he, in short, really a subjective idealist? The answer, I think, is no; but Peirce is anything but clear on the issue. In his manuscripts from 1873 (the "Logic of 1873") he returns to the question time and again, each time coming up with a different answer. Thus, in chapter 4 of the "Logic of 1873" Peirce begins by noting a dilemma arising from the common-sense conception of external realities acting causally upon our thoughts. In this conception there is a causal output from the physical world into a mental world, something which is contradictory to the principles of mechanics (MS, 367, pp. 17–18)—meaning, presumably, contradictory to the Law of Conservation of Energy. He then goes on to show how the dilemma is avoided in the realistic conception of reality already outlined, and finally raises the question of "whether there may not be some other reality which is external to us in some sense other than this" (*ibid.*, p. 23). This, he replies, is "a rather idle question," since all the facts which require the hypothesis of an external reality have been accounted for by his own simple hypothesis, and there is consequently no need for a more complex hypothesis to account for the same facts. Moreover, "it can mean nothing at all to say that any other reality than this exists" (*ibid.*). Here, it seems, actually existing external objects cannot be meaningfully designated as real, which makes one suspect that Peirce is a realist only by virtue of using the word 'real' in a rather peculiar sense.

In an alternate draft of the same chapter, Peirce begins by giving essentially the same answer: "There is a complete vacuity of meaning in saying that independent of all thought there exist such things as we shall think in the final opinion" (MS, 372, p. 7). Yet later in the same manuscript he makes it clear that he does not mean to deny the actual, present existence of real things, only to give an equivalent reformulation to the assertion of their existence:

> It is true that the belief is future and may not even be attained, while the reality actually exists. But the act of believing is one thing, the object of belief another. Nor need anyone who is familiar with the conceptions of physical science shrink from admitting that the existence of a present reality is in one sense made by a contingent event. Nobody hesitates to say that a leaden weight resting upon a table is really

heavy. Yet to say that it is heavy only means that if it is free to move it will approach the earth. (*Ibid.*, p. 13)

Likewise, according to modern physics, matter is nothing but the focus of force, and force only consists in the fact that if something happens something else happens: "Thus we find the physicists, the exactest of thinkers, holding in regard to those things which they have studied most exactly, that their existence depends on their manifestations or rather on their manifestability" (*ibid.*, p. 14). Here, to the best of my knowledge, we find the earliest formulation of the pragmatic theory of meaning (although it was certainly hinted at by 1868, as W. B. Gallie pointed out many years ago).[15] As we shall see in the next chapter, Peirce for a while equivocated over the all-important distinction between "manifestation" and "manifestability." If the reality of an object were to consist only in its manifestations, the conception of reality would be a purely subjective one. In the above quote, however, Peirce says ". . . or *rather* on their manifestability," which is surely something external to the individual mind.

And finally, in the manuscript "Of Reality" from about 1873, Peirce once more sketches the causal theory of the representative realists and comments:

This statement of the matter is entirely justified upon logical principles & perhaps no modern philosopher has questioned it. Yet I entertain no doubt that it is only another way of stating the fact that a fate leads every investigator to a predestined conclusion & not a solution of that paradox by means of any new fact. (MS, 373, p. 6; see also *CP*, 7.339–40)

What emerges from these manuscripts is this picture. To say that real objects actually exist externally to the mind and act upon the mind is both meaningful and true. A pragmatic analysis of meaning shows that this statement means that human opinion tends in the long run towards a final agreement on the reality of such objects. Those objects which in the final opinion are thought to be real are real now; and those objects which in the final opinion are thought to have existed now do exist now. What is purely vacuous is to say that the assertion of the existence of objects means something in addition to that which is brought out by this pragmatic analysis. There are still problems of interpretation, but these had better be postponed until our discussion of pragmatism in chapter 3.

Peirce's ambiguous attitude towards Kant is worth some attention. Later in life, after having discovered certain logical problems in the pragmatic analysis of meaning, Peirce was to decide that Kant was really a nominalist; in the 1870s, however, he regarded himself as a reformed Kantian, a Kantian without the thing-in-itself. In his 1871 review he admits to a species of phenomenalism; but, he adds, "it is the phenomenalism of Kant, and not that of Hume" (*CP*, 8.15). Kant's "Copernican step," he continues, "was nothing else than to consider every conception and intuition which enters necessarily into the experience of an object, and which is not transitory and accidental, as having objective validity. In short, it was to regard the reality as the normal product of mental action, not as the incognizable cause of it" (*CP*, 8.15). Without pretending to be a Kant scholar, I believe Kant would agree to the first of these statements, but not to the second. While Kant attributed objectivity to the phenomenal realm, his conception of the real was that of the *noumenon,* or thing-in-itself. In 1871, Peirce explicitly rejects the notion of the thing-in-itself, while at the same time embracing the notion of the noumenon:

> This theory of reality is instantly fatal to the idea of a thing in itself,— a thing existing independently of all relation to the mind's conception of it. Yet it would by no means forbid, but rather encourage us, to regard the appearances of sense as only signs of the realities. Only, the realities which they represent would not be the unknowable cause of sensation, but *noumena,* or intelligible conceptions which are the last products of the mental action which is set in motion by sensation. (*CP*, 8.13)

Thirty-five years later Peirce was to define the 'real' as "something noumenal, intelligible, conceivable, and utterly unlike a thing-in-itself" (*CP*, 5.553). And in 1878, in *Photometric Researches,* he was to define 'noumenal light' as "light considered purely as something in the external world," and 'phenomenal light' as "light considered as an appearance, and as a function of the sensation."[16] As appears from the context, the distinction is that between light as waves measurable by a spectroscope and light as observable illuminance measurable by a photometer. And, whereas light waves are not directly observable, spectral analysis is still an empirical procedure, so Peirce's noumenal light would seem to fall within Kant's phenomenal realm. Peirce was deeply conscious of the ethics of terminology, and time and again he reproached those who used the word 'real' in a sense different from that intended by Duns Scotus, who introduced the word into philosophy (e.g. in *CP*, 5.430, MSS, 438 and 440). Here, however, he seems *prima facie* to have broken his own rule by using Kant's technical term 'noumenon' in a sense widely different from Kant's.

Bruce Altshuler has pointed out that there is a sense in which Peirce's use of the word 'noumenon' is Kantian, in that it corresponds to Kant's negatively determined concept of the noumenon as a limit to our understanding.[17] Kant did not pretend to have a positive concept of the thing-in-itself; it is identified only as whatever lies beyond the limit to the understanding, as that of which we know nothing. As Kant put it in his *Critique of Pure Reason*: "The concept of the noumenon is thus a merely *limiting concept,* the function of which is to curb the pretensions of sensibility; and it is therefore only of negative employment."[18] The thing-in-itself is thus referred to only negatively, without being denoted by any defining characteristics; our concept of the thing-in-itself is a totally empty concept: "The problematic thought which leaves open a place for them serves only, like an empty space, for the limitation of empirical principles, without itself containing or revealing any other object of knowledge beyond the sphere of those principles."[19] Kant may have been speaking of a 'limit' only in the sense of a boundary or barrier; this, at least, is Altshuler's reading. Peirce more frequently uses the word 'limit' in a semantically different but empirically equivalent sense, namely in the mathematical sense of the limit of a function. The noumenon, for Peirce, is the object of true opinion, and the true opinion is that towards which inquiry converges as a limit. It may be recalled that Peirce's professional experience of truth-seeking largely consisted in determining the 'true' value of a magnitude as the limit towards which a series of observed values converged. How this concept can be applied to the convergence of opinion, rather than that of numerical values, has been shown by H. S. Thayer in his history of pragmatism: For any statement that is being investigated, the limit towards which opinion converges is the limit of convergence for the relative frequency of the number of assenters to that statement to the number of both assenters and dissenters.[20] So understood, Peirce's concept of the final opinion of inquiry as noumenal is empirically equivalent to Kant's negative concept of the noumenon; only, unlike Kant, Peirce denies that beyond the limit there is something of which we know nothing.

Peirce's realism, as we have seen, hinges on a concept of the real as the object of true opinion. The ambiguities noted in this concept of the real can be more clearly brought out and to some extent resolved through an examination of Peirce's concept of truth, to which we shall now turn.

d. Peirce's concept of truth

In 1868, as we have seen (section c, above), Peirce characterized real cognitions as "those which, at a time sufficiently future, the community will always continue to re-affirm" (*CP*, 5.311). In his 1871 review of Berkeley, he re-stated this view by characterizing the real as the object of the final conclusion "to which the opinion of every man is constantly gravitating" (*CP*, 8.12). There is implicit here a particular concept of truth, which in the 1871 review is made explicit:

> All human thought and opinion contains an arbitrary, accidental element, dependent on the limitations in circumstances, power, and bent of the individual; an element of error, in short. But human opinion universally tends in the long run to a definite form, which is the truth. Let any human being have enough information and exert enough thought upon any question, and the result will be that he will arrive at a certain definite conclusion, which is the same that any other mind will reach under sufficiently favorable circumstances. (*CP*, 8.12)

In 1901, in Baldwin's *Dictionary of Philosophy and Psychology*, Peirce was to re-state this conception of truth in the form of a more

explicit definition: "Truth is that concordance of an abstract statement with the ideal limit towards which endless investigation would
tend to bring scientific belief, which concordance the abstract statement may possess by virtue of the confession of its inaccuracy and
one-sidedness, and this confession is an essential ingredient of truth"
(*CP,* 5.565). As an example Peirce mentions π as the ideal limit
towards which 3.14159 . . . will approach through continued calcula-
tion of decimals, but to which no numerical expression will exactly
correspond. This is what we call an "ideal limit" theory of truth. So
understood, truth is clearly something absolute and objective, which
does not depend on actual human opinion, and that to which true
statements correspond is as real as anyone could wish. It may
therefore be taken as equivalent to the more familiar definition of
truth as correspondence of a belief (or a statement) with reality. And,
as a matter of fact, Peirce did not advance his ideal-limit theory as a
rival to the correspondence theory. His view was rather that the concept of an ideal limit reveals more fully what is meant by the concept
of correspondence. In Peirce's view, it is not *wrong* to speak of truth
as correspondence with facts; it just is not very informative (*CP,*
5.565 ff.; MS, 373, p. 6).

It should be sufficiently clear that around 1870 Peirce held truth
to be correspondence with reality—because that is how he defined
'reality.' To determine whether his conception of truth at this time
was an objective and absolute conception or a subjective and relative
one, we must avoid using the words 'real' and 'reality,' because it is
precisely the meaning of these words that we wish to throw light on.
We may interpret Peirce's early statements on truth as either a
"consensus" theory, which makes truth consist in some actual future
consensus and hence makes truth relative to human opinion, or else
as an ideal-limit theory, like the one he was to expound in 1901.
Which interpretation we choose depends on how we interpret two
key notions in his early formulations: the notion of "the long run"
and the notion of "community."

Some commentators have taken Peirce's conception of truth to
refer to a consensus reachable in a finitely long run, on the grounds,
among others, that the human race will presumably be extinct within
a finite time. This interpretation was suggested by Bertrand Russell,

who added that this would make truth "depend upon the opinions of the last man left alone as the earth becomes too cold to support life."[21] Russell rightly went on to conclude that this was not what Peirce had meant; but a similar interpretation has since been defended by John W. Lenz, who has argued that the expression "at a time sufficiently future" (in *CP,* 5.311) must refer to some point in time in the finite future.[22] If this were what Peirce intended, he would run into the following problem. Suppose some day human opinion has converged on a fixed value on every disputed question. For this value to represent the ultimate limit of convergence—that is, the truth—it will have to be upheld until, within a finite time, mankind becomes extinct. Since, as Peirce avers, there is an element of subjectivity, arbitrariness, and error in the opinion of any finite number of men, there will also be an element of error attached to the opinions of the last generation of men, since these opinions will have been held by only a finite number of men. Once it is granted that *any* finite number of men may be blinded by collective prejudices, we have no reason to exempt the last generation of men from this general rule. So, if Peirce's conception of truth were that of a limit reachable in a finitely long run, it would not yield a conception of reality as independent of human opinion, and Peirce's realism would be indistinguishable from the phenomenalism of Berkeley—or of Hume, for that matter.

There is, however, a fair amount of evidence that even in the years 1868 through 1871 Peirce thought of "the long run" as an infinitely long run. If so, then truth is identified with that unshakeable consensus towards which human opinion *would* converge, *if* inquiry were to go on for a sufficiently long time for opinion to converge towards a consensus which would thereafter never be broken, no matter for how long inquiry were then to continue. If we leave open the question of whether inquiry *will* go on long enough to establish such a consensus, the resulting conception of truth will be an objective and absolute one. This interpretation of the long run is, I think, the one which is required by Peirce's insistence that the final opinion is to be an opinion which is independent of all that is arbitrary and individual in thought (*CP,* 8.12). That this is also the interpretation which Peirce had in mind is indicated by his statement that agreement in the final opinion may be postponed "indefinitely" (*ibid.*), and that the real depends on the opinion of a community "without definite limits" (*CP,* 5.311). The same interpretation is indicated by Peirce's unpublished lecture notes on logic from 1870, where he says of the ultimate opinion: "Indeed this opinion is in one sense an ideal inasmuch as *more* experience & reasoning may always be had" (MS, 587, p. 5). Finally, in 1878 Peirce made this interpretation quite explicit by writing in his *Popular Science Monthly* articles that, even should the human race become extinct before the truth had been reached and then be replaced by another race of rational beings, then that race would ultimately converge on the true opinion (*CP,* 5.408). Truth is here obviously not made relative to human experience. It seems fair to conclude that the ideal-limit theory, to be made explicit in 1901, is already present in these early papers.

If, then, truth is something absolutely independent of human opinion and indefinitely beyond the grasp of human knowledge, how, one may ask, does it differ from a thing-in-itself? The answer is the one suggested earlier: truth does not differ from Kant's negative conception of the noumenon as a limit to our understanding. As Peirce was to make clear in his dictionary article in 1901, an essential ingredient of truth is the confession that our statements do *not* possess it (*CP,* 5.565). The concept of truth as a property actually possessed by a statement is a meaningless one, "an empty space" in Kant's formulation. The only truth of which we can have any conception, hence the only truth there can be, is that towards which we can attempt to bring our opinions closer, even though we cannot attain it, in the same way that we have a conception of π because we know how to bring 3.14159 . . . *closer* to π, even though we know that we can never make it equal π.

A second question arises: if Peirce in the years 1868 to 1871 held an ideal-limit theory of truth, why did he couch it in the terminology of "the community," thereby misleadingly suggesting a consensus theory? Part of the answer may lie in Murphey's suggestion, quoted in the last chapter (section f), that Peirce was really a romantic idealist who masqueraded as an empiricist in order to appear scientifically respectable. We might even reinforce Murphey's interpretation with some supplementary evidence. The consensus theory of truth, as it happens, was an extremely fashionable one among nineteenth-century scientists. Its classic expression is found in Sir John Herschel's *Preliminary Discourse,* published in 1831, which was something of a methodological catechism to natural scientists of Peirce's generation. In Herschel's words, "the grand and indeed only character of truth is its capability of enduring the test of universal experience, and coming unchanged out of every possible form of fair discussion."[23] The ability of experimental science to transcend national boundaries and command the assent of Germans, Frenchmen, and Englishmen alike was, according to Herschel, not just a contingent historical fact, but was part and parcel of what constituted scientific knowledge: "Knowledge can neither be adequately cultivated nor adequately enjoyed by a few . . . It acquires not, perhaps, a greater certainty, but at least a confirmed authority and a probable duration, by universal assent."[24]

In 1865, the same conception of scientific knowledge, if not of truth, was voiced by Claude Bernard, in his *Introduction to the Study of Experimental Medicine*: "Systems and doctrines are individual; they are meant to be immutable and to preserve their personal aspect. The experimental method, on the other hand, is impersonal; it destroys individuality by uniting and sacrificing everyone's particular ideas, and turning them to the advantage of universal truth as established with the help of the experimental criterion."[25]

Finally, in 1892, Herschel's consensus theory was to be repeated by Peirce's great adversary Karl Pearson, in his enormously popular *The Grammar of Science*: "The touchstone of science is the universal validity of its results for all normally constituted and duly instructed minds."[26] We need not, therefore, regard the consensus theory as a peculiarly Peircean doctrine, or seek any special reason why Peirce should have held to it. His adherence to it, it might seem, would be sufficiently explained by the supposition that he accepted as much as he could of the self-image of contemporary science so as to legitimize his form of realism in the eyes of his fellow experimentalists.

So far, Murphey's interpretation seems a plausible one. It receives further support from Altshuler's argument to the effect that Peirce's conception of truth not only does not need the concept of the community, but is in fact individualistic and anti-communitarian in the extreme. The function of the notion of an ideal, unlimited community is to eliminate the arbitrariness that attaches to the individual *qua* actual person and *qua* member of an actual community, so as to get at the purely rational agent who is free of all those biases and prejudices which form the warp and woof of man's social existence. Altshuler compares this idea to John Rawls's idea of the "veil of ignorance," which is meant to insure fair and impartial judgment, and he traces both ideas to Kant.[27]

Altshuler's argument is persuasive; identification with a community does seem to lead to extreme individualism as soon as the community is conceived of in sufficiently broad terms to turn it into an empty notion. Historically, the union of individualism and universalism in opposition to collectivism and cultural particularism can be traced back to the Stoics and Epicureans, of whom Alasdair MacIntyre has written, somewhat disapprovingly:

> The question now is not, In what forms of social life can justice express itself? or, What virtues have to be practiced to produce a communal life in which certain ends can be accepted and achieved? but, What must I do to be happy? or, What goods can I achieve as a private person? The human situation is such that the individual finds his moral environment in his place in the universe rather than in any social or political framework. It is salutary to observe that in many ways the universe is a more parochial and narrow environment than Athens was.[28]

In the same way, it may be argued, Peirce identified truth with the opinion of an ideal, unlimited community which never has existed and never will exist, i.e., with the opinion of an ideally informed and maximally rational individual, while couching this conception of truth in terms of consensus within a community because this is what contemporary scientists already believed truth to be.

Certain facts are not, however, accounted for by this interpretation. Peirce was not a professional philosopher interested in flattering the natural scientists of his day; he was himself a scientist, and a fairly self-confident one, who seems never to have doubted his own authority to speak on behalf of the "experimentalists" or "men of science," to use two of his own favorite expressions. As we shall see in chapter 4, he never hesitated to take on the most influential spokesmen of contemporary science, such as Kirchhoff, Bernard, and Pearson, more often than not exaggerating his differences with them. If he formulated his theory of truth in terms of the opinion of the community, there is *prima facie* reason to believe that he thought the notion of the community played an essential role within that theory. Likewise, although Altshuler is right in pointing out that the notion of an ideal, unlimited community is indistinguishable from the notion of individual rationality, we still need to account for the fact that Peirce habitually explained the notion of individual rationality in terms of the procedures of an *actual* community, namely the community of scientific investigators. So, for instance, Peirce wrote in 1868: "Hence, if disciplined and candid minds carefully examine a theory and refuse to accept it, this ought to create doubts in the mind of the author of the theory himself" (*CP,* 5.265). Similarly, in his article on "Scientific Method" in Baldwin's *Dictionary* in 1902, he was to write:

> The next most vital factor of the method of modern science [i.e. after the love of truth] is that it has been made social. On the one hand, what a scientific man recognizes as a fact of science must be something open to anybody to observe, provided he fulfils the necessary conditions, external and internal. As long as only one man has been able to see a marking upon the planet Venus, it is not an established fact. . . . On the other hand, the method of science is social in respect to the solidarity of its efforts. The scientific world is like a colony of insects, in that the individual strives to produce that which he himself cannot hope to enjoy. (*CP,* 7.87)

To Peirce, rationality consists in following the scientific method; this method, in its turn, is inherently social, inherently bound up, that is, with the life of an actual community. Peirce did not, then, draw individualistic conclusions from his reliance on the notion of an ideal community as the locus of truth. Yet such conclusions would seem to be logically inescapable, in which case Peirce would be guilty of a deep inconsistency, in operating with two incompatible notions of community. In concluding this chapter, I shall endeavor to show that this is not necessarily so.

e. Pragmatic realism: A preliminary statement

The full statement of Peirce's pragmatic realism must wait until after we have examined his pragmatic theory of meaning and its place within his theory of signs. At this point, the gist of the matter may be put as follows. To the user and the interpreter of a sign, there is no difference between what a sign means and what it refers to. For instance, the word 'force' is used to refer to forces; if pressed to identify the reference, the user can do so only by specifying what he means by 'force.' To the user, the reference is the meaning, which in turn consists in the observable results of possible actions, that is, in possible experimental results. To the student of the theory of signs, however, meaning and reference are distinct; from his vantage point it can be seen that the sign user will have success in his use of signs only if these signs do in fact refer. Physicists, for instance, can have some success in their manipulation of the sign 'force' only if there is some feature of the physical world which ensures that the same accelerations will occur under the same conditions, so that accelerations are experimentally reproducible and hence predictable.

Let us assume with Peirce that science progresses, and that it has progressed with astonishing success for a while. As spectators at the game of science, we may then attempt to explain this success by the hypothesis that there is a real, external world, and that science progresses through the application of a method which is so designed as to result in ever closer approximation to truth in the sense of agreement with this real world. If this is the only hypothesis on which the behavior of scientists can result in progress, it follows that it is rational for scientists to behave as they do only if they are motivated by a search for truth in this absolute sense, that is, only if the absolute concept of truth functions as a regulative idea for science. However, 'correspondence with reality' cannot be the *meaning* of 'truth' for the scientist who seeks truth. This notion has no methodological content; it does not tell the scientist anything about what to do in his research, or what to expect from his actions. Each one of his beliefs, no matter how erroneous, is a belief about what the facts are, so each belief is *eo ipso* a belief that it itself corresponds with reality. In the words of "The Fixation of Belief": "we think each one of our beliefs to be true, and, indeed, it is a mere tautology to say so" (*CP*, 5.375).[29] The scientist does not, indeed, believe that *all* his beliefs are true, but the notion of truth as correspondence does not tell him anything about which ones are true and which ones are not, or about how to go about finding this out.

From the vantage point of the observer the notion of truth as correspondence is adequate (although it will no longer do when applied to his own beliefs). The scientist needs an equally absolute notion of truth as a regulative idea, but an idea cannot regulate anything unless it is explicable in terms of experimental procedures and their outcomes. Of course the scientist, like everyone else, believes that his beliefs correspond with facts, but this is saying no more than that he believes what he does believe. This belief cannot act as a spur to further inquiry, or as a guide to direct that inquiry. The deadlock is broken by the ideal-limit theory of truth. The limit towards which inquiry will converge in the long run is an absolute notion, as absolute as that of correspondence with reality. It is also, to be sure, beyond any actual experience; still, it can be given a meaning by extrapolation from the experience of that finite process by which scientists have so far reached agreements, and of the experimental procedures involved in that process. Any agreement so far reached may be spurious, but it would be a fantastic coincidence if they all were; and the final agreement, if it ever will be reached, can be reached only by the further employment of those same procedures by which agreement has been reached in the past. As these procedures essentially involve social cooperation within limited, actual communities of investigators, the content of the notion of the ideal limit is that of the opinion of an ideal, unlimited community—a notion formed by extrapolation from actual experience of the lives of scientific communities. Although the ideal community is not identical with any actual community, yet the experience of actual communities gives meaning to the concept of an ideal community.[30] So Peirce's two notions of community are complementary, not incompatible.

In the above, I have made use of Peirce's distinction between the vantage point of the user of a sign and that of the student of signs— the vantage points of "semiosis" and "semiotic," respectively. From the point of view of the scientist's use of signs, meaning and reference are indistinguishable; the distinction can be made only when the sign activity called "science" is itself made the subject of a second-order, semiotic inquiry. As applied to scientists as sign users, this distinction is controversial in that it may seem to involve an appeal to the aprioristic vantage point of the omniscient observer who is capable of comparing the scientists' beliefs with the Real World. In recent years, W. V. O. Quine has emphatically denied that there is such a vantage point: the best knowledge we have of the real world, in Quine's view, is the knowledge furnished by contemporary science, and in particular by contemporary physics.[31] In this respect Quine has explicitly allied himself with John Dewey,[32] but his view is also reminiscent of Peirce's view as presented in chapter 1 of this book, to the effect that there is no independent vantage point from which to justify or criticize our entire body of beliefs. Where Quine differs from Peirce is in equating the vantage point of contemporary knowledge as a whole with the vantage point of contemporary physics; Peirce's position, set forth, e.g., in *CP*, 1.116–20, is that physics may well be the *best* contemporary knowledge, but it certainly does not constitute *all* of contemporary knowledge—merely a fraction of it, in fact. For one thing, the scope of our physical science to date is extremely limited and covers only a fraction of the world as we know it from everyday experience. In addition, most of us do not know enough of the physics of our day to be able to see the world as a whole through the spectacles of physics, and even the professional physicist derives most of his knowledge about the world—to the extent that such things can be measured—from sources outside the laboratory. The vantage point from which Peirce philosophizes includes not only a first-hand acquaintance with science, but also "those universal experiences which confront every man in every waking hour of his life" (*CP*, 1.246). What is implied, then, is not the unattainable vantage point of the omniscient observer, but the obviously attainable, extra-scientific vantage point of everyday experience. This, I might add in conclusion, is in fact the only vantage point from which we can even make sense of certain statements one might want to make concerning scientific progress. To some extent, to be sure, "progress" can be discussed and judged from the vantage point of science itself. So long as the theoretical framework of a particular science remains constant, scientists can and do employ this framework as their standard for measuring how far they have made progress on empirical problems arising within this framework. But when we say, for instance, that science has progressed since the Renaissance, we are not talking about this kind of progress. What we mean is either that there has been unbroken empirical progress across changes of theory, or else that the successive replacements of one theory by another have themselves been somehow progressive. From the vantage point of present-day physics the claim that there has been this kind of progress in physics is empty: it amounts to no more than the claim that present-day physics is superior to the physics of the past. And this claim is already implicit in the choice of contemporary physics as one's vantage point. If we are to grant, as practically all non-philosophers would, that physics has enjoyed several centuries of progress, we are making a statement which does not even make sense except on the assumption that an alternative vantage point, outside contemporary physics, is available to us.

This concludes my presentation of Peirce's early scholastic realism. I do not claim to have solved all the problems arising from this doctrine; some of them, indeed, will become apparent only through a closer examination of the pragmatic theory of meaning. This will occupy us in chapter 3, after which I shall return to Peirce's realism for a fuller exposition and a more detailed statement of my interpretation.

Chapter Three
Pragmatism as a Criterion
of Meaning

a. The pragmatic maxim: Original statement

THE REALISM EXAMINED in chapter 2 was already "pragmatic"; in the years 1868 to 1873 Peirce developed realism and pragmatism as two aspects of one and the same doctrine. The pragmatic theory of meaning did not, however, become a matter of public record until 1878, ten years after the first published statement of Peirce's scholastic realism. One cannot say everything at once; for convenience of presentation I have chosen to follow the chronology of publications. It should be stressed that this is nothing more than a matter of convenience; as is clear from the manuscripts considered in the last chapter, the chronology of publications does not reflect the chronology of Peirce's thinking.

In this chapter we shall examine Peirce's theory of meaning, as summed up in his "pragmatic maxim." For purposes of interpretation this theory will be explicitly compared with later attempts at formulating a verifiability criterion of meaning. Since this is hardly a novel approach, I trust I have learned enough from earlier attempts to avoid the more obvious pitfalls of this line of interpretation. I should note, however, the general objection recently voiced by Murphey that while comparison of Peirce with later thinkers may throw light on those later thinkers, it throws no light at all on Peirce.[1] It should be clear from the Introduction that I disagree with this; though an enthusiastic adherent of the historical approach to textual interpretation, I must stop short of extreme historicism. In order to interpret the thoughts of the past to a present audience the historian

of ideas must establish points of contact with two termini, two
contexts: that of the writer whom he is interpreting, and that of the
audience to whom he is interpreting. Thus he cannot rest content
with recording what X said, when he said it, and under what circumstances; he must also try to explain the meaning of what X said (not
merely X's subjective intentions, but also the logical consequences
implied by his statements), and he must also try to explain why we
should care.

The first published statement of Peirce's theory of meaning is to
be found in the popular article "How To Make Our Ideas Clear,"
published in *Popular Science Monthly* in 1878 as a sequel to "The
Fixation of Belief." Peirce here resumes his running argument with
Descartes in the form of a critical examination of the latter's notion of
"clear and distinct ideas." The conclusion is that Descartes's two criteria of clearness and distinctness do not suffice to distinguish different ideas or to pick out empty verbalisms which fail to express any
idea. For these purposes we need what Peirce calls "the third grade
of clearness"; this can be attained through the application of the
following maxim: "Consider what effects, that might conceivably
have practical bearings, we conceive the object of our conception to
have. Then, our conception of these effects is the whole of our conception of the object" (*CP*, 5.402).

When Peirce originally presented his paper to the Metaphysical
Club in 1873, he called this maxim the "pragmatic maxim," a term
which for popularization purposes he omitted from the published version. As we recall from chapter 1, one of the topics discussed in the
club was Alexander Bain's definition of 'belief' as "that which a man
is prepared to act upon," of which pragmatism was "scarce more
than a corollary" (*CP*, 5.12).[2] James, who revived the pragmatic
maxim in 1898, was to understand this definition to mean that belief
consists in action; Peirce, on the other hand, emphasized as early as
1878 that belief consists in a disposition or habit of action: "The
whole function of thought is to produce habits of action" (*CP*, 5.400).
A thought, then, is identified by the belief to which it leads, i.e., the
habit which it produces; two formulae which produce the same habit
are not, therefore, different thoughts, even though they may be
clothed in different words and accompanied by different feelings and

sensations. A habit, in its turn, consists of the totality of different actions which it might occasion, under all conceivable circumstances. So, if the total practical effect of a thought—or a concept—consists in the formation of a habit, then our conception of the effect—which constitutes the entire meaning of the concept first mentioned—will consist of a series of conditional statements describing what effects would result from our actions on all conceivable occasions if the concept were truly affirmed of its object. For our concept to have any pragmatic meaning both the antecedent and the consequent of each of these conditionals must be formulated in observational terms: "What the habit depends on is *when* and *how* it causes us to act. As for the *when*, every stimulus to action is derived from perception; as for the *how*, every purpose of action is to produce some sensible result" (*CP*, 5.400). This point was to be reiterated twenty-five years later, in one of Peirce's most eloquent passages: "The elements of every concept enter into logical thought at the gates of perception and make their exit at the gate of purposive action; and whatever cannot show its passport at both those two gates is to be arrested as unauthorized by reason" (*CP*, 5.212). Put more pedantically, the meaning of every concept, no matter how abstract, must be expressible with reference to the observable effects of actions which the predication of the concept of some object would occasion under circumstances describable in observational terms.

All of this is not yet as clear as one could wish; in fact, the title "How To Make Our Ideas Clear" is beginning to appear unintentionally ironic.[3] Later, as we saw in chapter 2, section a, Peirce was to express himself much more clearly by saying that an experimentalist (such as himself) would understand any statement whatever as meaning only that if an experiment of a given kind were to be carried out, an experience of a given kind would follow (*CP*, 5.411). Although experiments are not explicitly mentioned in the 1878 formulation of the maxim, still they must have been uppermost in Peirce's mind throughout the 1870s. Moreover, it is fairly clear from Peirce's illustrations of his maxim that this is the way in which reference to actions enters into the meaning of concepts. When we say, for instance, that a diamond is 'hard,' we mean that if we were to bring it under pressure by a great many other substances, it would not be scratched. When we say that a body is acted upon by a particular force, we mean that if certain conditions were to obtain, the body would undergo a particular change of velocity (*CP*, 5.404). Here, the concepts of hardness and force are defined contextually; what Peirce gives us is really the meaning of the statements containing these concepts. The meaning consists in the statement of those sensible effects which, on all conceivable (relevant) occasions for action, would follow from the truth of those statements. More precisely, the meaning consists in a series of conditional statements, each stating that if such and such action were to be taken, such and such a result would follow. To say that the meaning of a concept consists in its bearing upon action appears to mean, then, that it consists in its reproducible sensible effects. That this is what Peirce had in mind is fairly clear from passages such as the following, where he contrasts his own view with Kirchhoff's:

> In a recent admired work on *Analytic Mechanics* it is stated that we understand precisely the effect of force, but what force itself is we do not understand! This is simply a self-contradiction. The idea which the word force excites in our minds has no other function than to affect our actions, and these actions can have no reference to force otherwise than through its effects. Consequently, *if we know what the effects of force are, we are acquainted with every fact which is implied in saying that a force exists, and there is nothing more to know.* (*CP*, 5.404; italics added)

In sum, explicating a concept in terms of conceivable effects which can conceivably have a practical bearing amounts to explicating it in terms of sensible effects which can be produced or averted through actions, i.e., in terms of experimental consequences.

During the following twenty years Peirce did not write another word about pragmatism, and he does not seem to have attached any great importance to the maxim until 1898, when it was revived and introduced into print by James. Unlike Peirce, James gave the maxim a straightforwardly nominalist and instrumentalist bent: the meaning of a concept, in James's view, consists in the totality of those individual actions which the acceptance of the concept would lead us to perform. Thus, the acceptance of the concept 'God' would lead us to act as if there were a better life to come, the acceptance of the concept of 'free will' would lead us to make independent, deliberate choices, etc.—regardless of whether any definite sensible results of those actions would logically follow from the affirmation or denial of those concepts.[4] This interpretation was antithetical to Peirce's intentions on at least two counts. On the one hand, it tended to undermine the autonomy of pure science by making meaning depend upon practical effects in a sense of 'practical' which did not include 'experimental.' On the other hand, it relinquished those stringent logical and empirical requirements which Peirce had intended his maxim to convey.

Since James generously attributed the doctrine of pragmatism to his old friend Peirce, the latter was now obliged to re-examine the pragmatic maxim so as to elucidate his differences from James. These differences have now been clearly and concisely stated by scholars more qualified than I, and I have no wish to duplicate their efforts.[5] It will here simply be taken for granted that Peirce's maxim is not nominalist in the precise sense that James's is, that is, in the sense of making meaning consist in concrete, particular actions. But the maxim may be thought to be nominalist in a different manner. As it is formulated above, it bears a striking resemblance to the verifiability criterion of meaning later propounded by the logical empiricists of the Vienna Circle: "The meaning of a sentence consists in the mode of its verification."[6] Although, as one recent commentator has put it, one of the oddities about the appeal of the verifiability criterion is that no one has ever been able to state it,[7] the gist of it may be roughly summarized as follows. The meaning of a sentence consists in the set of observation sentences which confirm or disconfirm it. If two sentences imply the same set of observation sentences and prohibit the same set of observation sentences, they have the same meaning. If a sentence does not imply or prohibit any observation sentences, it is either tautological or meaningless. It should be added that though this is a radically *empiricist* criterion of meaning, few if any of the logical empiricists thought of the criterion itself as *empirical*. It was usually thought of as a tautology which was meant to function as a recommendation of usage or, in other words, as a persuasive definition of the word 'meaning.'[8] To that extent, it may be said to exemplify empiricism as an *a priori* philosophical doctrine, as opposed to what we might call empiricalness, or empiricism as a procedure of inquiry.

A great many philosophers have noted the resemblance of Peirce's maxim to the verifiability criterion. To the best of my knowledge, it was first pointed out in 1937 by Charles Morris, who described Peirce's program as "really a logical positivism,"[9] while at the same time stressing that the pragmatist criterion of meaning is broader than that of the logical empiricists, in so far as the former makes meaning consist in verifiability by the community, not by the individual knower.[10] Later, the resemblance between the pragmatic maxim and the verifiability criterion was noted by, among others, Arthur Burks and Ernest Nagel, and in 1968 it was asserted by A. J. Ayer that the two principles are for all practical purposes identical.[11]

There are good reasons both for and against interpreting Peirce's maxim as an early version of the verifiability criterion of meaning. The strongest reason against such an interpretation is that it ignores Peirce's theory of signs, according to which there can be no such thing as absolute precision and, consequently, no such thing as a criterion of meaning. We shall return to this theory in the next chapter. We may ignore it for the moment, because as we shall see, Peirce himself at times ignored it. But there are other reasons for being skeptical of the proposed interpretation. This interpretation would place Peirce's realism in jeopardy, since his realism appears to be both a rival account of meaning and an unverifiable one to boot.[12] And, it so happens that in this case Peirce has second-guessed his later commentators by offering his own interpretation of the pragmatic maxim; in so doing, he both considered and rejected an interpretation strikingly similar to the one later proposed by Ayer et al.

On the other hand, the direct textual evidence of the 1878 article is almost overwhelmingly in favor of the verificationist interpretation, which is furthermore supported by strong collateral evidence. So, while we have reason to be wary of the interpretation of Peirce as a precursor of logical empiricism, the interpretation has a certain *prima facie* plausibility and cannot be dismissed too quickly—not even this late in the day of Peirce scholarship. To show my own hand, the conclusion for which I shall argue in the following is that Peirce consistently espoused a verificationist semantics, according to which a language user can fully understand the words he uses in terms of expected outcomes of possible experiments, and only in those terms. This does not conflict with his view that the student of language use can and must understand those same words to refer to real entities, that understanding being further explicable in terms of second-level "experiments," etc. While this account has no room for a criterion of meaning, Peirce at times *also* put forth pragmatism as a verifiability criterion of meaning, and this strand in his thinking does conflict with his realism.

b. The verifiability criterion of meaning

Before attempting a detailed discussion of the relation of the pragmatic maxim to the verifiability criterion of meaning, we need to take a closer look at the latter, its underlying motivation, and the difficulties which were eventually to defeat it. Logical empiricism (originally "logical positivism") originated with a group of radical scientists and philosophers who met in Moritz Schlick's seminar in Vienna in the 1920s, and who gained world renown as the "Vienna Circle." The problem, What is meaning? is not one which confronted them out of the blue; it arose from a specific historical problem situation, and its solution was subject to definite boundary conditions. What the logical empiricists wanted was to unmask what they perceived as a socially pernicious abuse of language, namely the masquerading of myths and value judgments in the garb of statements of fact. Among those myths were theological doctrines, idealist metaphysics, the rhetoric of reactionary German nationalism, and, in the thirties, the rather more menacing rhetoric of the radical nationalism and racism of the Nazis. The logical empiricists were for the most part socialists, but they were skeptical of the dogmas of Marxism. Like Peirce, they perceived all inquiry, including inquiry into philosophy, as a social, cooperative enterprise. In the place of old myths they wanted to put a "unified science," formalized in a logically perfect, universal language, and capable of serving as a tool for the rational solution of social and political problems. In this respect they saw themselves as the direct descendants of the eighteenth-century *philosophes* and the nineteenth-century positivists. These affinities were commemorated in the name "logical positivism" and in the project of an "International Encyclopedia of Unified Science."[13]

The problem thus confronting the logical empiricists was how to show the superiority of science over the popular myths of the age. The truth of science as a whole is not something that can be scientifically proven. Nor could the myths be scientifically refuted; they were altogether too vague to be proven false. The solution hit upon was not only were the myths too vague to be proven false, they were too vague to *be* false; they were simply meaningless, and hence incapable of either truth or falsehood. Once this line of attack had been chosen, the constructive task facing the logical empiricists was that of developing an account of meaning which would satisfy the conditions that science is meaningful, while theology, idealism, nationalism, and Nazism are not. These conditions seemed *prima facie* to be met by the verifiability criterion which was derived from Ludwig Wittgenstein, though never actually endorsed by him. This criterion divided all statements into three classes. The statements of the natural and social sciences were meaningful because they could be empirically verified; unverifiable myths were nonsense; the philosophical statements of the logical empiricists themselves were analytical truths, or tautologies, as were the statements of logic and mathematics.

This solution turned out to be illusory. After about twenty years it became clear that there was no precise criterion of meaning which was both liberal enough to assign a meaning to all scientific statements and stringent enough to deny meaning to obviously nonsensical statements. This conclusion emerged from the cumulative impact of numerous objections, among them objections to the meaningfulness of the notion of analytical truth and objections to the project of formulating logical criteria of confirmation. We shall here look at only one objection, historically perhaps the decisive one, namely the failure of any proposed criterion to assign a meaning to dispositional terms, such as 'soluble.' This failure became apparent in the late thirties, and was formulated in the forties as the problem of "counterfactual conditionals." The problem may be illustrated in the following manner. Saying that a certain metal is soluble in a certain acid is as much as saying that, if it is submerged in the acid, it will dissolve. For any particular piece of metal at our disposal this statement is verifiable; we can perform the test and see whether the result follows. It might seem, therefore, that the lawlike statement 'Metal M is soluble in acid A' is translatable into an infinite series of conditional statements containing only observation terms, as follows: 'If the piece of metal M_1 ($M_2, \ldots, M_n$) is submerged in A, it will dissolve.' Since each of these statements is verifiable, such an analysis would seem to assign empirical meaning to the lawlike statement and thereby to the dispositional term 'soluble in A.' It might be objected that since the series of conditional statements is infinite, we can never enumerate them all, let alone verify them all, so the lawlike statement is not susceptible to complete verification, not even to a complete translation into verifiable terms. This may be granted, and it may be replied that so long as any one of the conditional statements can be verified, the dispositional term is given a meaning for every application of it which falls within the range of our experience—which is all that we want. But just this condition proved impossible to fulfill. If we postulate that the piece of metal M_1 is not, has not been, and will not be submerged in A, we would still want to regard the statement 'M_1 is soluble in A' as meaningful (and possibly true); but it makes no sense, given our initial postulate, to translate this statement by 'If M_1 is submerged in A, it will dissolve.' Nor is this conditional verifiable, given our postulate. What we mean by calling M_1 'soluble in A' can be expressed only by the counterfactual conditional 'If M_1 *were to be* submerged in A, it *would* dissolve.' Since we have already postulated that the antecedent condition is never fulfilled, this conditional statement is not verifiable.

The logical empiricists considered several possible ways out of this dilemma. The simplest and most obvious solution was to regard all conditionals as material conditionals, i.e., as conditionals which are false only when the antecedent is true and the consequent false, and are true in all other cases. In the propositional calculus these can be converted into disjunctive statements which in turn can be converted into conjunctions of categorical statements capable of direct verification. Thus the three following statements are equivalent, as is shown by their truth tables:

$$p \supset q \quad \equiv \quad {\sim}p \lor q \quad \equiv \quad {\sim}(p \ \& \ {\sim}q)$$

p ⊃ q	~p v q	~(p & ~q)
T [T] T	F T [T] T	[T] T F F T
T F F	F T F F	F T T T F
F [T] T	T F [T] T	[T] F F F T
F [T] F	T F [T] F	[T] F F T F

The three formulae stand for, respectively, 'If p, then q,' 'Either not-p or q or both,' and 'Not both p and not-q.' The tables beneath show the truth values ('T' for 'True,' 'F' for 'False') for the compound statements under all possible combinations of truth values for their component statements. Since the three statements are true under the same conditions and false under the same conditions, they are logically equivalent. By replacing equivalent with equivalent we can therefore turn our counterfactual conditional into the verifiable statement: 'It is not the case both that M_1 is submerged in A, and that it does not dissolve.'

The problem with this way out is that in a truth-functional analysis, *all* counterfactual conditionals will turn out to be true. This conclusion is highly counterintuitive, as was most clearly pinpointed by Nelson Goodman in 1946.[14] The statements 'If I strike the match, it will light' and 'Even if I strike the match, it will not light' are inconsistent with each other whether I strike the match or not, so there can be no circumstances under which both would be true. Still, in a truth-functional analysis, if I do not in fact strike the match, both statements will be true since both antecedents will be false. An awkward corollary is that if this analysis is applied to dispositional terms, it will turn out that any object whatever which is not, has not been, and will not be submerged in A, must be considered 'soluble in A,' which is clearly an undesirable consequence.[15]

An alternative solution, proposed by Rudolf Carnap, consisted in the use of so-called "reduction-sentences."[16] Instead of translating 'M is soluble in A' into an infinite series of conditionals one may, *on the condition that* $M_1, \ldots M_n$ are, have been, or will be submerged in A, replace 'M is soluble in A' by the series of *categorical* statements

'M_1 (M_2, . . . , M_n) will dissolve.' The lawlike statement is thereby reduced to a series of verifiable categorical statements, jointly constituting its meaning. The problem with this ingenious solution is the incompleteness of such an interpretation of dispositional terms. If, as before, we postulate that M_1 never has been, or ever will be submerged in A, then, in the statement 'M_1 is soluble in A;' the term 'soluble' is now left undefined. Thus the statement is no longer trivially true; rather, on Carnap's interpretation of the verifiability criterion, that criterion fails to assign any meaning to such a statement.

It will not do to say—as did for a while proponents of "weak verifiability"—that the fact that the statement 'M is soluble in A' has *some* verifiable consequences makes that statement itself verifiable, and thereby gives meaning to all its consequences.[17] The same thing can be said of the statement 'M is soluble in A, and the Absolute is lazy,' from which it would follow that 'The Absolute is lazy' is a meaningful statement. After rejecting this and other solutions the logical empiricists were in the end led to the conclusion that the interpretation of dispositional terms represents an insurmountable obstacle to a verifiability criterion of meaning. It is a tribute to the candor and the intellectual courage of the logical empiricists that no one has expounded the above objections with greater clarity and frankness than the logical empiricists themselves, or than Carl G. Hempel in particular.[18]

Although philosophical disputes may often seem to take place in never-never land, still the history of philosophy differs from a fairy tale in that it has no clear-cut endings—no happily-ever-afters. The denouement of logical empiricism may seem as definitive as that of any fairy tale; yet there is another way out of the problem of counterfactuals, one suggested by Goodman (1965), especially in chapters 2 and 4. Instead of defining dispositions in terms of counterfactual conditionals we may define the latter in terms of dispositions, and dispositions, in turn, in terms of scientific laws. Then, there is no longer a special problem of counterfactuals; instead, there is a problem of how to distinguish, in verifiable terms, between a law and an empirical generalization—such as 'All the coins in my pocket are copper'—*without* making use of the fact that laws support counterfactual conditionals while empirical generalizations do not. Whether this new problem is any easier to handle than the old one is, of course, a different question, one aside from the purpose of this brief historical sketch.

c. Pragmatism and logical empiricism

This excursus through the history of logical empiricism will serve as an indirect approach to the interpretation of Peirce's pragmatic maxim. This maxim, it was noted above, has often been seen as an early version of the verifiability criterion, and Peirce has accordingly been seen as a forerunner of logical empiricism. We have seen that the *prima facie* objections to this interpretation are so strong and so numerous that it cannot be accepted as telling the whole story about Peirce's pragmatism. It ignores Peirce's theory of signs, it makes his pragmatism inconsistent with his realism, and it is itself inconsistent with most of what Peirce had to say about pragmatism after 1898. Nor can we explain away the discrepancies by saying that Peirce was a logical empiricist in 1878 and later changed his mind. Peirce was a realist at least as early as 1868; realism and pragmatism are developed side by side in the 1873 manuscripts, and his commitment to realism is reaffirmed in the 1878 article "How To Make Our Ideas Clear" (*CP*, 5.407). Still, it is of interest to see just how much of the evidence the verificationist interpretation will accommodate. I shall argue that at least the original formulation of the pragmatic maxim in 1878 entails a commitment to a criterion of meaning which is indistinguishable from that of the logical empiricists, and which is vulnerable to precisely the same objections as the latter. Nor is this a mere slip of the pen on Peirce's part; although Peirce was later to disavow the original formulation, that formulation was in fact required by at least some of the philosophical goals which he intended his maxim to meet. And these goals, which were straightforwardly "positivistic," were to persist even in his later writings.

In his 1878 article Peirce makes no secret of the intention behind the pragmatic maxim; the intention, he tells us, is to provide a method for unmasking all sorts of empty and meaningless verbalisms masquerading as profundities: "It is terrible to see how a single unclear idea, a single formula without meaning, lurking in a young man's head, may sometimes act like an obstruction of inert matter in an artery, . . . Many a man has cherished for years as his hobby some vague shadow of an idea, too meaningless to be positively false . . ." (*CP*, 5.393). The purpose of the maxim, then, is to provide a method for exorcizing shadowy ideas. Peirce makes it reasonably clear that this purpose, in his view, can be attained only through a strictly empiricist criterion of meaning:

> Thus, we come down to what is tangible and conceivably practical, as the root of every distinction of thought, no matter how subtle it may be; and there is no distinction of meaning so fine as to consist in anything but a possible difference in practice. (*CP*, 5.400)

> I only desire to point out how impossible it is that we should have an idea in our minds which relates to anything but conceived sensible effects of things. Our idea of anything *is* our idea of its sensible effects; and if we fancy that we have any other we deceive ourselves, and mistake a mere sensation accompanying the thought for a part of the thought itself. (*CP*, 5.401)

As late as 1905, by which time Peirce was busy reconciling his pragmatism with scholastic realism, he explicitly reiterated the debunking intent behind the maxim. Pragmaticism, he now held, would show that "almost every proposition of ontological metaphysics is either meaningless gibberish, . . . or else is downright absurd" (*CP*, 5.412). For this reason, he conceded, pragmaticism was closely akin to positivism, and might aptly be termed "prope-positivism" (*CP*, 5.423).

It is clear from these quotes that *part* of the intention behind Peirce's maxim, both early and late, was identical to that behind the verifiability criterion of the logical empiricists. Peirce did not altogether share their goals; he was no enemy of theology, and he certainly did not wish to attack idealism although he did want to keep both theology and metaphysics demarcated from natural science. Nor was he in the same historical problem situation as his later kinsmen. Peirce was not confronted with the menace of twentieth-century irrationalism; he did not greatly care about politics, but to the extent that he did express any political beliefs, his was an attitude of contempt for the rottenness of contemporary liberalism from the point of view of an authoritarian, Humean kind of conservatism.[19] On the other hand, the nineteenth century was rife with precisely the sort of myths that the logical empiricists were later to combat, i.e., pretentious metaphysical systems and all-embracing ideologies which not only claimed the authority of "science," but which frequently presumed to settle questions internal to the sciences themselves. Hegelianism, Comtism, Spencerism, Social Darwinism, and scientific materialism are among the better known of the myths, and they are myths which Peirce specifically opposed on the ground that they threatened the integrity of science. Peirce, to be sure, placed positivism in the same category with these other myths;[20] but the word 'positivism' was already a pejorative term by the mid-nineteenth century. If positivism is the rejection of all metaphysics in the name of science as the only form of legitimate knowledge, then Mill, Bernard, and Mach, as well as the later logical empiricists, were positivists *because* they rejected positivistic metaphysics, not in spite of it. Peirce's critical attitude towards positivism does not in and of itself serve to distinguish him from others whom we call positivists; it was shared by all of them—with Comte as perhaps the only important exception.

So much, at this point, for Peirce's intent; now to the maxim itself. As we have seen (section a, above), the pragmatic maxim makes the meaning of any term consist in conceived sensible effects which can have a bearing on action, that is to say in conceived experimental consequences. These can be formulated only in a series of conditional statements; and, since far from all conceivable experiments are ever carried out, a large number of these conditionals will have unfulfilled antecedents, that is, they will be counterfactual. The verifiability of conditional statements depends upon the interpretation of their counterfactual instances. Peirce's interpretation of counterfactuals ought therefore to throw light on the relation of his maxim to the verifiability criterion.

In "How To Make Our Ideas Clear" Peirce does not appear to have consistently thought through the status of counterfactuals, and he offers at least two mutually incompatible interpretations. This is not in itself surprising. The later Peirce was, to my knowledge, the first thinker to take seriously the logical problem of counterfactuals; nobody else discussed the problem until the late 1930s, and it seems likely that these later discussions were due to a direct Peircean influence.[21] What is surprising, unless we take Peirce to be in part an early logical empiricist, is the fact that both his interpretations of counterfactuals in 1878 are interpretations which were later to be proposed by the logical empiricists in defense of their criterion of meaning.

The first of the two interpretations occurs in an analysis of the meaning of the term 'hard.' Peirce here claims that the idea of hardness only consists in the idea of a substance not being scratched when brought into contact with other substances, and that the term 'hard' therefore has no meaning when applied to substances which are not so brought into contact: "There is absolutely no difference between a hard and a soft thing so long as they are not brought to the test" (CP, 5.403). Thus it makes no sense to ask whether a particular diamond is hard or soft so long as it has not been brought under pressure. The observable facts are compatible with either predicate, and the meaning of the words 'hard' and 'soft' consists only in our idea of the observable facts. We may even speak of the diamond as growing hard with increased pressure and growing softer as the pressure subsides; this would be an awkward use of the words, but it would not militate against their meaning since they are not assigned any meaning in cases where their application does not signal any sensible effect:

We may, in the present case, modify our question, and ask what prevents us from saying that all hard bodies remain perfectly soft until they are touched, when their hardness increases with the pressure until they are scratched. Reflection will show that the reply is this: there would be no *falsity* in such modes of speech. They would involve a modification of our present usage of speech with regard to the words hard and soft, but not of their meanings. For they represent no fact to be different from what it is; only they involve arrangements of facts which would be exceedingly maladroit. (CP, 5.403)

Peirce's position here is strongly reminiscent of Carnap's, but it does in fact involve a more radical verificationism than that of the latter.

In Carnap's version of the verifiability criterion, dispositional terms are assigned a meaning only when applied to objects which are, have been, or will be brought to an experimental test. In Peirce's analysis, they have a meaning only when applied to an object actually undergoing the test. Once the diamond is put back on its bed of cotton, it becomes meaningless to ask whether the diamond is *now* hard or soft.

A somewhat cruder interpretation of counterfactuals follows immediately after the first one. Peirce's illustration is the apparent conflict between free will and determinism. When I have done something of which I am ashamed, I may wonder what would have happened under the contrary-to-fact condition that I had exerted my will power more than I in fact did. The answers given by the voluntarist and the determinist, respectively, may be formulated in two contrary and apparently incompatible counterfactual conditionals, namely, 'If I had exerted my will power, I should have resisted the temptation,' and 'Even if I had exerted my will power, I still should not have resisted the temptation.' In a pragmatic analysis, Peirce holds, the apparent conflict between these two answers disappears; both antecedents are false, hence both the conditionals are true: "There is no objection to a contradiction in what would result from a false supposition. The *reductio ad absurdum* consists in showing that contradictory results would follow from a hypothesis which is subsequently judged to be false" (*CP*, 5.403).

A minor point to be noted is that Peirce has here momentarily switched from speaking of conditionals to speaking of implications: in a conditional statement the antecedent is not a hypothesis from which the consequent follows. This does not affect the substance of his position, since to every implication there corresponds a conditional formula which must be valid for the implication to be valid. Thus the implication:

$$p \supset q$$
$$p$$
$$\underline{\hphantom{p}}$$
$$\therefore q$$

is valid if and only if the formula '$((p \supset q) \ \& \ p) \supset q$' is a valid formula. If we take the validity of the conditional to be the ground of the validity of the implication, we get involved in an infinite regress, as was shown by Lewis Carroll, who showed at the same time that we always *may* convert an implication into a conditional, if we so wish.[22] Saying that given a false hypothesis contradictory results will follow is then tantamount to saying that when we have two counterfactual conditionals sharing the same (false) antecedent but having mutually contradictory consequents, both will be true. That is, it is tantamount to treating the counterfactual conditionals as material conditionals. This position is vulnerable to precisely the same objection which confronted the early logical positivists, namely that since, in this analysis, all counterfactuals are trivially true, any dispositional term will truly apply to all objects which have not been brought to a relevant test. Here again Peirce interprets counterfactuals in a manner which would (if itself tenable) support a verifiability criterion of meaning, but which would serve no other apparent purpose.

So far, then, the pragmatic maxim in its original formulation appears practically indistinguishable from the verifiability criterion. I have already indicated that this matter of formulation is not just a slip of the pen. Peirce came later to regard it as just a slip, and there is some evidence that it might have been just that. It is necessary therefore to go over the evidence in more detail.

d. Peirce and the problem of counterfactuals

In 1873, the same year in which Peirce presented the pragmatic maxim to the Metaphysical Club, he also wrote the series of manuscripts known as the "Logic of 1873," containing what appears to be an alternate or preliminary draft of the articles which five years later were to appear in *Popular Science Monthly*. In these manuscripts Peirce clearly presupposes yet a third interpretation of counterfactual conditionals. This third interpretation is inconsistent with both interpretations found in the 1878 article, inconsistent with the verifiability criterion of meaning, but fully consistent with Peirce's scholastic realism. In the "Logic of 1873," Peirce writes the following, concerning the meaning of the term 'hard': "But though the hardness is entirely constituted by the fact of another stone rubbing against the diamond yet we do not conceive of it as beginning to be hard when the other stone is rubbed against it; on the contrary, we say that it is really hard all the time, and has been hard since it began to be a diamond" (*CP,* 7.340). This might be construed as just a comment on ordinary linguistic usage; it would be more awkward so to construe the following comment on the term 'force': "It exists only by virtue of a condition, that something will happen under certain circumstances; but we do not conceive it as first beginning to exist when these circumstances arise; on the contrary, it will exist though the circumstances should never happen to arise" (*CP,* 7.341).

If hardness and force both consist in the fact that certain sensible effects would appear under certain circumstances, while yet both exist even should those circumstances never in fact be realized, then the meaning of the terms 'hard' and 'force' depends upon the meaningfulness and irreducibility of counterfactual conditionals. In other words, it is here assumed, in contrast with the 1878 article, that counterfactuals are neither meaningless (as in the example of the diamond) nor reducible to material conditionals and therefore trivially true (as in the example of free will). That Peirce did at the time make this assumption is even clearer from the unpublished portion of the "Logic of 1873," which we considered in chapter 2. Peirce there said that the existence of forces "depends on their manifestations *or rather on their manifestability*" (MS, 372, p. 14; italics added). If there is to be any point in that distinction, the manifestability of a quality cannot simply consist in its manifestations, as it would under the interpretations of counterfactuals offered in the 1878 article. Potentiality or possibility must be essentially irreducible to any number of actual, observable events. Since this is a position which Peirce later came to advocate, it might be thought reasonable to infer that this was really his position all along, and that he just had a bad day while writing "How To Make Our Ideas Clear." Anyone with any experience in writing at length upon highly abstract matters has had moments when his hand wrote things which the mind did not register, and which thereafter have gone undetected through successive proof stages.

Moreover, in the 1878 article itself there are passages which throw doubt upon the interpretation which I put forth in the last section. On the question of whether gems on the bottom of the sea are brilliant or not, Peirce writes that this *"probably* makes no difference, remembering always that the stone may be fished up tomorrow" (*CP,* 5.409; italics in the original). This seems flatly to contradict the statement that there is "absolutely no difference" between a hard and a soft diamond so long as they are not brought to the test. The gems at the bottom of the sea have not in fact been fished up; hence the possibility that they *may* be fished up makes no difference to the question of whether they are brilliant, unless the meaning of that question be constituted in part by irreducible counterfactuals. This passage, then, conflicts with the explicit analyses given in the same article of the meaning of the terms 'hard' and 'soft,' but harmonizes well with the quite different analysis implicit in the 1873 manuscript.

On these grounds one might conclude that the pragmatic maxim, though originally formulated in a manner reminiscent of the verifiability criterion of meaning, was never seriously intended as such a criterion. It might even have been intended to function in a manner exactly opposite to that of the verifiability criterion. The gist of that criterion was that if we know that a statement has verifiable consequences, we thereby know that it is meaningful. But are verifiable consequences really more evident than meanings? One might think that, to the contrary, we need to understand a statement, i.e., know its meaning, before we can begin to deduce its logical consequences and inquire whether any of these are verifiable. If this is Peirce's view, the pragmatic maxim might turn out to be the reverse of the verifiability criterion: if we know that a statement is meaningful, we thereby know that it has experimentally testable consequences, whether or not we know what those consequences are, or how to test them. This appears to be the line taken by John F. Boler:

One source of confusion lies in what I think is the mistaken notion that pragmatism must be a reductionist theory. A reductionist pragmatism, as I understand it, contends that only actual events are real— powers and laws, abstractions of all sorts, are only shorthand expressions for actual events. . . . It seems to me that Peirce's pragmatism was never intended to be like this at all. For him the pragmatic maxim is a reformulation, intended to expose the structure of our conceptions and indicate their reference to actual events.[23]

What Boler calls "reductionism" is reasonably close, I believe, to what I have called "verificationism." I sympathize with Boler's opposition to such an interpretation of the pragmatic maxim, and I wish I could follow him, as it would greatly simplify the task of interpreting Peirce's later thought. As it is, and for reasons which I shall shortly set forth, I can follow Boler only part of the way. His is a proper interpretation of one strand in Peirce's thought, probably the main strand. Boler is right in holding that Peirce did not wish to dispense with abstractions but, on the contrary, wished to show that abstractions must be supposed real, because they are essentially involved in the only way in which we can speak of actual events. It does not follow that this was *all* that Peirce intended, or that all of his intentions were mutually compatible.

We have seen that Peirce's formulation of the pragmatic maxim in 1878 *is* reductionist: Peirce explicitly reduces the concept of force to the concept of acceleration, the concept of hardness to the concept of resistance to scratching under pressure, etc. The formulation is also explicitly verificationist: Peirce makes the meaning of a term consist only in those sensible effects which have a practical bearing, i.e., which can be reproduced by human action. Although Peirce states the maxim itself in subjunctive terms, in terms of effects that "might conceivably" have practical bearings, yet his illustrations— *vide* his analyses of hardness and of free will—make meaning consist only in those effects that do actually have practical bearings; those, that is, which result from experiments that are actually carried out. That Peirce in 1878 formulated a verifiability criterion of meaning can thus hardly be doubted. What the objections I have listed may indicate is that this formulation was a mere slip, foreign to Peirce's intentions. There are several reasons why such an interpretation will not hold water.

First, there is the direct, internal evidence of the 1878 article itself. We have seen that Peirce did not at the time propose a consistent interpretation of counterfactuals; indeed, there is no indication that he was at that time aware of counterfactuals as a special problem (even though he was obviously aware of the distinction between possibility and actuality). Still, he was obliged to deal with them by implication and, in so doing, he operated with two mutually inconsistent interpretations, one rendering counterfactuals meaningless and the other rendering them trivially true. So, if Peirce slipped in his formulation of pragmatism, he made two slips, not only one. This might not be unlikely; the curious thing, however, is that *both* his interpretations would, if they could be made to stick, meet the requirements of a verifiability criterion of meaning. If this were a result of mere carelessness of formulation, it would be a coincidence so striking as to strain one's credulity to the breaking point.

Second, this striking coincidence would be compounded with the second, utterly incredible coincidence that the interpretations of dispositional terms thus arrived at met the requirements of those plainly stated purposes for which the maxim was advanced. The purposes for which the logical empiricists needed a reductionist analysis of dispositional terms were purposes explicitly shared by Peirce. Peirce's intention, as we have seen, was to exorcize "vague, shadowy ideas, too meaningless to be positively false." And this is an intention which he never relinquished; as late as his 1905 articles in *The Monist,* he still held that the pragmatic maxim would show almost all of ontological metaphysics to be meaningless gibberish. Likewise, in a manuscript from 1905, Peirce stated the purpose of the maxim thus:

> It is expected to bring to an end those prolonged disputes of philosophers which no observation of facts could settle, and yet in which each side claims to prove that the other side is in the wrong. Pragmatism maintains that in those cases the disputants must be at cross-purposes. They either attach different meanings to a word, or else one side or the other (or both) uses a word without any definite meaning. (*CP,* 5.6)

Obviously, if every disposition could be shown to consist in its manifestations (not in its manifestability), this purpose would be attained; every question would be a question concerning observable facts.

Third—and, I believe, decisively—the logical doctrine of the truth-functional reducibility of conditionals to categoricals, which is implicit in Peirce's analyses of dispositional terms, is a doctrine which he explicitly defended at least from 1870 onward and which, on his own testimony, he did not abandon until 1903 (*CP,* 4.580). As one of the pioneers of modern symbolic logic, Peirce had early arrived at a truth-functional logic, in which conditional statements are reducible to disjunctives and these in turn to conjunctions of categoricals. The clearest statement of this reducibility is found in the article "Notation for Logic of Relatives," published in 1870:

> Every hypothetical proposition may be put into four equivalent forms, as follows:
>
>   If X, then Y.
>   If not Y, then not X.
>   Either not X or Y.
>   Not both X and not Y.
>   (*CP,* 3.140)

Of these, the first, third, and fourth forms are, of course, the formulae whose truth tables were given in section b, above. The second form is what we today call the "contraposition" of the first. In this analysis of conditionals, all counterfactual conditionals are trivially true. Subjunctive conditionals, therefore, are reducible to material conditionals, and there can be no difference between explicating the meaning of a concept in terms of subjunctive conditionals and explicating it in terms of verifiable, material conditionals. There can be no difference, therefore, between what might conceivably be the case and what actually is the case. We have seen that this is the conclusion which Peirce actually drew in "How To Make Our Ideas Clear."

As late as 1902, Peirce still held to this interpretation of conditionals, which he illustrated with this example: "But conditionals are only a special kind of *disjunctives.* To say, 'If it freezes tonight, your roses will be killed' is the same as to say, 'It either will not freeze, or your roses will tonight be killed.' A disjunctive does not exclude the truth of both alternatives, at once" (*CP,* 2.316n). Then, in 1903, Peirce realized that his earlier view of conditionals, and hence of dispositions, had been mistaken. This realization is detailed in the paper "Prolegomena to an Apology for Pragmaticism" and the address "An Improvement on the Gamma Graphs," both from 1906; in the latter,

Peirce dates the realization from his Harvard lectures in 1903. In this address, also, Peirce illustrates his point by demonstrating the ambiguity of the truth-functional representation of the statement "There is a man who, if he goes bankrupt, will commit suicide." We obviously want this statement to mean something different from the statement "There is a man such that, if he goes bankrupt, someone will commit suicide." Yet these two conditionals are truth-functionally equivalent. We shall not here introduce Peirce's graphic representation of the statements; his argument can be easily transcribed into the standard notation of the modern predicate logic. Such a transcription was made in 1962 by the Swedish Peirce scholar Hjalmar Wennerberg;[24] what follows is a slightly simplified version of Wennerberg's transcription.

Let us call the two statements 'p' and 'q,' let 'B' stand for 'goes bankrupt,' and let 'S' stand for 'commits suicide.' Then,

$$p: \exists x\, (Bx \supset Sx),$$

i.e.

$$\exists x\, (\sim Bx \lor Sx),$$

which is true if at least one man does not go bankrupt, or if at least one man commits suicide, and false if and only if

$$(x) \sim (\sim Bx \lor Sx),$$

i.e.

$$(x)(Bx \,\&\sim Sx),$$

i.e. if and only if every man goes bankrupt while no man commits suicide.

And,

$$q: \exists x \exists y\, (Bx \supset Sy),$$

i.e.

$$\exists x \exists y\, (\sim Bx \lor Sy),$$

which is true if at least one man does not go bankrupt, or if at least one man commits suicide, and false if and only if

$$(x)(y) \sim (\sim Bx \vee Sy),$$

i.e.

$$(x)(y) (Bx \& \sim Sy),$$

that is, once again, if and only if every man goes bankrupt while no man commits suicide.

This shows that 'p' and 'q' are true under precisely the same circumstances and false under the same circumstances; thus they are truth-functionally equivalent.

From this argument Peirce concluded that counterfactual conditionals cannot be treated as material conditionals, and consequently that possibilities cannot be reduced to series of actual events:[25]

> This reasoning is irrefragable as long as a mere possibility is treated as an absolute nullity. Some years ago, however, when in consequence of an invitation to deliver a course of lectures in Harvard University upon Pragmatism, I was led to revise that doctrine, in which I had already found difficulties, I soon discovered, upon a critical analysis, that it was absolutely necessary to insist upon and bring to the front, the truth that a mere possibility may be quite real. That admitted, it can no longer be granted that every conditional proposition whose antecedent does not happen to be realized is true, and the whole reasoning just given breaks down. (*CP*, 4.580).

Here we have it straight from the source that the original formulation of pragmatism did indeed involve both the unreality of possibility and the truth of all counterfactuals, both of which doctrines Peirce now abandons. Their interrelatedness is made equally clear: the truth-functional analysis of counterfactuals implies the unreality of possibility, and the denial of the latter necessitates denying the former as well. This is tantamount to acknowledging that the original version of pragmatism involved a reductionist empiricism of precisely the kind that was later to be advocated by the logical empiricists, and that this empiricism was organically linked with Peirce's early logical doctrines.

e. Pragmatism and realism: Later reflections

This concludes my case for interpreting the pragmatic maxim, in its original formulation, as a verifiability criterion of meaning. In 1878, as we have seen, Peirce had been a scholastic realist for at least a decade, but he did not at that time explicitly address the question of the compatibility or incompatibility of realism and pragmatism. Later in life, he grew acutely aware of the tension between realism and verificationism and he emphatically rejected certain versions of the latter. Thus, in 1903 we find him ridiculing the verificationisms of Auguste Comte, Henri Poincaré, and Karl Pearson, all of whom, according to Peirce, proposed to reduce the cognizable to the directly observable. Such a verificationism, Peirce notes, must reject the evidence of memory, since that which was observed yesterday is no longer observable today:

> Of course with memory would have to go all opinions about every-thing not at this moment before our senses. You must not believe that you hear me speaking to you, but only that you hear certain sounds while seeing before you a spot of black, white, and flesh color; and those sounds somehow seem to suggest certain ideas which you must not connect at all with the black and white spots. (*CP*, 5.597)

We can hardly avoid noticing that the verificationism which Peirce is caricaturing is uncomfortably close to the doctrine which he himself had defended twenty-five years earlier. Nor did this fact altogether escape Peirce's notice. From the year 1898, when James brought the pragmatic maxim to the attention of both Peirce himself and the rest of the world, Peirce devoted a great deal of time and effort to reinter-preting the maxim so as to reconcile it with realism. It has been said humorously—I forget by whom—that Peirce twice confessed to hav-ing made a mistake, and the second time he confessed that the first confession had been mistaken. The story is in fact slightly more com-plex.

In 1902, in an article in Baldwin's *Dictionary of Philosophy and Psychology*, Peirce admitted that his original formulation of the prag-matic maxim had been too "stoical," meaning too nominalistic (*CP*,

5.3). This admission was repeated in a letter to the Italian Mario Calderoni in 1905: "I myself went too far in the direction of nominalism when I said that it was a mere question of the convenience of speech whether we say that a diamond is hard when it is not pressed upon . . ." (*CP*, 8.208). That very same year, in his articles in *The Monist*, he described scholastic realism as an "essential consequence" of "pragmaticism" (as he now called it), and went on to claim that "it is the reality of some possibilities that pragmaticism is most concerned to insist upon" (*CP*, 5.453). Whether this was a reinterpretation or a revision of the original doctrine was left unclear, since the 1878 statement was described, in one and the same sentence, as "no doubt true" and "an abominable falsehood" (*ibid.*). It would seem to be a revision since, as we have just seen, in 1906 Peirce stated that he had recognized the reality of possibilities only in 1903. However, in a footnote added to "How To Make Our Ideas Clear" in 1906, we find Peirce retracting his 1902 admission that he had been too nominalistic (*CP*, 5.402, n3).

It is a moot question whether Peirce was covering his tracks, or whether his memory was getting hazy. As I have hinted several times, and as I intend to show in the next chapter, the fact is that Peirce all along had in mind something very different from a verifiability criterion of meaning—different, in fact, from any criterion of meaning. We have seen (section d, above) that as early as the 1870s Peirce equivocated over the reductionist implications of the pragmatic maxim; by that time, I believe, he had two incompatible maxims in mind, and he may be excused, therefore, if his later recollections of what he had originally thought were somewhat cloudy. In any case, no matter what Peirce thought was right or wrong about his original formulation, at least by 1905 he was convinced that he had a formulation of pragmatism which was in perfect harmony with scholastic realism.

In chapter 2 we started out by taking a brief look at the series of articles published in *The Monist* in 1905. In the second of these articles Peirce turned to the task of showing that scholastic realism, so far from being incompatible with the pragmatic maxim, is actually an essential consequence of the maxim properly understood. Scholastic realism was now defined as the doctrine that there are real objects which are general; and Peirce went on to emphasize that among these real objects must belong modalities, and especially that of possibility. How can this be?

Peirce's argument runs as follows: saying that a diamond is 'hard' means, according to the pragmatic maxim, nothing more than that *if* it were brought under pressure it *would* resist being scratched. This is a subjunctive conditional statement which holds also counterfactually; that is, it is true also of a diamond which never has been or ever will be brought under pressure. Since it is now granted that the meaning of counterfactuals cannot be explained truth-functionally, it follows that the meaning of the subjunctive conditional is not exhausted by any set of material conditionals. This, in turn, entails that if any subjunctive conditional be true, its conditional form will then be an essential component of the meaning of a true statement, and there must be some feature of reality which makes conditional statements true. The conditional form must itself have a real counterpart, a role which can be filled only by a real possibility:

> Pragmaticism makes the ultimate intellectual purport of what you please to consist in conceived conditional resolutions, or their substance; and therefore, the conditional propositions, with their hypothetical antecedents, in which such resolutions consist, *being of the ultimate nature of meaning,* must be capable of being true, that is, of expressing whatever there be which is such as the proposition expresses, independently of being thought to be so in any judgment, or being represented to be so in any other symbol of any man or men. But that amounts to saying that possibility is sometimes of a real kind. (*CP*, 5.453; italics added)

From the vantage point of his acceptance of real possibility Peirce reconsiders the example of the diamond used in his 1878 article. In the original discussion it was claimed that if a diamond were to be formed in a bed of cotton and then burn to coal before it could be tested for hardness it would be merely a verbal question whether that diamond were hard or soft or neither. Peirce now shrinks from unequivocally admitting that he made a mistake in the earlier article, but he disassociates himself clearly from the substance of the earlier statement: "No doubt this is true, except for the abominable falsehood in the word MERELY, implying that symbols are unreal. Nomenclature involves classification; and classification is either true or false, and the generals to which it refers are either real in the one case, or figments in the other" (*CP*, 5.453). Saying that a diamond is hard is to assert a subjunctive conditional, whose truth depends upon the truth of a general rule—for instance, "all objects formed from carbon in such-and-such a manner and presenting such-and-such an appearance, resist scratching." The hardness of the diamond consists only in the truth of this general rule; and if the rule is true the diamond is really hard, irrespective of its particular circumstances. Peirce concludes the discussion of this example with a rhetorical question which comes as close as possible to condemning the earlier statement, short of an explicit retraction: "Is it not a monstrous perversion of the word and concept *real* to say that the accident of the non-arrival of the corundum prevented the hardness of the diamond from having the *reality* which it otherwise, with little doubt, would have had?" (*CP*, 5.457).

Having made this apparent 180 degree turnabout, Peirce hurries to reaffirm the truth of the pragmatic maxim. As he now explains it, the purpose of the maxim is to turn empiricism against nominalism by (a) accepting the verificationist maxim that a statement can have no meaning other than its consequences for possible experiments, and adding (b) that these consequences can themselves be formulated only in irreducibly subjunctive conditionals. The conclusion is that if there are meaningful statements, then some subjunctive conditionals must be true and must refer to real modalities:

> For to what else does the entire teaching of chemistry relate except to the "behavior" of different kinds of material substance? And in what does that behavior consist except that if a substance of a certain kind should be exposed to an agency of a certain kind, a certain sensible result *would* ensue, according to our experiences hitherto. As for the pragmaticist, it is precisely his position that nothing else than this can be as much as *meant* by saying that an object possesses a character. He is therefore obliged to subscribe to the doctrine of a real Modality, including real Necessity and real Possibility. (*CP*, 5.457)

Such, in outline, is Peirce's 1905 argument for a peaceful coexistence between pragmatism and realism. There are, no doubt, several strands of argumentation compressed into these passages. In the next chapter we shall examine one strand which I find cogent and persuasive, but which presupposes a different interpretation of the pragmatic maxim. So long as the pragmatic maxim is regarded as a criterion of meaning Peirce has, in a sense, a 'valid' argument, but its validity is of a very special kind. As we find it in *CP*, 5.453 and 457, the argument is elliptically formulated; to exhibit its structure let me spell out what I take to be its individual steps:[26]

P1: The meaning of any statement consists only in the totality of its conceived sensible effects.

P2: The totality of the conceived sensible effects of any statement can be formulated only in subjunctive conditionals, on whose truth its meaning depends.

P3: There are true meaningful statements.

P4: Every meaningful component of a true statement corresponds to something real.

P5: That which corresponds to the subjunctive form is a modality.

C1 (from P1, P2, and P3): There are true subjunctives.

C2 (from P4, P5, and C1): There are real modalities.

One might not agree with all the premises in this argument; most people would, I believe, have reservations about the truth of P4. Surely *some* components of a true statement must correspond to something real; but if we say that *every* meaningful component must so correspond we inevitably land in a particularly objectionable version of Platonism, leading to an infinite regress. If the subjunctive form corresponds to something real merely because it is part of the meaning of a true statement, then the statement "The subjunctive form corresponds to something real" is true, and every meaningful component of it must correspond to something real. One meaningful component is the word 'corresponds'; hence this word must itself correspond to something. But if the correspondence of every true statement with reality must in its turn correspond with reality, each true statement will require an infinity of correspondences. This, in a slightly different formulation, is the oldest known objection to Platonism ("the third man"); it is found in Aristotle's *Metaphysics*,[27] and it was originally formulated by Plato himself, in the *Parmenides*.[28]

One may argue validly from false premises; let us disregard the truth or falsity of Peirce's premises and examine the validity of the argument. If one accepts P2, namely that the meaning of any statement depends on the truth of certain subjunctive conditionals, and that therefore (by P4) there must be something corresponding to the subjunctive form, then one is saying that the subjunctive form is a component of the meaning of a subjunctive conditional. But P1 says that the meaning of a statement consists only in its conceived sensible effects; and, although these sensible effects can be conceived only in the form of subjunctive conditionals, still the subjunctive form is not itself a conceived sensible effect. And this is as much as saying that P1 and P2 are mutually inconsistent. This is what I meant before by calling the argument 'valid,' putting the word in scare quotes. The argument is valid, but its validity is purely gratuitous; it is the kind of validity which belongs to any inference from inconsistent premises. Once you have an inconsistency among your premises, you can validly infer that modalities are real, or that they are not real, or anything else you please, since any statement whatever may be validly inferred from a contradiction.

We may recall at this point Peirce's view that no philosophical conclusion should be made to rest on a single chain of argument no stronger than its weakest link, but rather on a cable of intertwined fibers of argumentation mutually supporting one another. Peirce was probably under no illusion that this particular argument clinched the matter, and he had in any case better arguments in reserve. It is, however, my impression that Peirce's employment of this argument weakens rather than strengthens his case.

In this chapter I have regarded pragmatism as a criterion of meaning, which is how Peirce himself frequently presents it, and which is what he needs for some of the philosophical purposes underlying the pragmatic maxim. So understood, the maxim is itself untenable, it is inconsistent with the doctrine of the irreducibility of subjunctives, and it makes nonsense of the doctrine of realism. The semantic argument by which Peirce derives his realism from the pragmatic maxim boils down to the sort of gratuitous inference by which you may derive anything you like from inconsistent premises. If this were the whole story concerning Peirce's pragmatism, it would still be worth telling as a fascinating chapter of intellectual history. There is, however, a different story to be told, of even greater interest.

Chapter Four
Peirce's Pragmatic Realism

a. The theory of signs

UP TO THIS point, my conclusions have been largely negative. In chapter 2, Peirce's early scholastic realism was seen to involve his pragmatism as an essential component. In chapter 3, this same realism was seen to be undermined by the pragmatic maxim which, when interpreted as a criterion of meaning, makes nonsense of the notion of abstract entities. This pragmatism, it was further argued, is untenable in itself; and Peirce's later formulation of it, where he attempts to reconcile it with his realism, is inconsistent.

This book is not intended as a critique of Peirce; my intention is to exhibit the coherence of Peirce's thought rather than the numerous inconsistencies which can undoubtedly be found there. Thus these negative conclusions are no part of my main thesis; they are part of what I think intellectual honesty requires me to concede to possible objectors before I proceed to argue for my own thesis. Throughout chapter 3 I have tried conscientiously to act as the Devil's advocate; by now, that gentleman has received his due, and the time has come to embark on the case for the defense (even though it was James, not Peirce, who was elevated to sainthood).[1]

Although we have seen ample textual evidence that Peirce often thought of the pragmatic maxim as a criterion of meaning, this is not the only way in which he thought of it. In this chapter, we shall see that he also thought of it as a semantic theory which fully exhibits the meaning which a term has for its user, but which says nothing about the conditions for the successful employment of the term. Such considerations enter only on the level of pragmatics, which is an empirical study of how the sign user interacts with the world of experience by means of signs. Both Peirce's pragmatism and his realism, I shall argue, are chiefly intended as empirical hypotheses, the one belonging on the level of semantics, the other on the level of pragmatics. Within this framework, there can be no criterion of meaning; when we state what experimental consequences are implied by a given statement, we are making a fallible, empirical hypothesis. If we cannot find any experimental consequences, it may be due to our ignorance rather than to a lack of meaning in the statement. The insistence that a given statement is meaningless because it is untestable may easily serve to impede the progress of science. Thus Dalton's atomic theory and Mendel's gene theory were both initially condemned as metaphysical and unscientific because their testable consequences had not yet been formulated. Pragmatism claims only that we know what a statement means to the extent that we know what its experimental consequences are. Thus the pragmatic maxim itself, as well as the doctrine of scholastic realism, are intelligible to us only in terms of "experimental" consequences; since these hypotheses are hypotheses about signs, the relevant experiments cannot be physical experiments, but a certain kind of thought experiment.

In this initial statement, I have already used the technical terms "semantics" and "pragmatics," both of which belong to the vocabulary of the science of signs, a science of which Peirce was one of the founders. Peirce called this science "semiotic"; this name has a long and venerable history, especially in the history of medicine, where it was used to denote the science of symptoms. Its modern usage first appeared in the late eighteenth century and was firmly established through Peirce's writings.[2] There is today a growing interest both in semiotic as such and in Peirce's specific contributions to the subject; my exposition of his theory will, however, be limited to only so much as is necessary to reveal the respective roles of pragmatism and realism within his scheme of thought.[3]

Peirce's major writings on semiotic stem from the 1890s and early 1900s, but the hard core of his theory is found in the doctrine of thought-signs presented in his articles and manuscripts from 1867 and 1868. Peirce there argued that everything is a sign to the extent that it is capable of being understood as standing for something else. It was also part of his early doctrine that nothing can be known without being understood as standing for something else, that is, without being understood as a sign. Moreover, since nothing which cannot be known can be said to be real, it followed that everything which is real is a sign. Let us take a closer look at what is involved in being a sign.

In his University Lectures from 1865, Peirce stressed that a sign has a function in addition to the function of meaning: "It is important to distinguish between the two functions of a word 1st: to denote something—to stand for something and 2nd: to mean something—or as Mr. Mill phrases it—to *connote* something" (MS, 345, p. 6). In his 1868 articles, he elaborated this distinction in terms of a threefold distinction between the three "references" of a sign (a distinction set forth in 1867): "Now a sign has, as such, three references: first, it is a sign *to* some thought which interprets it; second, it is a sign *for* some object to which in that thought it is equivalent; third, it is a sign, *in* some respect or quality, which brings it into connection with its object" (*CP*, 5.283).

In the next three paragraphs (*CP*, 5.284–86), Peirce proceeds to explain these three references or, as I should call them, conditions for signification. First, the sign must be capable of being interpreted by a subsequent thought, which in turn can function as a sign and be interpreted by yet another thought, and so on *ad infinitum*—or until the process of interpretation is interrupted, for instance by death. Second, the sign must be capable of standing for some real, outward object; but, third, it must be capable of representing that object by means of previous thoughts. For instance, take for the object of the sign the person Toussaint; if I represent Toussaint to myself I must represent him as something of which I already have prior knowledge, for instance as a general. And I can represent him to myself as a general only by virtue of having already represented him to myself as a Negro, and before that again as a man (*CP*, 5.285). I take this to mean that although the sign functions as a sign only by representing a real object, it can do this only by functioning as an interpreter of earlier, more general signs, and by being itself interpretable in terms of later, more determinate signs. By the way, we can already glimpse how the pragmatic maxim fits into the scheme: it exhibits how the sign functions to the thought which interprets it; *to that thought*, the object is equivalent to the interpreted sign. It does not follow that the two are equivalent to someone surveying this whole process of interpretation.

Having spelled out this trivision, Peirce goes on next to emphasize the distinction between the representative function of a sign and the material conditions for its having a representative function. This distinction is essential to his theory as I interpret it in this chapter. There are two kinds of material conditions. In the first place, there are what Peirce calls the "material qualities" of the sign: "As an example of such qualities, take in the word 'man,' its consisting of three letters—in a picture, its being flat and without relief" (*CP*, 5.287). In the second place, there is what Peirce calls the "pure demonstrative application" of the sign:

> In the second place, a sign must be capable of being connected (not in reason but really) with another sign of the same object, or with the object itself. . . . The usefulness of some signs—as a weathercock, a tally, etc.—consists wholly in their being really connected with the very things they signify. . . . This real, physical connection of a sign with its object, either immediately, or by its connection with another sign, I call the *pure demonstrative application* of the sign. (*CP*, 5.287)

Now the representative function of the sign, Peirce emphasizes, depends upon, but does not consist in, either its material qualities or its pure demonstrative application. To grasp the distinction, consider the example of the weathercock. This contraption signifies the direction of the wind by means of a direct physical connection with the wind. But this physical connection is not signified or represented by the weathercock; the weathercock simply signifies the direction of the wind, it does not signify its own mode of signification. A person who was ignorant of how a weathercock functions could still understand that it points out the direction of the wind; that is, he could fully understand the meaning of this sign without having any idea what kind of sign it is, or by what means it is capable of representing its object. Furthermore, a make-believe weathercock which is manually adjusted to the direction of the wind by a meteorologist would have exactly the same meaning as a real weathercock. But it would not be a weathercock, nor would it be the kind of sign that a weathercock is. In Peirce's terminology, it would be a *symbol,* not an *index.* So the meaning of a sign and the material conditions for its having that meaning can both be known independently of each other and exist independently of each other—although some material conditions must obtain for the sign to signify at all. To anticipate, the meaning of a sign may consist entirely in experimental consequences, while the reality of universals may at the same time be a condition for its having that meaning.

The weathercock is obviously a rather special kind of sign; most linguistic signs are not indices, but symbols, whose meanings are fixed by convention, not by a physical connection with the object referred to. These signs, too, must have a pure demonstrative application, in Peirce's view, but in this case the connection is indirect. To use my example, the manually operated make-believe weathercock can signify the wind direction only by virtue of there being real weathercocks. Similarly, according to Peirce, all symbols presuppose indices, i.e., signs which are physically connected to the object of reference.

So far Peirce in 1868. In the 1890s Peirce devoted himself more fully to the elaboration of a general theory of signs, which he now labelled "semiotic." In his writings from this period we find his famous distinction between "types" and "tokens," as well as his classification of signs into "icons," "indices," and "symbols"—a trivision originally introduced in 1867 (see *CP,* 1.558; 2.247–49). These terms have by now become part of the standard vocabulary of semiotic. Of more immediate interest to us are his distinction between "semiotic" as a science and "semiosis" as its subject matter, and the two tripartite distinctions between the three dimensions of semiosis and the corresponding three levels of semiotic.[4]

By semiosis or "sign-action," Peirce does not mean the purely physical manipulation of signs, the emission of sounds, the inscription of ink marks, etc., that is, the "verbal behavior" of more recent psychological behaviorism.[5] What he has in mind is the action of signs understood *quae* signs, where the sign users are just the physical vehicles for the signs. Insofar as signs act as signs, their action can be described only in terms of the three conditions of signification:

> All dynamical action, or action of brute force, physical or psychical, either takes place between two subjects . . . or at any rate is a resultant of such action between pairs. But by "semiosis" I mean, on the contrary, an action, or influence, which is, or involves, a cooperation of *three* subjects, such as a sign, its object, and its interpretant, this tri-relative influence not being in any way resolvable into actions between pairs. (*CP*, 5.484; c.1906)

There is a crucial difference between dyadic and triadic relations. A dyadic relation—such as a relation of cause and effect, or of action and reaction—just *is*; it may be described, but it cannot be judged or evaluated. Triadic relations, on the contrary, are essentially open to evaluation; a sign may represent its object to its interpretant rightly or wrongly, truly or falsely, better or worse. These normative terms imply the possibility of correction and improvement. It is an essential property of semiosis, therefore, that it can be corrected and improved upon, something which can happen only if the semiosis is itself made a subject of discourse (that is, of a second-order semiosis) and explicitly criticized. So, the capacity of discourse to function as the subject of second-order discourse is an essential prerequisite for discourse to function as semiosis:

> For thinking is a kind of conduct, and is itself controllable, as everybody knows. Now the intellectual control of thinking takes place by thinking about thought. All thinking is by signs; and the brutes use signs. But perhaps they rarely think of them as signs. To do so is manifestly a second step in the use of language. (*CP*, 5.534; c.1905)

It is an essential characteristic of language that it can itself be talked about and thinking about signs as signs, by means of second-order signs, is the province of semiotic.

We have seen that there are three conditions of signhood, and that sign action or semiosis is a relation between three terms. Correspondingly, the science of semiotic has three branches, each studying one of the three terms involved in semiosis. The clearest statement of these trivisions is found in a manuscript from 1897:

A sign, or *representamen,* is something which stands to somebody for something in some respect or capacity. It addresses somebody, that is, creates in the mind of that person an equivalent sign, or perhaps a more developed sign. That sign which it creates I call the *interpretant* of the sign. The sign stands for something, its *object.* It stands for that object, not in all respects, but in reference to a sort of idea, which I have sometimes called the *ground* of the representamen. . . . In consequence of every representamen being thus connected with three things, the ground, the object, and the interpretant, the science of semiotic has three branches. (*CP*, 2.228–29)

Peirce next enumerates these three branches of semiotic: pure grammar, logic proper, and pure rhetoric, corresponding to what we today call, respectively, syntactics, semantics, and pragmatics.[6] Of the third branch, pure rhetoric or pragmatics, Peirce says that "its task is to ascertain the laws by which in every scientific intelligence one sign gives birth to another" (*CP*, 2.229), having shortly before defined "scientific intelligence" as "an intelligence capable of learning by experience" (*CP*, 2.227). Pragmatics, we may say, is the study of how thoughts are modified by the sign user's interaction with the world of experience. This study must take into account both what a sign refers to and the meaning it has for its user. In addition, however, it examines how the user's understanding of the sign affects the realization of his goals and purposes, and how it is in turn modified by the experience encountered in the course of purposive action. The pragmatic maxim tells us only how the sign is understood by its user; this is part of the story of how that understanding is modified by experience, but it is not the whole story.

b. Pragmatism, realism, and semiotic

The hard core of Peirce's semiotic was formulated in the years 1867–68. Certain elements of the doctrine of thought-signs set forth in the anti-Cartesian articles of 1868 bear a striking resemblance to the pragmatic maxim and may be plausibly seen as a preliminary formulation of the maxim. Such, for instance, is the doctrine that the meaning of a thought-sign consists in the infinite train of subsequent thoughts in which it may be interpreted, so that "the meaning of a thought is something altogether virtual" (CP, 5.289). It is plausible, therefore, to regard the early doctrine of thought-signs, later elaborated as the science of semiotic, as the intended frame of reference for the pragmatic maxim. In that case, the maxim cannot be understood as an intended criterion of meaning. Even if the maxim fully exhibits the sign user's understanding of the sign, it does not yield a criterion of meaning by which we can divide statements into two classes, meaningful and meaningless. The sign user's understanding, namely, is modified by further experience and is not complete until there is nothing left to experience. Hence the precise meaning of a sign is something which we can ascertain only when we have attained omniscience; indeed, only then will the sign have a precise meaning. This was partly acknowledged in the 1878 article, where Peirce hinted that, even if we know that the meaning of a term consists in the totality of its conceivable experimental consequences, still we never do know the totality of those consequences (CP, 5.409). Novel instruments or improved logical analysis may uncover novel consequences tomorrow. What was more or less implicit in 1878 was to be made explicit in a letter from Peirce to Lady Welby in 1903. Here he wrote: "Perfect accuracy of thought is unattainable— theoretically unattainable. And undue striving for it is worse than time wasted. It positively renders thought unclear."[7]

A few acknowledgements are in order at this point. The interpretation of the pragmatic maxim just sketched was originally impressed upon me by Bruce Altshuler, who later developed it in detail.[8] Although Altshuler's detailed textual exegesis is pioneering work, in its broad outlines the interpretation has various antecedents. It was hinted at in 1949 by Wiener,[9] and made more explicit in 1952 by Gallie.[10] But the clearest statement of this interpretation was made in 1962 by Hjalmar Wennerberg, who pointed out that, in Peirce's theory, the meaning of a proposition does not remain constant but grows more precise with the growth of scientific knowledge, specifically with the discovery of laws of nature which permit us to attribute novel experimental consequences to a given property. Wennerberg gives the following apt quotation from Peirce: "How much more the word *electricity* means now than it did in the days of Franklin; how much more the term planet means now than it did in the time [of] Hipparchus" (*CP*, 7.587; c.1867). According to Peirce, Wennerberg goes on, "we can analyse a proposition better if we increase our knowledge of laws of nature, and a philosophical theory is always liable to be upset by future discoveries of science."[11] While this appears to me an entirely just paraphrase of Peirce's view, it is curious to note that Wennerberg concludes that this result of Peirce's theory of meaning constitutes an objection to it. The only reason he gives is that Peirce's theory "blurs the important distinction between logical analysis and empirical research."[12] If my reading is at all correct, Peirce does not blur this distinction in the least; he unconditionally denies that there is any such distinction. Wennerberg's book was published in 1962 and was thus presumably written before the appearance in the same year of Thomas Kuhn's *The Structure of Scientific Revolutions*.[13] At the time, the legitimacy of the distinction in question may have seemed self-evident; today, few thinkers familiar with the history of science would deny that scientific terms change their meanings through changes in scientific theory. What is controversial is only whether such changes are progressive or arbitrary. This does not make Peirce's position equivalent to Kuhn's; Peirce held that scientific terms grow more precise through the progress of knowledge, hence their changes of meaning have a definite direction, that of greater precision. By maintaining, for instance, that the term 'mass' in Einsteinian physics is incommensurable in meaning with the term 'mass' in Newtonian physics, Kuhn appears to deny that meanings change in the direction of increased precision, and his conclusion seems to be that the meanings of scientific terms change in an essentially arbitrary manner which can be ascertained only by historical research. What remains common to the views of Peirce and Kuhn is the insistence that the meaning of a scientific term depends on the contemporary state of scientific knowledge (including scientific theory). Thus, in order to know what the word 'electricity' meant in 1830, for instance, we need to know what was known about electricity in 1830. Today, this seems almost a truism; less than twenty years ago it seemed almost self-evidently false.

In the light of all the considerations advanced in chapter 3, it seems fair to say that when Peirce formulated the pragmatic maxim in "How To Make Our Ideas Clear" in 1878, he was motivated by conflicting purposes and ended by disregarding his own theory of signs—partly, perhaps, thinking it too esoteric to be taken into consideration in a popular article. Not until 1902, in re-thinking the pragmatic maxim, did Peirce assign it a role within the framework of his semiotic and suggest the beginnings of a pragmatic argument for realism:

> The doctrine appears to assume that the end of man is action—a stoical axiom which, to the present writer at the age of sixty, does not recommend itself so forcibly as it did at thirty. If it be admitted, on the contrary, that action wants an end, and that that end must be something of a general description, then the spirit of the maxim itself, which is that we must look to the upshot of our concepts in order rightly to comprehend them, would direct us towards something different from practical facts, namely, to general ideas, as the true interpreters of our thought. (*CP*, 5.3)

At least two interesting ideas are introduced here: one is the idea that the pragmatic maxim must itself be pragmatically understood in terms of its consequences; the other is that such a pragmatic analysis of the pragmatic maxim would reveal general ideas. The restriction of the pragmatic maxim to the semantic dimension of semiosis is made fairly explicit in a manuscript from about 1905. Having claimed that the maxim exhibits the meaning of a sign, Peirce continues: "The object of a sign is one thing; its meaning is another. Its object is the thing or occasion, however indefinite, to which it is to be applied. Its meaning is the idea which it attaches to that object, whether by way of supposition, or as a command, or as an assertion" (*CP*, 5.6; see also MS, 345, p. 6 [1865] and MS, 587, pp. 1–2 [1870–71]).

In a letter to Lady Welby in 1909 Peirce was to change his terminology slightly and refer to the meaning as the "immediate object," as opposed to the "dynamoid object," or reference of the sign: "It is usual and proper to distinguish two Objects of a Sign, the Mediate without, and the Immediate within the Sign. Its Interpretant is all that the Sign conveys; acquaintance with its Object must be gained by collateral experience. The Mediate Object is the Object outside of the Sign; I call it the *Dynamoid* Object. The Sign must indicate it by a hint; and this hint, or its substance, is the *Immediate* Object."[14]

   To understand what Peirce is doing, it is important to be clear about one thing he is not doing. He is not proposing a Fregean kind of "sense-reference" semantics, within which we are supposed to be able to give each sign both a meaning and a reference.[15] Peirce was fully cognizant of the objection which was to be eloquently put by Russell in his criticism of Frege, namely, that within one and the same language the reference of a term can be picked out only through the meaning of that term, and the meaning of the term can be specified only through a description of its reference.[16] As early as 1868, Peirce wrote that a thought "is a sign for some object *to which in that thought it is equivalent*" (*CP*, 5.283; italics added). In 1909, Peirce says that all that a sign conveys is its meaning, and that the (immediate) object of the sign, insofar as it can be gathered from analyzing the sign, *is* merely that hint by which the sign indicates its (dynamoid) object, that is, the (immediate) object is the meaning. The "dynamoid object" is not given in and through the meaning of the sign; acquaintance with it must be gained by "collateral experience." In Peirce's semantics, then, sense and reference are identical, since they must of necessity be so to the sign user. To find any other object of reference besides the meaning, we must step outside of semantics and make an empirical study of the sign user and his interaction with his environment, i.e. of pragmatics.

   There is, however, a closer and more recent parallel to Peirce's account of meaning and reference, namely the "new theory of reference" associated with the names of Keith Donnellan, Saul Kripke, and Hilary Putnam. Especially striking is the parallel with the account given by Putnam who, in several papers, has argued that the reference of "natural-kind terms" is not fixed by their meaning.[17] For instance, by the word 'gold' I intend to refer to the same thing that metallurgists refer to by this word, but I do not know the criteria by which they determine whether or not something is gold. Of course I have a set of criteria which enable me to use the word, and these may be said to constitute its meaning for me; Peirce would say that these criteria, together with the results of their application, constitute the "immediate" object of the word. Yet when I want a gold wedding ring, I want a ring which metallurgists would recognize as gold, not merely one which *I* would recognize as gold.[18] A dishonest jeweller would not get far by pleading in court that, since I could not tell the difference between gold and brass, he concluded that by the word 'gold,' I intended to refer to brass. The "dynamoid" object, in Peirce's terminology, is *real* gold, irrespective of whether I possess criteria for recognizing real gold. Recently, in his book *Meaning and the Moral Sciences,* Putnam has pushed this analysis further and has developed a general theory of the relation between meaning and understanding. On this theory I understand a term when I possess criteria for its use, and the concept of reference contributes nothing to the analysis of linguistic understanding. But I cannot explain the contribution which language use makes to my total activity without the notion of objects to which terms refer. Language is in this respect similar to any other tool: I can use electric light simply by knowing how to flip the switch and without knowing the first thing about electricity. But I cannot explain how my switch-flipping produces light without invoking the notion of electricity. Comparing Wittgenstein's early theory of language as a picture with his later theory of language as use, Putnam concludes that both may be correct, though for different purposes:

> The picture theory *was* wrong as a theory of understanding, for reasons that Wittgenstein himself very well brought out; but not totally wrong as a theory of language functioning. It *is* essential to view our theories as a kind of 'map' of the world, realists contend, if we are to explain how they help us guide our conduct as they do. But the 'use' theory is *also* right as an account of how language is *understood*. . . . Talk of use and talk of reference are parts of the total story, just as talk of switch-flipping and talk of electricity flowing through wires are parts of a total story.[19]

By comparison, though Peirce did not exactly look on signs as tools (the agent and the end being signs as well), he did regard semiosis as essentially a purposive activity. To act purposively, the agent need know only the interpretant, not the dynamoid object of the sign—indeed, he can know the object only through some interpretant—but he will not be able to attain his purpose unless there by a dynamoid object. As we saw from the letter to Lady Welby, knowledge of the object, as an external object, can be had only from collateral experience; and, as we saw from the 1902 quotation, it is when we apply the spirit of the pragmatic maxim to the maxim itself that our attention is directed towards general ideas. It is, then, when we regard the pragmatic maxim as an empirical hypothesis concerning the semantics of the language of science that we recognize the need for universals as a supplemental hypothesis in our total semiotic theory. So understood, the pragmatic maxim is neither a postulate nor a definition of the word 'meaning,' but an empirical hypothesis explaining how language users understand their own language. And, in that case, realism too is an empirical hypothesis, purporting to explain how language users, by using language in the precise way in which they do use it, succeed in attaining their goals to the extent that they do so succeed.

It should probably be noted at this point that there is a problem of how to test pragmatism taken as an empirical hypothesis. Peirce clearly thought it an empirical fact that when experimental scientists use words, they understand them pragmatically, that is to say experimentally. This indeed can be tested. We can ask a physicist what he means by 'force' and, if Peirce is right, we will be told that a force is an acceleration. Also, we can make a metaphysical statement to a physicist, and unless he can come up with some testable consequences following from our statement, he will pronounce himself baffled as to what we mean. So far, so good. But Peirce certainly often appears to think of pragmatism as a theory of language understanding in general, or at least as a theory of our understanding of all theoretical language; as such, it should apply to metaphysicians as well as to experimentalists. In this generalized version pragmatism may indeed still be testable; a possible counterexample would be the case of two metaphysicians debating some undecidable question with every appearance of understanding each other. Yet Peirce does not treat this case as a counterexample; his view is, rather, that in such a case the parties erroneously believe they understand each other, whereas in fact neither of them is saying anything at all intelligible. Now if two metaphysicians think they understand each other, the assertion that they do not in fact do so appears, in the absence of evidence, as nothing but a dogmatic apriorism. We noted in chapter 3 that there are conflicting purposes behind the pragmatic maxim; what I want to note here is how these conflicting purposes may endanger its testability. Peirce wants his maxim to be *both* an empirical theory of language understanding *and* a criterion by which to outlaw certain types of discourse as unintelligible; this latter purpose, it is now apparent, renders the maxim immune to a wide range of possible counterexamples by which it might be tested. This is of interest to note as an example of how the empiri*cist* strain in Peirce's thought is continually at odds with the empiri*cal* strain in his thought. Once this problem has been noted, it should be added that there are various gambits open by which the testability of the maxim may be saved. Peirce might, for instance, have opted for the view that the maxim is to be tested against the obvious cases of meaningful discourse (natural science), and that it can thereafter be applied as a criterion to decide doubtful cases (metaphysics). Or he might have granted that when people believe that they understand each other, they really do so. Each option would incur its own liabilities. In the former case, Peirce would have landed in a to him unpalatable scientism akin to that of Bernard or Mach; in the latter case, his pragmatic maxim would have been robbed of its critical bite. I am not sure whether Peirce ever finally decided between these two options. Be that as it may, the problem of testing pragmatism appears to me to be peculiarly Peirce's problem; there is not in principle any insurmountable difficulty in devising a relevant test, nor is there any great doubt about the philosophical liabilities attached to each of the two modes of testability suggested. I propose therefore to leave this question aside and turn to the more difficult and far more interesting question of how *realism* can be thought to be testable.

There is a great deal of evidence that Peirce thought of realism as an explanatory theory and as an empirically testable theory. There is disagreement among philosophers as to how these two properties are related; what it seems safe to say is that in order to be an acceptable explanation, a theory must explain certain facts which are the case, but if it explains only what is known to be the case few people would think of it as a good explanation. A good explanation is one which explains, in addition, something which may or may not be the case; we do not know which, but by putting the explanatory theory to the test of experience we can find out. In 1868, as we saw in chapter 2, Peirce presented realism as part of an explanation of the presumed fact that we sometimes have reason to change our opinions. We have such a reason, Peirce held, if we may believe that by that means we will eventually reach a true opinion. We might take this to mean that there is an observed drift towards relative stability of belief through error-elimination, and that this phenomenon is explained by the hypothesis of a long-run convergence towards truth through the same method of error-elimination. This is the hypothesis which in chapter 2 I labelled "scientific realism." In the "Logic of 1873," Peirce adduces another observed fact which requires explanation, namely the puzzling fact that "observations however different yield one identical result" (*CP*, 7.335). In the version which has appeared in the *Collected Papers,* he grants that this strange fact is explained by the hypothesis that external things act upon our senses ("representative realism"), but adds that this is a weak explanation and not necessarily the most appropriate one (*ibid.*). In alternate, unpublished drafts Peirce expressed doubts as to whether the hypothesis of representative realism is even meaningful, and concluded that all it can mean is that which is more simply expressed by the hypothesis that there is a universal tendency in human thought towards an ultimate, true opinion. These two facts, then, of relative stability and relative consensus of opinion are explained by the hypothesis of a drift towards a long-run stable consensus.

As I have mentioned, Peirce did not distinguish between the two hypotheses of scholastic and scientific realism. Later in this chapter we shall see how he derived the former from the latter; at this point we shall note that he held scholastic realism to be an empirically testable theory. So, in his 1905 articles, where he maintained that pragmaticism must insist upon the truth of scholastic realism, he also claimed that once the pragmatic maxim had swept away all ontological rubbish, what would remain of philosophy would be "a series of problems capable of investigation by the observational methods of the true sciences" (*CP*, 5.423). And the methods of the true sciences, Peirce frequently insists, are the methods of hypothesis and experimental testing (e.g. *CP*, 1.120, 2.635, 5.197, 5.598, 7.220). Perhaps the strongest and clearest formulation of the requirement that even an ontological hypothesis be empirically testable is found in a letter from 1908, where Peirce replies to Lady Welby's query whether the reality of God is to be proved by testing or by mathematical demonstration: "I reply that the question of the truth of religion being a question of what *is* true, and not of what *would be* true under an arbitrary hypothesis, such as those of pure mathematics, the only logical proof possible is the testing. . . . I maintain that "testing" is the sole logical proof of any question concerning Real objects."[20] We may note that Lady Welby's question arose from Peirce's 1908 article in the *Hibbert Journal*, "A Neglected Argument for the Reality of God" (*CP*, 6.452–93), where Peirce makes it clear that although God is *real,* he is not *actual.* God is not, then, an individual person or thing, but is real in the sense, presumably, that the individual things which do exist act in conformity to a rational purpose. (In *CP*, 6.494 ff., Peirce further emphasizes that although God is real, he does not exist.) This is, of course, a debatable view; my purpose is not, however, to digress into theology, but only to illustrate what Peirce meant by "proof." In the letter to Lady Welby, while discussing the reality of God, Peirce proceeds to generalize to all "Real objects"; hence we may safely take him to mean that the reality of any universal can be proved only by testing.

In 1903, Peirce actually proposed an experimental test of scholastic realism. In his Harvard lectures that year he posed the question whether general principles are really operative in nature, and proposed to approach the question by means of what he was sure his audience would regard as "a very silly experiment" (*CP*, 5.93). He then held up a stone and asked: How do I know that the stone will drop when I let it go? That the stone will drop is not in question; the question is how one can know this before it actually happens. Peirce's answer is the obvious one, that he knows this by prediction from the general law that heavy objects always fall when unsupported (*CP*, 5.95). More precisely, of course, it is predicted from the law of universal gravitation together with the appropriate initial conditions. But this law may be construed in two different ways, nominalistically or realistically. In the first case, the law is just a shorthand summary of a sequence of particular events which have been observed to be conjoined with a certain regularity in the past. In the second case, the law asserts that the observed past regularity is just a particular manifestation of a universal regularity to be found in nature; that is, it asserts that there is a real universal. The point of Peirce's "silly" experiment is to decide between these two options.

On the first hypothesis, Peirce claims, since there is nothing more asserted by the law than the actual occurrence of certain conjunctions of events in the past, the law tells us nothing about the future. On this hypothesis, therefore, it is entirely a matter of chance whether the past conjunctions of events will repeat themselves in the future; we should thus be willing to make an even bet that the stone will not drop on this novel occasion—an occasion which, in the nominalist view, does not fall within the scope of the regularity asserted by the law. But no one in his right mind would make such a bet; both Peirce and his audience know that the stone will drop. Peirce's argument is that they can know this only on the assumption that the chance hypothesis is false and that the opposite, realist hypothesis is true. Knowing something about the future by inference from past events is possible only if those past events count as evidence of a real law of nature which, by virtue of being universal, applies also the future: "The fact that I *know* that this stone will fall to the floor when I let it go, as you must all confess, if you are not blinded by theory, that I *do* know—and you none of you care to take up my bet, I notice—is the proof that the formula, or uniformity, as furnishing a safe basis for prediction, is, or if you like it better, *corresponds to,* a reality" (*CP*, 5.96). Remembering Peirce's later letter to Lady Welby, it would be uncharitable (and probably mistaken) to take the word "proof" here in the sense of deductive demonstration; rather, it must mean the test, as in "The proof of the pudding is in the eating." Next, Peirce drops the stone with a triumphant "I told you so!" and proceeds to draw the expected conclusion, namely that: "A thousand other such inductive predictions are getting verified every day, and one would have to suppose every one of them to be merely fortuitous in order reasonably to escape the conclusion that *general principles are really operative in nature.* This is the doctrine of scholastic realism" (*CP*, 5.101).

There are various ambiguities in this formulation of Peirce's "experimental proof of realism," as it has come to be called; some of these have been admirably brought out by Manley Thompson.[21] What we must note is that the experimental evidence which Peirce cites in favor of realism is not the particular event that this stone actually drops. There are two pieces of evidence. One is that everybody in the audience knows (by induction) that it will drop; the other is that a thousand such inductive predictions get verified every day. The drop of this stone is of interest as an instance of this class of phenomena. As such, it provides inductive confirmation of realism and inductive disconfirmation of nominalism, while it does not in the modern sense of the word 'prove' anything either way. Let us take a closer look at the logic of the test situation.

Realism says that *there are* laws of nature. But a law of nature does not *exist* as an individual thing which we may produce for inspection through an experiment. The reality of the law consists in that infinite class of individual occurrences of events through which the law may manifest itself. To prove its reality we should have to prove the truth of a universal statement, which is impossible. A universal statement may be disproved by counterexamples; hence the reality of any one proposed law of nature may be empirically disproved. But we cannot disprove the statement that there is, somewhere, a real law of nature, since this would also entail proving a universal statement; it would involve the claim that all possible laws of nature have been tested. The realist hypothesis, then, can be neither proved nor disproved, because it is really neither a universal nor a particular statement; strictly analyzed it is a statement embodying mixed quantifiers—although its precise formalization would involve too complex a notation to be worth attempting here. How, then, can it be put to an empirical test?

The answer is, I think, that the realist hypothesis can be inductively confirmed or disconfirmed by large classes of events. In this respect it is like a probabilistic hypothesis, which does not predict or rule out any particular event, but which is testable by statistical evidence. The parallel is not exact, since there may, of course, be laws of nature of which we have no inkling; still, we would have no reason to believe in the reality of laws of nature unless we had evidence of the reality of specific laws of nature. So the fact that Peirce can produce one well-confirmed law of nature is essential. The one he chooses is the law of gravitation; the fact that his audience is unwilling to bet on the fall of the stone is evidence that this is a well-confirmed putative law of nature. The actual fall of the stone is an instance of the broad class of events which confirm predictions from well-confirmed laws of nature. Hence this event counts as inductive evidence that well-confirmed laws of nature produce predictions which tend to get verified more often than not. This confirms the realist hypothesis, whereas it disconfirms the nominalist hypothesis, according to which such predictions should be defeated as often as not. Now what if the experiment had turned out differently? What if either Peirce's audience had accepted his bet, or the stone had remained suspended in the air after he let it go? Neither event would have forced Peirce to surrender his realism—or, more precisely, neither event could logically have forced him to do so. In the first case, he might have concluded that all Harvard students are thoroughly irrational; he left himself that loophole: "if you are not blinded by theory . . ." In the second case, he might have concluded either that the law of gravitation is not a real law of nature or that there were some unknown initial conditions at work. But if time and again he were to repeat his experiment with different audiences and different putative laws of nature, if each time his audience were to accept his bet, or if the stone were to drop (or whatever would count as a positive outcome) on the average only one half of the time, then it would eventually be irrational for Peirce to defend realism. So understood, Peirce's test is genuinely experimental, but it is part of an inductive, statistical test, it is not a crucial experiment.

The reader will note that Peirce's realist hypothesis is not here held to be testable in the sense specified by Karl Popper's "falsifiability criterion," a criterion which suffers from problems of its own.[22] There are other ways of construing testability; Putnam, for instance, has argued that the capacity for empirical confirmation is a sufficient requirement of testability.[23] If of two rival hypotheses only one is experimentally confirmed, then this counts as evidence against its rival, even if the latter cannot be falsified in a strict sense. Putnam's views are in this context of particular interest, since he has gone on explicitly to characterize realism as in this sense an empirical hypothesis. What the realist hypothesis states, according to Putnam, is that science converges towards truth in the Tarskian sense of correspondence with facts ("scientific realism" in our terminology). This hypothesis entails that the principle of charity is applicable to the history of science; that is, that, even though our descriptions of the world be incommensurable in meaning with past descriptions, still those past descriptions can be understood as having the same reference as ours, so that our descriptions can meaningfully be called *better* descriptions of the same world. If this condition were to fail, if the principle of charity were found to be inapplicable to the history of science, we should be forced to accept the "meta-induction" that no term now used will be found in the future to refer.[24] In such a case, then, we should have empirical grounds for giving up the realist hypothesis, and that is all that is needed for the hypothesis to count as empirical. Like Peirce, Putnam does not make testability depend on the possibility of a crucial experiment, but on the possibility of the accumulation of inductive counterevidence.

If this is the sense in which Peirce held realism to be an empirical hypothesis, how does this hypothesis fit into his theory of signs as outlined earlier in this chapter? Within that theory, as we saw, the pragmatic maxim figures as a semantic hypothesis; as such, it says that scientific statements are fully intelligible in terms of experiments and their outcomes. In 1905, Peirce went on to point out that this is as much as saying that words are meaningfully employed only on the condition that experiments can actually be carried out. This, in turn, implies both an actually existing world, in which the experimenter acts and is acted upon, and something of a general description, namely the experimenter's plan and purpose, without which his actions would not constitute an experiment. After describing the various phases of an experiment, Peirce concludes: "While the two chief parts of the event itself are the action and the reaction, yet the unity of essence of the experiment lies in its purpose and plan, the ingredients passed over in enumeration" (*CP*, 5.424).

We can now pull the various threads together. The scientist understands scientific statements in terms of possible experiments and expected experimental outcomes, that is, purely in terms of action and reaction. To the semiotic onlooker, studying the pragmatics of the language of science, it is evident that scientific terms can be used and understood only to the extent that certain experiments can be carried out. One condition for the execution of an experiment is the plan or purpose in the mind of the experimenter; he can, of course, manipulate lab equipment with no purpose whatever in mind, but such random manipulation does not constitute an experiment. For the experimenter to attach a purpose to his experiment, he must have reason to believe that experimental results are reproducible; i.e., that inductive predictions will tend, on the whole and for the most part, to be verified. A belief in predictive reliability is therefore a pragmatic condition for attaching an intelligible meaning to scientific terms; and this belief, in turn, involves a belief in universal regularities, manifesting themselves in reproducible experimental phenomena. The reproducible phenomena *per se* are compatible with nominalism as well; but realism explains why experimental results tend to be reproducible and predicts that they will go on being reproducible in a higher than random proportion of cases; nominalism does not. Hence, unless the realist hypothesis were true; science would be an idle game with no point or purpose to it.

This last point indicates in what way realism may be held to be an empirically testable hypothesis. If we can have empirical evidence for or against the claim that science is *not* an idle game—that it does in fact produce true predictions and contribute to the success of our total conduct—we shall *eo ipso* have empirical evidence for or against realism, which explains this presumed fact. I cannot resist pointing out, in passing, the parallel between this argument and the argument for realism later developed by R. G. Collingwood independently of Peirce. In 1933 Collingwood argued that logicians are committed to the existence of propositions and arguments, because their existence is a precondition for the pursuit of logic.[25] Although this type of argument was later to be made fashionable through the influence of Wittgenstein and Austin, at the time it fell on deaf ears. To my knowledge, it was noted only by Gilbert Ryle, who simply dismissed it as unintelligible.[26]

To conclude this section, the test of realism discussed above is not a very strong test, nor is it the only one Peirce considered. Realism has been invoked as an explanation of the predictive success of science, and we have seen that it explains this success in the sense that it predicts it. Hence it can be tested by the set of phenomena for which it has been invoked as an explanation. For it to be an interesting, non-trivial explanation it must predict, in addition, some other set of phenomena which are capable of independent testing. We shall see in the remainder of this chapter that Peirce's realism does yield additional predictions—predictions about the manner in which science progresses. But before we turn to this further elaboration of realism, we have to digress for a few pages and face some hard problems concerning the whole project of testing hypotheses with the scope of the realist hypothesis.

c. Problems of testability

Apart from all the problems surrounding the notion of testability in general, there are special problems attached to the idea of testing hypotheses about science as a whole.[27] Peirce formulates his realism as the hypothesis that there are real universals, or real laws of nature; my argument has been that, pragmatically speaking, this means that the reality of laws of nature is a precondition for the success of science. The problems then arise, how do we identify "science," and what are the criteria for its "success"? These are not idle questions; if, for instance, we follow a well-trodden path and define science by reference to empirical test procedures, the realist hypothesis becomes self-referential (that is, partly a hypothesis about itself), and attempts at testing it may easily generate tautology or self-contradiction. The problems may be illustrated through a few exercises in science fiction.

Suppose we were to abandon induction altogether and rely instead on predictions made by shamans, and suppose these predictions were to be fulfilled about half the time and defeated about half the time. Suppose, furthermore, that we were to apply the name "science" to the activity of the shamans. In this hypothetical situation, "science" would have no predictive reliability; the fact which realism is invoked to explain would no longer be a fact, and hence realism would no longer be an acceptable explanation. Would we really be forced to give up realism in this hypothetical situation—or, rather, would we *now* recognize such a situation as a refutation of realism? Of course not. We should say that realism is a hypothesis about *science,* not about whatever somebody might choose to call "science," and shamanism is not science, no matter what you choose to call it. What, then, is science? The most likely answer is that it is an activity pursued according to a particular method, for instance a method such that if there be laws of nature, this method will discover them. But if we define science in this manner, the presumed fact that science progresses turns into a tautology and, once again, there will be nothing for realism to explain. The method, therefore, must be specified independently of the result to which it leads. As we shall see in chapter 5, Peirce devoted a great deal of effort to giving such an independent specification of the scientific method, and he did apparently hold it to be a contingent fact that the method thus specified leads to the discovery of laws of nature. But is this enough to ensure that it is a contingent fact that *science* leads to this result? What would we say if we were to discover empirically that some procedure hitherto followed by science does not in fact lead to the desired goal? Obviously that that particular procedure is not part of the scientific method. So science is neither an ideal method, nor the method which happens to be followed by scientists; what, then, is it?

In addition to the problem of identifying science, there is the problem of identifying success. Let us give a slightly different twist to my story about the shamans. In the above, I assumed that we can determine how often the shamans' predictions are fulfilled; that is, there is a vestige of induction left in the picture. Let us now assume instead that we not only rely upon the shamans' predictions for practical action, we also take their word for what does and does not count as a fulfillment of a prediction. And, no matter what happens, the shamans tell us that their predictions have been fulfilled (we will assume all their predictions to be sufficiently vague to permit this);

so, their method is, for all we know, one hundred percent successful in producing true predictions.

Now consider two possibilities. In the first case the shamans are nominalists; in fact, they answer perfectly to Peirce's image of the nominalist. That is, they observe whatever happens and formulate empirical generalizations; but they do not invent theoretical entities or formulate laws of nature, let alone attempt to make predictions from such laws. Their position is that whatever has happened with perfect regularity in the past has a fifty-fifty chance of happening in the future. Still, they enjoy perfect predictive success, since they alone specify the conditions for such success. In this situation, how could one refute the shamans' claim that their predictive success refutes realism, understood as the hypothesis that real laws are a precondition for predictive success? If one could not, would it then be rational to give up realism as a refuted hypothesis?

In the second hypothetical case, all laws of nature have been empirically refuted, and all the predictive reliability of science (as we now know it) has been lost. Surely this is the sort of situation in which we should be rationally compelled to surrender realism. But suppose now that the shamans are realists. They simply retain all the refuted laws of nature and continue to make predictions from them. Since they are still eminently successful on their own terms, how could one possibly persuade them that realism is false?

The point of these fictional tales is a serious one. The conditions under which we would be compelled to give up realism are, so it would seem, conditions under which all inductive procedures are failed, and under which we are therefore not empirically compelled to anything. Hence the conditions appear to be inconsistent. Alternatively, we might be rationally compelled to surrender realism in situations where there is absolutely no evidence against it, which makes nonsense of the notion of rationality. The more general point illustrated by these predicaments is this: no matter what happens in the historical development of science, the scientific community may at any one time measure its scientific past by the yardstick of present-day science. By that standard, of course, present-day science will always be superior to the science of the past, and the history of science will always exhibit "progress" up to the present. In the absence of an independent standard with which to compare present-day science, we might find ourselves forced to conclude that the assertion that science has progressed will always be trivially true, no matter what happens. In that case, this assertion will not be an empirical statement, and there will then be no possible empirical evidence for or against realism.

Although I do not presume to have a definitive solution to these difficulties, a way out may perhaps be found along the following lines. The "real" science which is referred to in the realist hypothesis is the scientific tradition; this tradition is what Max Weber called a "historical individual," like "the Protestant ethic" or "the spirit of capitalism".[28] As an individual entity, science is not identified by an analytical definition, but is rather indicated by an ostensive definition. Say we have a set of Kuhnian "paradigms,"[29] or generally acknowledged examples of scientific methods and scientific achievements; we can then point to these paradigms and say that science is this sort of activity. Realism will then be a hypothesis about a contingent relationship between the paradigm methods and the paradigm achievements. If these paradigms were to change, as was envisaged in my hypothetical stories, then the meaning of the realist hypothesis would change; thereby, of course, its empirical content would change and perhaps disappear. When someone claims that realism is an empirical hypothesis, he does not mean that certain words have a definite empirical content, come what may. Least of all would Peirce hold anything like this; we have already seen that it is part of his pragmatism that words change their meaning over time. The claim that realism is an empirical hypothesis can mean only that the words in which this hypothesis is expressed have a definite empirical content so long as they have the meaning currently attached to them.

In my shaman stories we have no difficulty deciding under which conditions realism would have to be surrendered, so long as realism is understood to be a hypothesis about that which we today mean by "science." That is, not the science of today, but that activity which we today call "science," an activity which has been going on for centuries. The problem in my hypothetical stories is that the agents in those stories do not so understand realism, because they have a different paradigm of science. If such paradigm changes are among the conditions for the falsity of realism, then realism cannot be empirically refuted (something which has already been granted anyway, because of the logical form of the realist hypothesis), nor, it would seem, rationally surrendered. But no hypothesis would be refutable under the conditions we have considered, yet we would not accept the implication that there is no such thing as an empirical hypothesis. Realism remains empirical in this sense, that we can today envisage conditions under which we should have empirical grounds for surrendering it—even if, under those same conditions, we should not be sufficiently rational to do so. Moreover, even after a paradigm change there is nothing to prevent people having sufficient historical consciousness to know what we meant by "science," and hence to determine retrospectively what empirical grounds we had for believing or not believing in realism. Thus the conditions for the falsity of realism would not be inconsistent; they would merely exclude rational dissuasion from realism.

It is not clear, however, that the situation is as bleak as this. If science is a historical individual, then realism, if it is true at all, must be true of our scientific past, as well as of the present. If we can determine by reference to paradigm cases what elements in our intellectual history do and do not count as science, then the history of science provides a testing ground for realism, and then there are empirical procedures which we may employ here and now to determine the truth or falsity of realism. Once again, since the realist hypothesis contains mixed quantifiers the testing cannot take the form of straight falsification by crucial experiment. If, however, all or most of the recognized achievements of science have been nominalistically inspired, then we should have strong grounds for rejecting realism. Equally interesting are the acknowledged scientific failures. Even though we might not be able to recognize it if science as a whole were to regress permanently, still we do recognize individual regressive episodes in the history of science, and we may inquire into their methodological origins. We shall see towards the end of this chapter that this is the sort of test which Peirce himself undertook to carry out. Before we turn our attention to Peirce's highly interesting case studies, however, we need to explore the content of his realism a bit further and put some flesh and blood on the skeletal formulation so far considered.

d. Scientific and scholastic realism

As a theory of how scientists understand theoretical terms, pragmatism has certain definite methodological implications for the construction of scientific hypotheses. These are made explicit, e.g., in a paper on "The Logic of History" in 1901 and the Lowell Lectures in 1903. The former paper contains a discussion of hypothesis formation—what Peirce calls "abduction"—in which is offered this pragmatic justification of three proposed requirements for the construction of hypotheses:

> Now the only way to discover the principles upon which anything ought to be constructed is to consider what is to be done with the constructed thing after it is constructed. That which is to be done with the hypothesis is to trace out its consequences by deduction, to compare them with results of experience by induction, and to discard the hypothesis, and try another, as soon as the first has been refuted; as it presumably will be. (*CP*, 7.220)

The three requirements which Peirce proposes are: testability, explanatory adequacy, and economy. Only the third requirement is further discussed in this immediate context. It turns out, perhaps a bit surprisingly, that the most economical hypothesis is the one which recommends itself to the human mind as the most reasonable one. This is so because the number of possible hypotheses is always practically infinite, so that we cannot hope to get nearer the truth by random guessing. We can get nearer to the truth only if the mind is somehow preadapted to the order of nature, so that we have an instinctive tendency to guess at the truth. If there is such an instinctive tendency, we will save a great deal of effort and expense by first trying the hypothesis which instinctively recommends itself; if there is not, we might as well give up the whole enterprise of science:

> Science will cease to progress if ever we shall reach the point where

there is no longer an infinite saving of expense in experimentation to be effected by care that our hypotheses are such as naturally recommend themselves to the mind, and make upon us the impression of simplicity—which here means facility of comprehension by the human mind,—of aptness, of reasonableness, of good sense. For the existence of a natural instinct for truth is, after all, the sheet-anchor of science. (*CP*, 7.220)

We shall return to the idea of a natural instinct for truth in chapter 5. Of greater interest for immediate purposes are Peirce's first two requirements, which in the 1901 paper are stated thus:

In the first place, [the hypothesis] must be capable of being subjected to experimental testing. It must consist of experimental consequences with only so much logical cement as is needed to render them rational. In the second place, the hypothesis must be such that it will explain the surprising facts we have before us which it is the whole motive of our inquiry to rationalize. (*CP*, 7.220)

These two requirements are not further elaborated in the pages that follow; we shall turn therefore to the Lowell Lectures of 1903 for an elucidation of details. Peirce here repudiates the idea, which he attributes to Comte, Poincaré, and Pearson, that "a *verifiable* hypothesis . . . must not suppose anything that you are not able directly to observe" (*CP*, 5.597). He then proceeds to state his own, contrary view: the further a hypothesis is removed from what is directly observable, the richer will be its content, and the greater the number of its testable consequences:

If I had the choice between two hypotheses, the one more ideal and the other more materialistic, I should prefer to take the ideal one upon probation, simply because ideas are fruitful of consequences, while mere sensations are not so; so that the idealistic hypothesis would be the *more verifiable,* that is to say, would *predict more,* and could be put the more thoroughly to the test. (*CP*, 5.598)

The requirement of testability, apparently, is reduced to that of explanatory power. Precisely this requirement speaks in favor of speculating about theoretical entities and against hypothesizing purely in terms of what is directly observable. The conclusion is that precisely the methodological requirement of testability demands that we presuppose the existence of entities other than those which we are able to observe, or those which can be regarded as fictitious constructs substituting for descriptions of what we observe. This is as much as to say that a belief in the existence of a real external world, as postulated by scientific realism, is a presupposition of experimental science.

This kind of argument is by now becoming familiar to us. The scientist understands theoretical terms with reference to the experimental consequences of the theories in which these terms are embedded; if he knows all the possible experimental consequences of the theories employing, for instance, the term 'force,' then he understands this term perfectly. But he never does know all the possible experimental consequences of any theory; we cannot tell today what experiments might or might not become possible tomorrow. Scientific progress consists in, among other things, expanding the range of our experimental capability; it is in this way that we get to know nature better. If hypothesis formation is to serve this purpose, we ought to select those hypotheses which have the maximum number of experimental consequences which we are not yet able to test. That is, we ought to choose those hypotheses which have the greatest explanatory power, those which are richest in deductive consequences, whether or not all these consequences now appear to us to be testable. In the terminology of semiotic, if the semantics of the language of science is verificationist, then it is a fact of the pragmatics of this language that the sign activity which constitutes science is progressive only if it progresses towards a proliferation of verifiable statements. This, in turn, can be effected only if explanatory power, rather than ascertainable testability, be taken as a criterion for the selection of hypotheses for investigation. High testability is, then, a goal of inquiry and hence a requirement for the goodness of a hypothesis; for this very reason, however, current testability cannot be the criterion of a good hypothesis. The criterion must be explanatory power, something which entails that scientists, in order to advance science, must be realists at least to the extent of believing in the existence of a theory-independent reality of some sort.

Several scholars, among them A. J. Ayer,[30] have indicated a parallel between Peirce's requirements for the construction of hypotheses and Popper's "falsifiability criterion." This parallel is indeed worth noting, especially as Popper has also repeatedly equated degree of falsifiability with degree of explanatory power.[31] But the parallel should not be overworked; Popper, as far as I understand him, makes falsifiability the criterion of explanatory power, while Peirce's approach is the reverse, making explanatory power a criterion of testability. Moreover, as we have seen (section b, above), on Popper's criterion Peirce's realism would be purely metaphysical and *a priori,* something which Peirce clearly did not intend. Peirce has numerous affinities with Popper, but he was not simply a proto-Popperian.

Peirce's argumentation, as it has been presented so far in this section, need not entail more than a fairly austere scientific realism, i.e. a belief that science progresses by approximation towards correspondence with the "real" world, with no special commitment as to what the constitution of that world is. In the remainder of this section we shall examine how Peirce makes the step from scientific realism to scholastic realism, i.e., to the doctrine that the real world contains real universals. Before we proceed, however, a few words need to be said about the kind of universals Peirce had in mind. Earlier in this chapter we saw that Peirce believed in the reality of laws. He argued, for instance, that, because the laws governing the hardness of diamonds and the falling of stones are irreducible to sequences of particular occurrences of events, it follows that these laws are real, and that hardness and heaviness are themselves real, in so far as they consist in the operation of those laws. This much might be admitted, and one might still refuse to countenance another class of universals, namely theoretical entities. Hardness and heaviness are familiar to us all from everyday experience; we might grant their reality and still feel uneasy about the reality of electrons, protons, neutrons, and all the other strange entities which populate the universe of modern physics. Peirce, however, held his scholastic realism to entail the reality also of some theoretical entities, namely, those entities which are embedded in true theories.

Peirce's argument proceeds from the premise that one essential step in the process of "abduction" is the classification whereby a particular group of phenomena come to be regarded as a single *expla-*

nandum. In stressing the role of classification, Peirce is following in the footsteps of his Harvard teacher, the zoologist Louis Agassiz, and of the British philosopher William Whewell, who had held that the "colligation of facts" is an essential step in theory formation.[32] This process of colligation, Peirce holds, involves the grammatical conversion of the predicates of several subjects into one second-order subject, which then becomes the subject of the explanatory hypothesis. This grammatical conversion, which Peirce calls "hypostatic abstraction," is described thus in an article in *The Monist* in 1906:

> That wonderful operation of hypostatic abstraction by which we seem to create *entia rationis* that are, nevertheless, sometimes real, furnishes us the means of turning predicates from being signs that we think *through,* into subjects thought of. We thus think of the thought-sign itself, making it the object of another thought-sign. Thereupon, we can repeat the operation of hypostatic abstraction, and from these second intentions derive third intentions. (*CP*, 4.549)

In a manuscript from 1902, this example is given:

> Thus, we transform the proposition, "honey is sweet", into "honey possesses sweetness." "Sweetness" might be called a fictitious thing, in one sense. But since the mode of being attributed to it *consists* in no more than the fact that some things are sweet, and it is not pretended, or imagined, that it has any other mode of being, there is, after all, no fiction. (*CP*, 4.235)

Similarly, Peirce had already written, in his 1871 review of *Berkeley*: "It is perfectly true that all white things have whiteness in them, for that is only saying, in another form of words, that all white things are white" (*CP*, 8.14).

So far the notion of hypostatic abstraction appears fairly trivial, and it may seem to have little bearing on the reality of universals. It is well known that we can turn predicates into subjects by grammatical conversion, or by "semantic ascent" in Quine's terminology,[33] but there is no special problem about giving a nominalist account of the meaning of the resulting general term. Indeed, Peirce himself gives such an account in the two passages last quoted. His argument for universals, however, hinges on the claim that this operation, albeit semantically trivial, is yet pragmatically essential in the process of abduction. This is repeatedly emphasized by Peirce, who goes so far as to characterize hypostatic abstraction as "the one sole method of valuable thought" (*CP*, 1.383).[34] And he pushes the thesis to its extreme by illustrating it with the least favorable example possible, namely Molière's infamous *virtus dormitiva*. In Molière's comedy a medical student is asked by his examination board why opium makes people go to sleep; his answer is that it is because opium has a "dormitive power." Molière and his audiences thought this was a great joke on the scholastic manner of explaining phenomena by "occult powers"; the joke is, of course, that the statement "Opium has a dormitive power" says no more than the statement "Opium makes people go to sleep," which is just the fact that stands in need of explanation.

Peirce repeatedly returns to this example, and his various pronouncements on it are *prima facie* somewhat puzzling. So, for instance, in his 1871 review he seems to agree with Molière: "To say that people sleep after taking opium because it has a soporific *power*, is that to say anything in the world but that people sleep after taking opium because they sleep after taking opium?" (*CP*, 8.12). Having answered this question in the negative in 1871, Peirce seems to answer it in the affirmative in 1902, in the same manuscript from which I quoted earlier:

> Now it is very easy to laugh at the old physician who is represented as answering the question, why opium puts people to sleep, by saying that it is because it has a dormitive virtue. It is an answer that no doubt carries vagueness to its last extreme. Yet, invented as the story was to show how little meaning there might be in an abstraction, nevertheless the physician's answer does contain a truth that modern philosophy has generally denied: it does assert that there really is in opium *something* which explains its always putting people to sleep. (*CP*, 4.234)

Now, surprisingly, the joke is on Molière! The apparent discrepancy between the two statements can undoubtedly be easily explained by the time lag between them; too easily, because the discrepancy is in fact only apparent. Peirce does not say in 1902 that the statement "Opium has a dormitive virtue" says anything more than "Opium always puts people to sleep." What he does say is that the former statement says something more than does the nominalistic construction of the latter statement as referring only to a sequence of particular events. The two formulations are semantically equivalent, and so they are interchangeable at the level of describing the observable phenomena. But they are not pragmatically equivalent: it is not indifferent to the future course of research—including the future discovery of novel phenomena—which formulation is chosen as a hypothesis. Hence, when we describe and explain the pragmatics of science, the two formulations are not interchangeable.

This point is lucidly stated by Boler:

> If someone suggests that there is a real connection between taking opium and going to sleep, that there is "something about opium" which accounts for the fact that people always go to sleep after taking it (5.534), then, although such a suggestion "carries vagueness to its last extreme" (4.234), at least it starts me on the way to an explanation. It suggests, for example, that I might study the chemical structure of opium and other soporifics to explain what this "something about" opium is.[35]

So long as nothing more is known about opium than that it puts people to sleep, the hypostatic abstraction "dormitive power" means nothing more to the investigator than a statement of this fact. But it may acquire a richer meaning, which the mere statement of the fact cannot do. That is, we do in fact understand the two statements in the same way, but we may come to understand the theoretical statement at a deeper level. Once the investigator believes that there really is in opium a dormitive power, he will set about trying to discover all its experimental consequences, and he may discover some of these in the form of chemical properties and reactions which were not implied by the original statement of the fact to be explained.

All of this may be granted as true, and yet might be dismissed as trivial. A nominalist may grant that the meanings of theoretical terms change with empirical discoveries and still he might object that if the full meaning of these terms at any one stage of investigation consists in the experimental consequences known at that stage, then theoretical terms may be granted a heuristic value without the supposition that at any stage they refer to anything more than the experimental consequences known at that stage. Thus the term 'dormitive power' may be fruitful because it mediates between the known and the unknown experimental consequences. That is, the supposedly mistaken belief that the term 'dormitive power' means something more than the sum of experimental consequences already in hand might act as a spur to discovering further experimental consequences. But we discover this fruitfulness only after the previously unknown consequences have become manifest—so at no time need we suppose the term to refer to anything more than its known experimental consequences.

(At this point, one might start wondering about the good faith of our imaginary nominalist. If 'virtus dormitiva' implies no more than the phenomena already observed, it is a redundant concept. The moment it is shown to be a fruitful concept, it is taken to refer only to the phenomena we now observe. Either way, we do not need universals. As Collingwood was to put it in his critique of Ayer, it is a game of "Heads I win, tails you lose.")[36]

Peirce's answer is that theories possess more than a merely heuristic value. Science progresses through the proposal of hypotheses and through their subsequent elimination by inductive testing. Since the number of possible hypotheses which will explain any finite set of observations is infinite, the elimination of any finite number of false ones will get us nowhere nearer the truth unless the number of hypotheses has been antecedently limited to a finite number of near-true ones. This is why, as noted before, scientific progress presupposes a natural instinct for guessing at the truth. This instinct cannot be unerring; we manifestly make many false guesses, and this is why inductive testing is essential.[37] But, among those theories which have not been overthrown by experience, we have no empirical reason to prefer our theories to that infinite number of theories which it has not entered our minds to formulate, let alone to test. So, in the classification of phenomena and the therein implied choice of a particular kind of hypothesis, we make (highly fallible) truth claims which are not themselves tested and are not reducible to the set of empirical assertions resulting from testing, but on whose truth the success of the entire testing-process depends:

The chemist assumes that when he mixes two liquids in a test-tube, there will or will not be a precipitate whether the Dowager Empress of China happens to sneeze at the time, because his experience has always been that laboratory experiments are not affected by such distant conditions. Still, the solar system is moving through space at a great rate, and there is a bare possibility that it may just then have entered a region in which sneezing has a very surprising force. (*CP*, 5.8)

The hypothesis that the Empress' sneezing influences the chemical reaction in our laboratory is a testable hypothesis, but it is one which we do not bother to test, because we should make no progress if we had to test *all* such remote hypotheses. Peirce's point here is similar to the one recently popularized by Goodman, who has pointed out the paradox that we do not seriously consider hypotheses like "All emeralds are grue," when 'grue' is so defined that this hypothesis has the same evidential support as "All emeralds are green," yet predicts that all future emeralds will be blue.[38] This choice of a scheme of classification, on which the progress of science essentially depends, is not in the nature of an IOU to be cashed in by experimental phenomena. The predicate 'grue' is not given a chance to prove its mettle, any more than is the Dowager Empress' sneeze.

Yet our decision to exclude such bizarre hypotheses is in a way an IOU, although one redeemable in a different currency from hypotheses within science. The progress of science towards truth depends on our making the right choice of a classificatory scheme; hence, in Peirce's view, a classificatory scheme is true or false and hence, also, the universals postulated in such a scheme are real or unreal (*CP*, 5.453). But this means that our decision on classification can be cashed in by the future progress of science, and that scholastic realism (as asserting the reality of some universals) has the empirical import that if our general terms fail to refer to real entities, science will cease to progress.

The empirical nature of the realist hypothesis is, as I have argued, problematic because, among other things, it cannot be falsified. Still, as I have also argued, the history of science may provide evidence for or against realism. We have generally acknowledged paradigms of progress and stagnation in science; if, for instance, all or most of the progress has been due to purely empirical generalization, while all or most of the stagnation has been due to a futile search for imaginary entities, then we should have overwhelming empirical grounds for rejecting realism. It is appropriate to close this chapter with a brief consideration of Peirce's own contribution to the testing of realism by the case-study approach.

e. The test of realism

From his theory that science progresses only on the assumption that there are real laws of nature, and only through the discovery of such laws, Peirce drew the corollary that nominalism has impeded scientific progress in the past and will do so in the future, unless checked. Nominalism "blocks the road of inquiry" by prohibiting investigation into the reality underlying the phenomena—the only kind of investigation that can lay bare the laws of nature and hence prove fruitful of experimental consequences. Now this corollary of scholastic realism is a historical hypothesis; if true, it is true *a posteriori,* and its truth or falsity can be ascertained only by inquiry into the history of science. Peirce's vast—and largely unpublished—researches into this subject cannot here be reviewed; we shall merely look at a few of the historical cases cited in his published papers. The first example concerns the nominalism of Auguste Comte. Towards the end of the article "How To Make Our Ideas Clear," Peirce issued this warning against prejudging the future course of science:

> Who would have said, a few years ago, that we could ever know of what substance stars are made whose light may have been longer in reaching us than the human race has existed? Who can be sure of what we shall not know in a few hundred years? Who can guess what would be the result of continuing science for ten thousand years, with the activity of the last hundred? (*CP,* 5.409)

Comte's name is not here invoked; but a later use of the same example—the composition of the stars—suggests what Peirce had in mind. In the manuscript on "The First Rule of Reason" from about 1899, Peirce sets forth his famous rule, "Do not block the way of inquiry," which ought to be "inscribed upon every wall of the city of philosophy" (*CP*, 1.135). He then proceeds to enumerate various violations of the rule; one of them is the sin of asserting that something or other can never be known. This is Peirce's example:

> When Auguste Comte was pressed to specify any matter of positive fact to the knowledge of which no man could by any possibility attain, he instanced the knowledge of the chemical composition of the fixed stars; and you may see his answer set down in the *Philosophie positive*. But the ink was scarcely dry upon the printed page before the spectroscope was discovered and that which he had deemed absolutely unknowable was well on the way to getting ascertained. It is easy enough to mention a question the answer to which is not known to me today. But to aver that that answer will not be known tomorrow is somewhat risky; for oftentimes it is precisely the least expected truth which is turned up under the ploughshare of research (*CP*, 1.138)

In this example, the joke is on Comte, the philosopher who made himself ridiculous by posing theoretical boundaries to the progress of science, only to see these boundaries immediately transgressed by science. Here, also, Peirce's right to speak on behalf of science is beyond question; spectral analysis was one of his professional specialties. In the second example we shall look at, the case of Claude Bernard, the situation is both more serious and more complex. Here, Peirce holds, nominalism was actually taken seriously by the scientific community, so that it came to function as a real obstacle to scientific progress. Bernard appears as the *bête noire* in two passages in the "Lessons From the History of Science" from about 1896. In the first of these passages Bernard's nominalistic metaphysics is contrasted with Louis Pasteur's experimentalism:

> At that time the medical world was dominated by Claude Bernard's dictum that disease is not an entity but merely a sum of symptoms. This was pure metaphysics which only barricaded inquiry in that direction. But that was a generation which attached great value to nominalistic metaphysics. Pasteur began with the phylloxera. He found it influenced the "optical activity" of the sugar. This pointed to a ferment and therefore to an entity. He began to extend the doctrine to other diseases. The medical men, dominated by the metaphysics of Claude Bernard, raised all sorts of sophistical objections. But the

method of cultures and inoculation proved the thing, and here we see
new ideas connected with new observational methods and a fine
example of the usual process of scientific evolution. (*CP*, 1.109)

The second mention of Bernard occurs immediately afterwards, in a
list of "*a priori* dicta," illustrating the baneful influence of such dicta
on the progress of science. First on the list of Bernard's dictum that
disease is not an entity, which is once more dismissed as "a purely
metaphysical doctrine" (*CP*, 1.110).

This case, I said, is more complex than that of Comte. Bernard
was one of the most prominent physiologists of the nineteenth century
and is widely regarded as the founder of experimental physiology. He
must also be credited with one of the classic expositions of the experimental method, and he, too, roundly condemned the intrusion of *a
priori* dicta into science. Moreover, I have found no evidence that
Bernard ever wrote that disease is not an entity but merely a sum of
symptoms. In Peirce's *CP*, 1.109 there is a footnote reference to
Bernard's *Leçons de pathologie expérimentale*, 2me lec,on, but
without a page reference. In that lecture, Bernard twice verbally
equates disease with a series of symptoms, but in each case the
context makes it clear that the contrast is not between symptoms and
an underlying entity. In the one case, the point is that a disease does
not consist in a single symptom; in the other case, the point is that
symptoms can be experimentally induced by means of knowledge
of general physiological laws, and that diseased phenomena are
therefore not different in kind from normal physiological phenomena.[39] Finally, in the very same lecture Bernard explicitly defined
'disease' as "a troubled or exaggerated physiological phenomenon,"[40]
something which to a physician means something rather different
from merely a sum of symptoms. Peirce's denigration of Bernard
might appear, therefore, as itself an example of the aprioristic hubris
towards science so often exhibited by philosophers. Peirce was not a
professional philosopher, but neither was he a professional
physiologist—even though the physiological psychology of his day
was well within his sphere of competence.

What is true, however, is that Bernard held life to be nothing
but the sum of vital phenomena, and that this followed from his

aprioristic determinism, according to which there could be no such thing as spontaneous or creative vital forces, which were not themselves subject to causal determinism. In his *Introduction a l'étude de la médecine expérimentale,* Bernard repeatedly endorses determinism as an *a priori* principle.[41] In the same work, he condemns as futile the attempt to find the cause of particular vital phenomena in some underlying "vital force," citing specifically Pasteur's theory of ferments as an example of this kind of futile speculation.[42] So, although Peirce may be guilty of quoting Bernard out of context, his analysis seems to have been fundamentally correct.

It may be added, in further corroboration, that while Bernard opposed Pasteur's vitalism, he also held the biochemical reduction of physiology to be in principle impossible, thus occupying a dogmatic intermediate position between vitalism and reductionism. Moreover, Bernard turned to methodology only after he had made his chief experimental contributions to science, and at roughly the time when his interests turned from science to politics. He did his experimental work chiefly in the 1840s and '50s, his *Médecine expérimentale* was published in 1865, and in 1869 he became a senator. The historian of science Nils Roll-Hansen has argued that Bernard's methodological writings were largely motivated by reasons of research policy, specifically by the desire to establish physiology as an autonomous academic discipline.[43] For this purpose Bernard formulated a "practicalist" methodology which denied the possibility of reducing physiology to chemistry on the ground that this was not within the practical possibilities of experimentation—then or in any foreseeable future. Peirce's view of Bernard's influence as reactionary and obscurantist is substantially confirmed by Roll-Hansen: "The fate of Bernard's methodology of biology can teach us to beware of the prejudice that what is obviously impossible today will remain so in the future."[4]

In the case of Bernard, then, Peirce seems to be right that his nominalism was aprioristic, and that the undisputed progress effected by Pasteur took place in spite of Bernard's influence. It should be added that Bernard and Pasteur were roughly contemporaries (Bernard 1813–78; Pasteur 1822–95); both had done their most pioneering work by the mid-sixties, and both were dead by the time Peirce wrote his "Lessons From the History of Science." By this time, also, the verdict of the scientific community was in, and it was in Pasteur's favor; in writing about Bernard, therefore, Peirce wrote as a historian of science. He was not siding with Pasteur and joining issue with Bernard; the issue was already decided, and the decision gives evidential support to Peirce's realism insofar as the latter is a historical hypothesis.

Of course one or two case studies do not prove a thing; such case studies have a point, however, if we hope that by the gradual accumulation of evidence a clear pattern will eventually emerge and force a decision for or against realism. We cannot know *a priori* that this will happen. If no pattern were ever to emerge, we should eventually have to conclude that the issue between realism and nominalism is a pseudo-problem. That this possibility must be left open is quite in tune with Peirce's pragmatism: we can learn only empirically what a statement (e.g. the realist hypothesis) means, and also whether it means anything. Realism might turn out to be meaningless, but this can only be learned inductively and it cannot be conclusively known until we have attained omniscience.

We have already seen, however, that realism is not only a hypothesis about past history; it is about science as a historical entity which still exists, hence it entails predictions about the future fate of this entity for as long as it shall continue to exist. The verification of such predictions will presumably have greater evidential weight than *ex post facto* interpretations of past events. It is important to note, however, that the predictions will have to be of a rather special kind. If it is part of the realist hypothesis that we cannot foretell today what we may or may not discover tomorrow, then obviously the future course of science is to that extent unpredictable. This does not mean that the future course of science is in all respects unpredictable. If future discoveries are unpredictable, we can predict the fate of those (in the future) who would predict the future course of discovery and who base methodological prescriptions on such predictions. We can predict that such people will at best be surprised by the course of scientific progress, and that at worst, to the extent that they gain an influence over the actual pursuit of science, they will impede such progress. They may, of course, happen to be right in particular predictions, but this will have to happen by pure chance, and the probability of it is infinitesimal since there is presumably an infinity of possible discoveries for science to make. We may predict, therefore, that most of the time the predictors will be wrong.

Peirce did make one such prediction, one which was dramatically verified after it had been made; too late, in fact, for Peirce to say "I told you so." The prediction was made in the course of a critique of the methodological ideas of Karl Pearson (1857–1936), a British statistician who turned biologist and became Britain's acknowledged authority on hereditary studies until the breakthrough of neo-Mendelian genetics around 1915. His major philosophical work, *The Grammar of Science*, was published in 1892, and its second edition, which appeared in 1900, was reviewed by Peirce in *Popular Science Monthly* in 1901. Throughout Peirce's later writings there are scattered polemical asides against Pearson;[45] there is, however, only one attempt at serious criticism, namely in the 1901 review.

In his book Pearson had proposed a Social Darwinist justification of the scientific enterprise; the purpose of science, he claimed, is to "lead to more efficient citizenship and so to increased social stability."[46] To this doctrine Peirce objected, "First, that it is historically false, in that it does not accord with the predominant sentiment of scientific men; second, that it is bad ethics; and, third, that its propagation would retard the progress of science" (*CP*, 8.135). Pearson had maintained, furthermore, that laws of nature are purely mental constructs and not real facts; that science only describes the *how* of things while the why must remain forever a mystery; and that science only gives a *résumé* of past events, while prediction of the future remains a matter for belief.[47] All of these doctrines come under fire in Peirce's review. The first doctrine simply involves a misunderstanding of the word 'real' whereby concepts and ideas are arbitrarily excluded (*CP*, 8.144–52). The second doctrine is dismissed as pure obscurantism: "The author says that the *why* of things remains a mystery. . . . But according to my notions there can be no mystery in the universe, in the sense of a real fact to which no approach to knowledge can ever be gained. For a reality is an idea that insists upon proclaiming itself, whether we like it or not" (*CP*, 8.156). The third doctrine, that the sole business of science is to describe past events, is likewise dismissed: "It would be a maxim utterly blighting to all further progress of science, were it accepted, since it is only by predictions that men are led to devise new experiments" (*CP*, 8.155). In sum, Peirce's case against Pearson is that the latter's positivist methodology is a piece of obscurantism which is a false description of the science of the past, and which, if accepted by scientists, would impede the growth of science in the future.

Like Bernard, Pearson falls victim to being unfairly quoted out of context.[48] In all essentials, however, Peirce's criticisms were to be borne out by Pearson's subsequent career. Pearson's interest in heredity dated from the early 1890s when he, together with Weldon, founded the "biometric" school of biology. This neo-Darwinian school was dedicated to the statistical study of heredity on the level of overt traits, or "phenes" in a later terminology; its central doctrine was the "law of ancestral heredity" (attributed to Francis Galton), which held that overt traits are inherited with a specifiable statistical regularity. Within a few years this was to become the authoritative opinion in Britain; Pearson and Weldon were both prominent members of the Royal Society; in 1907 Pearson became the director of Francis Galton's eugenics laboratory, and in 1911 he became Galton Professor of Eugenics and head of the department of applied statistics at University College in London. However, from 1900 on, the biometric doctrine was challenged by the neo-Mendelians, led by William Bateson, who claimed that the statistical rules of heredity operate on the "occult" level of genes, not on the overt level of phenes. The exact ontological status of genes was unclear then as now. Genes were depicted as beads on a string, the whole string constituting a chromosome; this was a convenient graphic representation which was taken about as literally as Bohr's solar system model of the atom. The leading Mendelians, such as Bateson and Johannsen, never actually believed that genes were discrete material particles. Today, the gene is identified as a segment of a DNA-molecule, which makes it a material entity, though not necessarily a discrete one. Be that as it may, the controversy between Mendelians and biometricians did not revolve around the question of what a gene is; the question was rather that of the explanatory value of postulating such unobserved entities at all. The received view of this controversy has been that the Mendelians did not succeed in explaining the statistical results obtained by the biometricians, because of mathematical problems which were not solved until 1918 by R. A. Fisher. Recently, however, it has been documented by the historian of science Bernard Norton that Pearson himself solved these mathematical problems as early as 1909, then explained away his own result in an *ad hoc* manner and continued his opposition to Mendelism on purely *a priori* grounds.[49] Norton concludes that Pearson's opposition to Mendelism was motivated not by scientific reasons but by his "*Weltbild*," according to which the statistical regularities observed among phenomena are ultimate and not reducible to underlying laws or causes on the level of unobservable entities:

> Like many would-be banishers of metaphysics, Pearson himself had certain views which are themselves best characterized as metaphysical. For one with these views, the Mendelian mode of describing phenomena seemed unattractive. This metaphysics might perhaps be best described as a statistical *Weltbild,* and was perhaps most carefully expounded in Pearson's third (1911) edition of *The grammar of science*—though it can be traced back to an earlier period.[50]

This apparently straightforward verification of Peirce's prediction may seem too pat to be true. And, in a way, it is. Norton's paper is, as I mentioned, a challenge to the received view of the biometry controversy. In his paper Norton points out that Pearson's own version of the story was unquestioningly accepted by his student Cyril Burt, the father of modern studies on the inheritability of intelligence. "In science as in everyday life," Norton concludes, "Authority looms large."[51] It is also to the point that the article on Pearson in the *Encyclopedia of the Social Sciences* is an almost unqualified eulogy.[52] Once again, we are faced with the problem of testing the realist hypothesis; the specific problem here being that the history of science, like all history, tends to be written by the victors. The history of biology is written today by neo-Mendelians, while the history of the social sciences is written by Pearson's intellectual grandchildren, and neither group is likely to characterize its own scientific tradition as regressive. So, while Norton and other historians of biology regard Pearson's influence as regressive, this judgment is not unanimously shared by the entire scientific community. While recognizing this problem, I do not, however, think it warrants the epistemological conclusion that the question of whether a particular tradition is progressive or regressive is empirically unresolvable. A neo-Mendelian and an IQ-psychologist share a number of paradigms of scientific progress; there is nothing in principle to prevent both from examining the biometry controversy in relation to the same set of paradigms, and there is no *a priori* reason why they should not reach the same conclusion. One reason no universal consensus on the historical question has yet been reached is that the *scientific* question of the inheritability of IQ (a phenotypic trait) has not yet been settled. If this scientific question can be empirically resolved, so can the historical question whose answer will tell for or against realism. And, when it is claimed that realism has an empirical content, it is hardly claimed that it is more empirical, or better testable, than theories in the empirical sciences themselves.

In this chapter I have tried both to make a *prima facie* exegetical case for the interpretation of Peirce's realism as an empirical hypothesis about science as a historical entity, and to make philosophical sense of this hypothesis by present-day standards (I will not say criteria) of empirical significance. While I think both tasks belong within the sphere of responsibility of the historian of philosophical ideas, some readers may feel that I have strayed unduly far into the sphere of purely philosophical argumentation. For the remainder of this book, we shall stay safely within the confines of intellectual history in order to supplement and extend our exegesis of Peirce's thought.

Chapter Five
Convergence and Its Conditions

a. Peirce's apriorism

IN PRECEDING CHAPTERS I have characterized realism variously as the doctrine that universals (or at least some universals) are real, and as the doctrine that science progresses by convergence towards truth, in the absolute sense of correspondence with reality. The former realism is what Peirce calls "scholastic realism"; the latter is what I have called "scientific realism." In chapter 4 it was argued that Peirce validly infers his scholastic realism from his scientific realism in conjunction with the pragmatic maxim. The structure of the argument was that if, as a matter of fact, science converges towards truth through the partial experimental verification of universal hypotheses, then those hypotheses must refer to something beyond the experimental effects by which they are tested, namely to real laws of nature. The chief evidence for this conclusion was that in the eyes of scientists an experience does not count as an experimental result unless it is believed to be indefinitely reproducible, a belief which is logically warranted only if there be real, universal laws of nature. Nothing in this argument depends on the assumption that science necessarily converges towards truth; that assumption would actually be incompatible with the main argument as here presented. Peirce's view is that we have empirical evidence that convergence has taken place and will take place in the future; this view implies that convergence is something which might conceivably not take place.

It has been argued further that if we follow Peirce's recommendation and go on to apply the pragmatic maxim to the doctrine of realism, then that doctrine turns out to be a meta-hypothesis about scientific research, testable by the history of science. Increased predictive reliability and increased consensus among the scientific community are held to be facts which are explained by the hypothesis that the truth is susceptible of being gradually uncovered through the exercise of reason and the growth of experience. This is admittedly a slightly free rendering of Peirce, who is not altogether consistent on this issue; but it is the only way I can think of to make sense of his 'experimental proof' of realism. It also receives additional corroboration from the fact that Peirce himself found it worthwhile to defend his realism with historical case studies, something which would be pointless had he conceived of realism as an *a priori* truth.

In this chapter I shall attempt to reinforce the exegetical case for the above interpretation by discussing some *prima facie* powerful objections. Peirce's realist doctrine of convergence towards truth is frequently, indeed typically, expressed by the thesis that the scientific method is 'self-corrective' (e.g. *CP*, 2.588, 2.703, 2.729, 2.776, 2.781, 5.384, 5.385, 5.582, 5.590, 6.40, 6.41). This doctrine which, following Laurens Laudan, I shall call 'SCT' (the Self-Corrective Thesis), has been widely held to have been proposed by Peirce as a necessary truth, which he attempted to establish by *a priori* demonstration. Furthermore, it has been argued that this attempt failed, for at least two reasons. Thus, for instance, Laudan and Georg Henrik von Wright have argued that Peirce, while professing to establish the self-corrective nature of scientific method in general, in the end argued the thesis only with regard to the rather special case of statistical induction, without offering any reason for believing that the other methods of science are reducible to this particular form of inference.[1] Moreover, it has been argued by John W. Lenz and Edward H. Madden that Peirce's argument for the self-correctiveness even of statistical induction is trivial and that his version of SCT is simply analytically true.[2]

Working on the assumption that there are indeed inconsistencies in the corpus of Peirce's writings, I feel no obligation to refute these criticisms of Peirce. On the contrary, I am persuaded that these criticisms are by and large justified, up to a point. But I do feel obliged to show that they are not as important as might appear, and that they do not tell the only story compatible with the textual evidence. Specifically, I think one misses a great deal by singling out

Peirce's "theory of induction" or "justification of induction" as special topics for discussion. Peirce, in my view, does not have a justification of induction in the modern, post-Russellian sense. He has a logical theory of statistical inference, according to which statistical inferences are self-corrective, if any inductive inferences are. And he has a theory of scientific inquiry according to which there are certain factual assumptions which must hold for inquiry to converge towards the truth—i.e., for any inductive procedures to be self-correcting. According to this theory, also, the long-term convergence of inquiry towards truth allows for indefinitely wide short-term deviations from the truth. The theory is so constructed as to make room for the claims of non-scientific knowledge to legitimacy, without placing arbitrary boundaries to the future course of inquiry. As I claimed in chapter 1, this dual purpose is attained by arguing that the scientific method is such that, as a matter of fact, it will lead us towards truth, while there is no logical guarantee that it will do so in any finite short run. The time has come to substantiate this claim by showing how Peirce's arguments concerning induction and hypothesis formation support it.

To begin with, it would be pointless to deny that Peirce does advocate SCT as a necessary truth. The literature referred to above abounds in quotations like the following: "Nor must we lose sight of the constant tendency of the inductive method to correct itself. This is of its essence. This is the marvel of it" (CP, 2.729). "Induction is that mode of reasoning which adopts a conclusion as approximative, because it results from a method which must generally lead to the truth in the long run" (CP, 1.67). Induction "is a method of reaching conclusions which, it it be persisted in long enough, will assuredly correct any error concerning future experience into which it may lead us" (CP, 2.769). "Induction must mean that operation which induces an assent, with or without quantitative modification, to a proposition already put forward, this assent being regarded as the provisional result of a method that must ultimately bring the truth to light" (CP, 5.590).

This strand of apriorism and necessitarianism in Peirce's thought would be utterly perplexing were it not for John W. Lenz' discovery that Peirce's thesis is not only a necessary truth known *a priori*, it is analytic to boot. Lenz' argument is that since, for Peirce, 'truth' is only the final opinion on which the community of investigators will ultimately agree, and since the 'real' is only the object of true belief, it follows analytically that whatever is real will sooner or later reveal itself in the course of inquiry.[3] Lenz makes an impressive exegetical case for this interpretation, quoting such statements as:

> Now, since if there is anything real, then (on account of this reality consisting in the ultimate agreement of all men, and on account of the fact that reasoning from parts to wholes is the only kind of synthetic reasoning which men possess) it follows necessarily that a sufficiently long succession of inferences from parts to wholes will lead men to a knowledge of it, so that they cannot be fated on the whole to be thoroughly unlucky in their inductions. (*CP*, 5.351)[4]

If the analytic quality of this statement is not obvious enough, it is surely inescapable in the following—which Lenz does not quote—in which Peirce rejects the claim that induction needs to postulate a uniformity of nature:

> Any fact, then, which might be supposed postulated, must either be such that it would ultimately present itself in experience, or not. If it will present itself, we need not postulate it now in our provisional inference, since we shall ultimately be entitled to use it as a premise. But if it never would present itself in experience, our conclusion is valid but for this fact being otherwise than assumed, that is, it is valid as far as possible experience goes, and that is all that we claim. (*CP*, 6.41)

If the reader by now experiences a sense of déjà vu, the following quote from Lenz should produce total recall: "Peirce must mean that reality is the object of that opinion which, after some finite point in time, the community of investigators would continue to hold."[5] Must he? Lenz supports his claim by quoting from the 1868 article which we examined in chapter 2, section d. My argument there was that although Peirce may be ambiguous on just this point, on the whole the textual evidence favors an absolute notion of truth, which is defined as the opinion which would result from a process of inquiry indefinitely prolonged, and which is coextensive with the notion of truth as correspondence with fact. This latter notion, I argued, is required to make sense of Peirce's scholastic and scientific realism, as well as his fallibilism, while the relative notion of truth as an opinion reachable in a finite process of inquiry represents an anomalous strand of aprioristic phenomenalism which is flatly incompatible with fallibilism, and which turns both realist doctrines into tautologies. This aprioristic strand is present in Peirce's thought, and it crops up in his various formulations of pragmatism, thereby generating those confusions which I attempted to unravel in chapter 3. I am not surprised, therefore, to find that this strand reappears in Peirce's discussions of induction and scientific progress, and hence I have no quarrel with Lenz, who has the merit of having identified this strand of apriorism more clearly than anyone else I know of. But the Peirce who interests me is the thinker whose central philosophical concerns were those of realism and fallibilism. Once it has been established that Peirce peripherally embraced doctrines thoroughly alien to his central concerns, and once we have examined the reasons he did so, I do not think there is much to be gained from a further investigation into those anomalous doctrines.

To clarify the present point: I take Peirce's ideal-limit theory to hold that if on any one question inquiry converges towards a limit, then that opinion towards which inquiry converges is the truth concerning that question. The limit is not known today or in any finite future; nonetheless, the concept of such a limit is given an empirical meaning by extrapolation from the course of inquiry to date into the indefinite future. To say of a statement that it is true today then means that it coincides with that opinion towards which inquiry will eventually converge; in Peirce's view this was equivalent to saying that the statement corresponds with the facts of the matter. It should be noted that this definition does not assert that inquiry will converge towards a limit; on the contrary, in 1909 Peirce explicitly stated that there might conceivably be no convergence, and hence no truth. So far as SCT simply claims that inquiry will eventually converge, this claim is quite distinct from Peirce's definition of 'truth,' and it is not rendered analytic by that definition. However, when Peirce claims that inquiry will converge towards truth, *insofar as there is any truth,* this claim is more suspect, and Lenz seems to have good grounds for concluding that this claim is analytic—true by virtue of

Peirce's definition of 'truth.' I agree with Lenz that it would be analytic for Peirce to claim that inquiry will converge towards such truth as there is. But Peirce also claims that some convergence has already taken place, and he predicts that it will continue to take place in the finite future. It is these non-analytic claims I wish here to examine.

Lenz' objection, then, is one which has by implication already been dealt with in chapters 2 and 3. Before looking at some other objections, let us examine Peirce's argument for SCT, and specifically his argument for the self-corrective character of induction. This argument is set forth in a number of papers, of which the most important are: "The Doctrine of Chances" and "The Probability of Induction," both from 1878, "A Theory of Probable Inference" from 1883, "The Doctrine of Necessity Examined" from 1892, and "The Logic of History" from about 1901. My focus will be on the argument as it is set forth in the first three of these papers. Peirce here appears to be attempting a probabilistic justification of induction in general, and it has been objected, as noted above, that all he succeeds in doing is giving a circular justification of statistical induction in particular. Granted, once again, that such an interpretation is borne out by part of the evidence, I wish to propose, and explore the textual evidence for, an alternative interpretation which supposes that what Peirce actually does in these papers is pretty much what he intended to do. Before proceeding, it might be well to stress once again that, all other considerations aside, this type of interpretation is the one favored by time-honored principles of textual interpretation.

b. The probability of induction

The first thing which we shall note, and which has been amply shown by Thomas A. Goudge,[6] is that Peirce's probabilistic theory of induction is in large measure designed to refute the older, subjectivist view of probability advocated by Laplace and Quetelet among others. According to this 'Laplacian' view, probability is a measure of our relative ignorance of events; it is thereby also a measure of degree of evidential support for a belief, and hence also a measure of the degree of reasonable trust to be placed in a belief. In this way, the calculus of probability turns out to be interpretable as an inductive logic, capable of justifying all inductive conclusions by assigning to them different degrees of reasonable trust.

As opposed to this subjectivist or 'conceptualist' view of probability, Peirce champions the 'materialist' view originated by John Venn.[7] This is, in effect, what we today call the 'relative frequency' view of probability, which in our century has been developed primarily by Richard von Mises and Hans Reichenbach.[8] According to this view, probability is the measure of the relative frequency of occurrences of an event in a long series of occurrences. Taking as an example a finite sequence of tosses with a coin, the relative frequency of heads turning up is the number of occurrences of heads divided by the number of all the tosses; or, more generally expressed, the number of favorable cases divided by the number of all cases, favorable and unfavorable. In an infinite sequence of occurrences, no such fraction can be found, and the probability is here taken to be the limit towards which the ratio of favorable cases to all cases sampled will approximate in the long run. This limit is determinable to within an error of an arbitrarily small positive fraction by Bernoulli's theorem (or the 'Law of Large Numbers'), which says, in effect, that by taking a sufficiently large sample of any sequence, we can make the probability that the sample ratio will come within an arbitrarily small positive fraction of the sequence ratio as close to one as we please. Since this and other theorems of the probability calculus are valid only for infinite sequences, it is customary today to define 'probability' with respect to infinite sequences only; hence probability is more exactly defined as a limit of relative frequencies, rather than simply as a relative frequency.

In "The Probability of Induction," from 1878, Peirce explicitly endorses Venn's materialistic view, i.e., the relative-frequency view, and explicitly rejects the subjectivist view, as it had been formulated by Augustus de Morgan (*CP*, 2.682). Peirce does not, to be sure, adopt the event terminology which has become standard in relative-frequency theory. Following Locke,[9] he defines probability as a property of classes of inferences, specifically as the ratio of the number of cases in which members of that class of inferences will lead from true premises to true conclusions, to the total number of cases in which that class of inferences is employed. This definition is set forth in "The Doctrine of Chances," published the same year:

> In the long run, there is a real fact which corresponds to the idea of probability, and it is that a given mode of inference sometimes proves successful and sometimes not, and that in a ratio ultimately fixed. . . . We may, therefore, define the probability of a mode of argument as the proportion of cases in which it carries truth with it. (*CP*, 2.650)

As Goudge points out,[10] the relative frequency of transmission of truth in a class of inferences is equivalent to the relative frequency of occurrences of an event, so that Peirce's terminology can be easily translated into the event terminology. When Peirce chose his somewhat roundabout formulation, the point was, I suppose, to avoid the pitfall of assigning a definite probability to single occurrences and, hence, to particular inductive predictions. Peirce's point is, I take it, that to the extent that probability pertains to induction, it attaches to classes of inferences, not to particular inferences, let alone to particular inductive conclusions.

This position is argued in the form of the following criticism of Laplace's "Rule of Succession." According to the Rule, if m is the number of all the favorable cases observed, and n is the number of all the unfavorable cases observed, then the probability of a favorable result of the next trial is

$$\frac{m + 1}{m + n + 2}.$$

In an example used by Quetelet, if an inhabitant of the ancient Mediterranean world were to arrive at the Bay of Biscay and watch the tide rise every half-day on m successive half-days, he would know with a probability of

$$\frac{m + 1}{m + 2}$$

that the tide would rise again on the next half-day (*CP*, 2.682; also *CP*, 7.215). Now, on the very first half-day, Peirce points out, $m = 0$. That is to say, there is an even probability of the occurrence of an absolutely unknown event; or, in other words, any constitution of the universe is as probable as any other. And, while this assumption miraculously produces knowledge (of probabilities) out of total ignorance, it renders inductive knowledge in principle impossible.

The latter claim is argued as follows. The equiprobability of all possible constitutions of the universe can be represented by large equal numbers of black and white balls randomly distributed in a number of urns, each one representing a possible constitution of the universe. In this arrangement, the black and white balls will occur with different frequencies in the various urns, and if we sample each urn by drawing with replacements, we will be able to infer different frequencies of the occurrence of white balls, ranging from 0 to 1. Still, since we are drawing with replacement, each draw will be independent and the probability, for any one particular draw, of drawing a white ball will be unaffected by the results of any previous draws. Although we learn the frequency of white balls, and hence the probability of drawing a white ball, by making a number of draws, still that probability remains the same for each particular draw. If we suppose with Quetelet that the probability of drawing a white ball on the very first draw were one half, then the probability of drawing a white ball will remain one half for any one draw, no matter how many trials we have made. So, on this supposition no reasoning from past to future experience is possible, and hence the Rule of Succession is inconsistent. Far from providing us with a calculus of induction, it renders induction in principle impossible: "In short, it would be to assume that Nature is a pure chaos, or chance combination of independent elements, in which reasoning from one fact to another would be impossible" (*CP*, 2.684). In fact, Peirce holds, we do reason from past to future experience; but what the argument shows is that we cannot do so by assigning to the future occurrence of an event a definite probability based on the relative frequency of its known past occurrences.

Peirce does hold, however, that by defining probability as a property of classes of inferences, we can in a sense use it as a measure of the validity of inductive inferences. The validity of a class of inferences consists in its conformity to a true leading principle of inference. The truth of a leading principle, in its turn, consists in its leading us from true premises to true conclusions either in all cases, as in necessary inference, or in a majority of cases, as in probable inference. The Law of Large Numbers is a leading principle which will lead from true premises to true conclusions in a majority of cases; induction can therefore be shown to be a valid type of inference if it can be shown to be made in accordance with the Law of Large Numbers as its leading principle. Peirce at times claims that this constitutes the justification for all types of induction (*CP,* 1.93–94); at other times he flatly denies this (*CP,* 7.215). Be that as it may, the fact is that he argues the claim only with regard to one particular type of induction, namely statistical induction; it is this argument that I wish to examine.

As presented in the 1878 article "The Probability of Induction," Peirce's argument is somewhat ambiguous. The conclusion is that while in reasoning from a population ratio to a sample ratio we can assign a definite probability to the inference, in the converse case we both can and cannot: "It appears, then, that in one sense we can, and in one sense we cannot, determine the probability of a synthetic inference" (*CP,* 2.698). The negative conclusion here is clear enough. No definite probability attaches to the conclusion of an inference from sample to population, in the sense in which it attaches to a conclusion drawn from population to sample. In the latter case we can determine numerically the frequency of truth transmission in the class of exactly similar inferences, i.e., inferences from the same population to other samples—or, what comes to the same, to a gradually enlarged sample. No such determination is possible when we infer from sample to population; from any one random sample we may not get the ratio even approximately right. But Peirce does think that we can attach a probability to inductive inferences in a different sense, namely as a measure of the "degree of trustworthiness of our proceeding" (*CP,* 2.693). I am not quite sure how to take this, but what Peirce seems to have in mind is that although we cannot attach a definite probability to the class of exactly similar inferences, i.e., inferences from various samples to the same population, still we can attach a probability to the class of all inferences from samples to populations (ibid.). If this is the proper interpretation, it is at any rate a view which he had given up by 1883.

In the latter year Peirce published the paper "A Theory of Probable Inference" in the Johns Hopkins *Studies in Logic,* where he explored the grounds of validity of statistical deduction and induction. The form of statistical deduction is given as follows:

The proportion *r* of the *M*'s are *P*'s,
S', *S''*, *S'''*, etc., are a *numerous* set, taken at random from among the *M*'s;
Hence, *probably* and *approximately,* the proportion *r* of the *S*'s are *P*'s.

(CP, 2.700)

For any one sample of *S*'s from among the *M*'s the inferred ratio may be wide of the mark; but as the number of samples drawn approaches infinity the ratio of true inferences from population to sample to all such inferences approaches one. Hence probability is properly ascribed to inferences from population to sample. The validity of statistical deduction, then, consists in its conformity to the Law of Large Numbers as a leading principle. This principle is stated by Peirce thus: "The principle of statistical deduction is that these two proportions—namely, that of the *P*'s among the *M*'s, and that of the *P*'s among the *S*'s—are probably and approximately equal" (*CP*, 2.702). Understood as a leading principle of inference, this means that for a sufficiently large number of samples—or for a sufficiently large sample—the ratio of approximately true inferences from population to sample to all such inferences will be close to one.

So far this is fairly straightforward. Mathematically exact statements inevitably sound awkward when expressed in ordinary English; the argument could be formulated differently and no doubt more gracefully, but at least the meaningfulness of ascribing frequentist probabilities to statistical deductions is clear enough. More complicated is Peirce's further claim that the validity of statistical induction consists in its conformity to the same leading principle. Referring to the above-mentioned leading principle and to the deductive inference considered above, Peirce says: "If, then, this principle justifies our inferring the second proportion from the known value of the first, it equally justifies our inferring the value of the first from that of the second, if the first is unknown but the second has been observed" (ibid.). How can this be? Let us consider Peirce's example of the form of statistical induction:

S', S'', S''', etc. form a numerous set taken at random from among the M's,
S', S'', S''', etc. are found to be—the proportion p of them—P's;
Hence, *probably* and *approximately* the same proportion, p, of the M's are P's.

(Ibid.)

In the case of statistical deduction, the Law of Large Numbers validated the inference by assigning to it a definite numerical probability. No such probability can meaningfully be attached to statistical induction, for two reasons. In the first place, the probability described above is defined as a property of r—that is, of the population ratio—and not as a property of p—that is, of the ratio observed in some arbitrarily chosen random sample. In the second place, the probability of statistical induction *cannot* be defined as the relative frequency of occurrences of the truth of p, since there is only one population ratio for p to be true or false of. It will not help to insist that, given a sufficiently large random sample, p and r are identical. They are probably identical; and, as Gordon Pinkham has pointed out, if we treat r as a constant and p as a variable, we may assign a probable value to p; if, on the other hand, p is our only known constant, it makes no sense to assign a probable value to r.[11] Assuming the value of r to be identical to the known value of p is tantamount to assuming the whole population to have been sampled, so that there is no induction to perform. In conclusion, no numerical probability can be meaningfully assigned to an inductive inference.

This conclusion, which in a way follows from Peirce's critique of the Laplacians in 1878, but which he then shrank from explicitly drawing, is articulated with all desirable clarity in 1883. Statistical induction, Peirce now makes clear, is validated not by the assignment of any definite probability to p, but by the fact that, through prolonged sampling, p will be replaced or gradually corrected so as eventually to approximate to r:

The nature of the probability in the two cases is very different. In the statistical deduction, we know that among the whole body of the M's the proportion of P's is p; we say, then, that the S's being random drawings of M's are probably P's in about the same proportion—and though this may happen not to be so, yet at any rate, on continuing the drawing sufficiently, our prediction of the ratio will be vindicated at last. On the other hand, in induction we say that the proportion p of the sample being P's, probably there is the same proportion in the whole lot, or at least, if this happens not to be so, then on continuing the drawings the inference will be, not *vindicated* as in the other case, but *modified* so as to become true. (*CP*, 2.703; italics in the original)

Has Peirce then given a probabilistic justification of induction? It would seem he has not. After all, we always do make particular inductive inferences, and one thing we might want to know from a theory of induction is why we should ever want to make one particular inductive inference, rather than another—say, when we know one sample ratio and we also know that an enlarged sample might produce a widely different ratio. Even statistical deduction may lead us astray in any one particular case, but such inferences are rational because we know, at least, that they will lead us right more often than wrong. In the case of statistical induction, we do not even know this; all we know is that, in the end, prolonged sampling will inductively correct all the errors into which induction has led us. This seems to be a justification for exhaustively examining every population in which we are interested, rather than a justification for making predictions from samples.

Peirce's reply is that the assignment of a definite numerical probability to inductive inferences, even if it could be made, would not in fact get us any further. Knowledge of a probability is helpful in the case of deductive inferences, because the ratio from which we draw the inference licenses a large number of conclusions, which will be true or false of the actual world. It is interesting, therefore, to know the relative frequency of occurrences of truth transmission among our conclusions, even if we do not know what specific conclusions are true. But in inductive inference the observed ratio licenses only one conclusion; any talk of the probability of that conclusion, in the sense of relative frequency, can refer only to the proportion of possible universes in which that conclusion would be true, "something which we should have a right to talk about if universes were as plentiful as blackberries" (*CP,* 2.684). In the actual world, the 'probability' of an inductive conclusion, in this sense, would be absolutely worthless. So there is simply no way of justifying particular inductive inferences by ascertaining their degree of trustworthiness or otherwise reducing the inherent risk in making such inferences. In a sense, then, Peirce's 'solution' to the problem of induction consists in showing the problem to be insoluble.

c. Two conditions of self-correction

So far, then, Peirce's conclusions are essentially negative. These conclusions constitute a rebuttal of the Laplacian view of probability, and they remain pertinent objections to later inductive logics.[12] But there is a great deal more to Peirce's theory of induction; his positive conclusions, so far as I understand them, must be construed as answers to the question: Granting induction to be on the whole successful, under what factual conditions is this possible? Or, as Peirce, paraphrasing Kant, formulated the question in "The Probability of Induction": "How are any synthetic judgments at all possible?" (*CP,* 2.690). Peirce follows Kant in holding that the answer must be sought by finding out what is universally true of experience and is therefore involved in the conditions of experience (*ibid.*). However, as I shall argue, unlike Kant, Peirce does not seek the transcendental conditions of all possible experience as an explanation of the success of induction; rather, he seeks to explain this success by finding the contingent conditions of the specifically human experience of pursuing empirical science. To that extent, he proceeds 'pragmatically,' that is empirically.

This subject can best be approached through considering two important provisos contained in Peirce's theory of statistical inference. The first proviso is that sampling must be random; the second is that the character whose ratio we seek must be predesignated—that is, chosen in advance of the sampling. The requirement of random sampling is stated as follows: "The rule requires that the sample should be drawn at random and independently from the whole lot sampled. That is to say, the sample must be taken according to a precept or method which, being applied over and over again indefinitely, would in the long run result in any one set of instances as often as any other set of the same number" (*CP*, 2.726). Randomness is here defined in terms of a "sampling device," as Ian Hacking puts it. A random sample is not defined, either directly or indirectly, by its composition; it is not a 'fair' or representative sample. Such a definition would make all statistical inferences circular, since a random sample would then by definition approximate to the composition of the population. To make statistical inferences non-trivial, we must define randomness independently of the composition of the sample, in terms of a method of which we know *empirically* that it will tend in the long run to produce fair samples. And, as Hacking points out, the claim that a sample is random is itself a statistical hypothesis; that is, it can be established only by a statistical inference.[13]

One implication of this requirement is that there seems to be a circularity in Peirce's justification of statistical inference. As we saw, the Law of Large Numbers justifies an inference from population to sample, provided the sample is a random one; that is to say, the validity even of statistical deduction depends on the validity of the prior statistical induction by which we establish the randomness of the sample. This circularity has been spelled out by E. H. Madden, who concludes that Peirce really must presuppose something like Laplace's 'antecedent probability' or J. S. Mill's 'uniformity of nature,' both of which assumptions Peirce himself declared unwarranted and unnecessary.[14]

Madden further points out a second circularity in Peirce's justification of statistical induction. He takes as his point of departure the circumstance that the prediction from the sample ratio to the population ratio will be, not vindicated, but corrected by further sampling. The ratio will indeed be corrected, Madden grants, and in the end p will be equal to r; but by this time the sample will have exhausted the whole population, and hence we shall be using the conclusion of the inference as one of its premises: "At last, unfortunately, can only mean here: when the need for any inference has passed because there is nothing left to infer to. That is to say, the more nearly certain we become of the accuracy of our ratio, the less use we have for it, for the more nearly exhaustive is our examination of the class." [15]

No doubt, part of Peirce's intention was to show the epistemic validity of inductive inference. I have no special stake in proving him successful on this score, and I suspect that Madden's criticisms are to the point here. Nonetheless, since Madden formulates his criticisms in a somewhat sweeping manner, I feel bound to point out that Peirce's argument has important aspects which are not touched by these criticisms. To consider the second circularity first, this criticism would be pertinent to Peirce's thesis of the self-correctiveness of induction only if he had held the degree of trustworthiness of inductive conclusions to increase with prolonged sampling. The degree of trustworthiness is indeed something which self-correction teaches us only when it is too late—when our trust has already been superseded by knowledge. But, as we have seen, Peirce did not hold this view of self-correction; the long-run self-correction of prolonged sampling is meant to establish only the degree of trustworthiness of the inductive procedure; inductive predictions, so long as they remain predictions, remain also irremediably uncertain. Peirce might be faulted for failing to account for the fact that we do trust inductive predictions, and that we trust them more the larger our sample. But this would be quite a different criticism from Madden's.

With regard to the first circularity, I want to argue once again that although this would indeed be a circularity in a proposed justification of statistical inference, such as Peirce at times proposed, it is not a circularity in a proposed explanation of the presumed fact that statistical inferences are, on the whole, successful. As we shall see, this explanation involves the hypothesis of uniformities in nature, along with other hypotheses. But these hypotheses are not assumptions, and they do not justify the use of inductive methods; such methods are justified only by their success in application. Random sampling, in Peirce's view, is an existential condition which must hold for statistical inference to succeed, but it need not be known to hold. In fact, it cannot be known to hold because there is no prescribed method of random sampling. Sampling is "a real art"

(*CP*, 2.727), which requires, in addition to method, such virtues as honesty, industry, and ingenuity. Peirce's view is not, then, the circular one that the validity of statistical method presupposes the validity of a prior application of the same method in the sampling process. The point of his requirement of random sampling is, rather, that statistical inference can succeed only on the factual condition that the investigator is so constituted as to possess the honesty and skill required to practice the art of sampling—with or without a reliable method. If this factual condition fails, so does statistical inference. And this, of course, is consistent with my hypothesis that Peirce's self-corrective thesis is an empirical hypothesis about the scientific activity.

Similar conditions for the success of statistical inference appear in Peirce's discussion of his second requirement, that of predesignation. Unless the character whose ratio we seek has been chosen before we draw a sample, there will be no reason whatever to believe that the sample ratio will give us any clue to the population ratio. To illustrate this point Peirce chooses for his sample the names and ages of the first five poets mentioned in Wheeler's *Biographical Dictionary*:

> Aagaard, died at 48.
> Abeille, died at 76.
> Abulola, died at 84.
> Abunowas, died at 48.
> Accords, died at 45.

Peirce then shows that these ages have a number of mathematical properties in common: in each case the difference between the two digits, divided by three, leaves a remainder of one; the first digit raised to the power of the second and divided by three, leaves a remainder of one; the sum of the prime factors, counting one as a prime factor, is divisible by three. "Yet," he goes on, "there is not the slightest reason to believe that the next poet's age would possess these characters" (*CP*, 2.738; see also *CP*, 1.96).

The point here is not, as one might at first think, that the properties selected are arbitrary, inessential properties which for that reason do not yield predictions. It is, after all, only by making and testing predictions that we learn which properties are significant and which are not. We do not know *a priori* that there is no connection between a man's vocation and certain mathematical properties of his age; we know this only from experience—albeit, admittedly, experience of a very general sort. The point of Peirce's example is the quite different one that the properties were selected only after the sample had been examined, and furthermore that they were chosen only because they were shared by all the members of the sample. The sample cannot now serve as evidence for inferring that the same properties will be shared by the whole population. This is so because the statement that the members of the sample share these properties is not an informative statement, given that the properties have been specifically chosen because they were shared by the whole sample. All that the statement tells us is that the sample exhibits the properties which it does exhibit; in short, it tells us nothing and it cannot serve as a premise in an inductive inference. In general, once we have a random collection of objects, it requires only a little patience and ingenuity to discover all sorts of properties shared by all, or at least a significant proportion, of these objects. Pseudo-scientific cranks are generally expert at this sort of exercise. Yet we have no grounds whatever to infer that properties thus discovered will be present in even approximately the same proportion in an enlarged sample. So induction has no hope of success unless the property sampled for has been selected prior to sampling.

This rule, Peirce points out, is equivalent to the older rule, "that a hypothesis can only be received upon the ground of its having been *verified* by *prediction*" (*CP*, 2.739). Given a body of observations, it will always be possible to account for them by any number of incompatible hypotheses, of which no more than one can be true. No hypothesis, therefore, is confirmed by observations made before it was formulated; confirmations can come only from new observations which have resulted from predictions from the hypothesis. The equivalence of these two rules, we may note, is not accidental. As Peirce gradually came to see, induction is simply the experimental testing of predictions made from a hypothesis. This is most explicitly stated in his "Logic of History" from about 1901:

Having, then, by means of deduction, drawn from a hypothesis predictions as to what the results of experiment will be, we proceed to test the hypothesis by making the experiments and comparing those predictions with the actual results of the experiment. . . . This sort of inference it is, from experiments testing predictions based on a hypothesis, that is alone properly entitled to be called *induction*. (*CP*, 7.206)

The success of induction, then, depends upon its being performed as a test of predictions deduced from an antecedently formed hypothesis. The deduction and induction involved in the testing of the hypothesis have only the function of transmitting truth; hence, if they are to lead us to true conclusions, the hypothesis must have been formed in such a manner as to produce truth. The rules for hypothesis formation—"abduction" or "retroduction," as Peirce at different times calls it—were briefly considered in the last chapter; the account there given must now be supplemented.

d. The problem of abduction

The need for a set of rules for abduction stems from the circumstance that not only is induction impossible without some prior abduction, but inductive self-correction is impossible unless the abductions are made in such a way as to converge towards the truth. This circumstance is illustrated by the example of the five poets. In Peirce's sample there were three mathematical properties shared by the numbers representing their ages at death. If these were all the poets whose ages we knew, we might use these three properties to formulate three different hypotheses concerning the ages of all poets. These hypotheses would probably be quickly refuted by an enlargement of the sample, but a more important thing to note is that the three hypotheses would be mutually incompatible: by further sampling any one of them might be confirmed and the others refuted. Yet all three of them are compatible with the original sample. Now let us ask what will happen when we enlarge our sample; the choice among the three original hypotheses will be quickly determined (presumably, they will all be refuted), but the new sample will in its turn be compatible with a number of rival and incompatible hypotheses. No matter how far we carry the inductive process—short of examining the whole population of poets—we will be left with a sample which permits of incompatible hypotheses, and hence permits of false hypotheses. When we deal with infinite populations (or even finite populations which it is practically impossible to examine exhaustively), induction will not determine our choice among hypotheses unless the range of permissible hypotheses has been antecedently limited through the process of abduction. This thesis of the empirical underdetermination of choices among hypotheses was taken over by Peirce, with acknowledgement, from his old mentor Augustus de Morgan (see *CP,* 1.450). A similar, though more radical thesis of underdetermination was advanced by Peirce's contemporary Pierre Duhem; this thesis was later emphasized by Quine and is therefore commonly referred to as the "Duhem-Quine thesis."[16]

There are at least two possible views of what the implications of underdetermination are for the relation between theories and experience. An extreme view is that since observations do not uniquely determine our choice among hypotheses, it follows that such choices are made on non-empirical grounds, and that scientific theories are therefore at bottom pure fictions or conventions. This, it is fairly clear, is a view which Peirce would have found unpalatable. A more moderate view is that since observations do not logically compel us to accept or reject a hypothesis, it follows that scientific reasoning involves something more than just experience plus logic. This more moderate view would, I believe, be acceptable to most scientists and philosophers, Peirce included. However, the moderate view, thus baldly stated, is sadly incomplete; it virtually cries out for an answer to the question, what is that "something more" in scientific reasoning? In the remainder of this chapter Peirce's theory of abduction will be presented as at least in part an answer to this question. We have already noted, in chapter 4, some of Peirce's methodological requirements for abduction. We shall now note two other sets of requirements, logical and factual.

In his early writings Peirce tended to emphasize the logical requirements for abduction (or "retroduction" or "hypothesis").

Thus, for instance, in the paper "Deduction, Induction, and Hypothesis" from 1878, Peirce draws the distinction among these three forms of inference in purely logical terms. Initially, he adopts the terminology 'rule,' 'case,' and 'result' for, respectively, the major premise, the minor premise, and the conclusion of a syllogism of the form Barbara. Deduction is then defined as the inference of a result from a rule and a case; induction as the inference of a rule from a case and a result; and hypothesis as the inference of a case from a rule and a result. Peirce gives this example of his schemata:

DEDUCTION

Rule. — All the beans from these bags are white.
Case. — These beans are from this bag.
Result. — These beans are white.

INDUCTION

Case. — These beans are from this bag.
Result. — These beans are white.
Rule. — All the beans from this bag are white.

HYPOTHESIS

Rule. — All the beans from this bag are white.
Result. — These beans are white.
Case. — These beans are from this bag.

(*CP*, 2.624)

This classification, as Peirce frequently acknowledges, is inherited from Aristotle; and the terms 'abduction' and 'retroduction' are different attempts at latinizing Aristotle's 'apagogé,' which is defined as the search for a minor premise.[17] It may seem initially puzzling that hypothesis is characterized as inference to a case, that is, a minor premise. Surely scientific hypotheses serve as major premises for deducing experimental predictions. This is so; but the inference by which a hypothesis is tested is different from the inference by which it is arrived at. To use one of Peirce's examples, if we want to test Kepler's laws of planetary motion, we use the conjunction of these laws as our major premise from which, together with the record of astronomical observations (minor premises), we deduce an astronomical prediction (conclusion). For Kepler, however, the laws of planetary motion were the point of arrival, not of departure. He started out from Tycho Brahe's record of astronomical observations, together with the conviction that the motions of the heavenly bodies had to exhibit a certain "harmony" or "inaudible music." His problem was that of constructing a minor premise which would permit him to retain the harmony hypothesis as his major premise and to deduce the record of observations as his conclusion. After numerous trials and failures Kepler eventually solved his problem with the minor premise that the planets move in elliptical orbits. Peirce makes it clear that we need a hypothesis only when we want to explain some surprising fact, and no fact is surprising unless it clashes with a prior expectation. To Kepler, a number of Brahe's observations were surprising because they did not fit the hypothesis of circular orbits, which appeared to Kepler as the most harmonious type of motion. The function of a hypothesis, such as Kepler's elliptical hypothesis, is to render the surprising fact unsurprising, by showing it to follow from our prior expectation, as a major premise, together with a novel minor premise: "Hypothesis is where we find some very curious circumstance, which would be explained by the supposition that it was a case of a very general rule, and thereupon adopt that supposition" (*CP*, 2.624).

What this suggests is that the logical form of abduction (to wit, the inversion of induction) is only a minimum requirement, intended to ensure that the hypothesis will at least be a possible explanation. This minimum requirement does not begin to grapple with the problem which was seen to occasion the need for a method of abduction, namely the problem of limiting the range of permissible hypotheses. Indeed, the thesis of underdetermination can be simply restated in terms of Peirce's logic of abduction: given a major premise and a conclusion, if there is any minor premise which will validly mediate between them, there is an infinite number of such minor premises. Hence the mere fact that a proposed hypothesis serves as a minor premise only shows that it is a possible explanation; this fact does not in and of itself give us any reason to believe that the hypothesis is the true explanation.

The late Norwood Russell Hanson, in a number of papers, defended Peirce's theory of abduction as a "logic of discovery," characterized solely in terms of syllogistic inversion.[18] This line of argument, according to what has been said, must be doomed to founder on the thesis of underdetermination. Peirce himself realized, increasingly in later years, that the logical form of abduction would not in fact get him very far, and that abduction could aid induction only on the condition that certain factual assumptions were to hold. Induction is possible at all only if the range of permissible hypotheses is limited, and inductive self-correction is possible only if the limited set of hypotheses includes within it a true, or near-true, hypothesis. Inductive self-correction, Peirce concluded in his "Lessons from the History of Science" in about 1896, is possible only if there is in fact a natural tendency to guess the truth: "It is certain that the only hope of retroductive reasoning ever reaching the truth is that there may be some natural tendency toward an agreement between the ideas which suggest themselves to the human mind and those which are concerned in the laws of nature" (*CP*, 1.81).

And from the same paper: "Retroduction goes upon the hope that there is sufficient affinity between the reasoner's mind and nature's to render guessing not altogether hopeless, provided each guess is checked by comparison with observation. It is true that agreement does not show the guess is right, but if it is wrong it must ultimately get found out" (*CP*, 1.121). Inductive self-correction, then, is dependent for its success on the factual assumption of a natural tendency to make correct guesses.

This line of thought is developed at great length in Peirce's later writings. Looking at various texts from the period 1898 though 1901, we reach the following account. The function of a hypothesis is to explain surprising facts, and explaining a fact means rendering it unsurprising (*CP*, 7.202). For scientific explanation to be possible, the universe must be such that the facts presented to us admit of being rendered unsurprising, admit of "rationalization," as Peirce calls it:

> The hypothesis is that the facts in hand admit of rationalization, and of rationalization by us. That we must hope they do, for the same reason that a general who has to capture a position or see his country ruined, must go on the hypothesis that there is some way in which he

can and shall capture it. We must be animated by that hope concerning the problem we have in hand, whether we extend it to a postulate covering all facts, or not. (*CP*, 7.219)

The first factual assumption, then, is that the facts admit of rationalization or, as it was put in chapter 4, that nature exhibits real regularities. The analogy of the general shows, once again, how Peirce's factual assumptions are intended to function. The assumption that victory is somehow possible is not needed in the justification of a particular strategy; conversely, if the strategy is called into question, the general cannot justify it by making this assumption. Moreover, the assumption itself concerns a contingent matter of fact, and it can be established only empirically—only by making the attack. But the attack must be made anyway; otherwise, the country is lost. So, for the general, prior to the attack, the possibility of victory is not known empirically, and it can under no circumstance be known *a priori*. But in the context of the general's decision making it need not be known; it can make no difference whatever to his decision. Still, it is a factual condition which must hold in order for him to succeed. If a general has succeeded in capturing an apparently invincible enemy stronghold, we can subsequently explain his success only by the hypothesis that the stronghold was, in fact, vulnerable in some specifiable respect, and this hypothesis must then be compared with empirical evidence. Likewise, to the experimental scientist the existence of real regularities is not known either empirically or *a priori*; and the postulate of such regularities is neither necessary nor sufficient to justify his activities. If there are no regularities, science is bound to fail and it makes no difference what hypotheses the scientist adopts or what experiments he performs. And even if there are somewhere real regularities, he may well be wasting his time pursuing imaginary regularities—just as the general may waste his opportunities by pursuing a wrong strategy. Still, there must be real regularities for the scientist to succeed in his efforts; if, therefore, we take a certain measure of inductive success to be an observed fact, this fact, which is *prima facie* quite miraculous, can be explained only on the hypothesis that there are, in fact, real regularities. The testing of this hypothesis, as I indicated in the last chapter, is problematic, though not necessarily impossible.

e. The investigator as a condition of knowledge

There is a second factual condition specified in my last quote from Peirce. It is not enough that the facts admit of rationalization; they must admit of rationalization by us. That is to say, we must be so constituted as to be able to guess at the regularities actually there. The regularities cannot be inferred inductively from observation, because induction already presupposes near-true hypotheses. We must guess, then; but how do we guess? The view that first leaps to mind is that, if our guesses are not guided by induction, they must be purely blind or random, and all approximation towards truth must be due to error-elimination at the subsequent stage of inductive testing. This view was advocated in 1896 by Peirce's friend James, who derived it, with acknowledgment, from Stanley Jevons.[19] It was later popularized by Karl Popper and enjoyed a considerable vogue until it was undermined by, among other things, Quine's revival of Duhem's underdetermination thesis, but it still remains an influential view.[20] But Peirce could not avail himself of this way out since, as we have seen, he had already discovered underdetermination, and hence realized that convergence towards truth must take place at the stage of hypothesis formation, if it is to take place at all. And the probability is overwhelmingly against any such convergence taking place through chance guessing in the brief span of time in which men have pursued science:

> How was it that man was ever led to entertain a true theory? You cannot say it happened by chance, because the possible theories, if not strictly innumerable, at any rate exceed a trillion—or the third power of a million; and therefore the chances are too overwhelmingly against the single true theory in the twenty or thirty thousand years during which man has been a thinking animal, ever having come into any man's head. (*CP*, 5.591; see also *CP*, 1.172 and *CP*, 5.587)

Chance guessing, then, cannot explain convergence. How, in that case, is it that convergence can take place through any kind of guessing? It can take place, Peirce replies, in two ways. In the first place, biological evolution may have produced an instinct for making rough guesses at those truths the knowledge of which would have an immediate survival value. But in the second place, since the theories of the mature sciences are neither rough nor of immediate survival value, instinct must at a certain stage have been supplemented with intellectual and moral self-control. Science is the fruit of instinct tempered by virtue.

The role of instinct is stressed especially in the relatively early writings, such as "A Theory of Probable Inference." Let us return briefly to the topic which impelled us to make this survey of abduction, namely, the requirement of predesignation. Peirce illustrates the importance of this requirement with the following science-fiction story. Suppose that a creature from a different planet, with knowledge of English and mathematics, but with an evolutionary history different from ours, were to be presented with a United States Census Report. He would be able to discover innumerable statistical correlations of values, not one of which would be very likely to be projectible onto an enlarged sample of data. Among the things which he might infer from the Census Report of 1872 is a significant geographical correlation between the amount of rainfall in January and the level of illiteracy. There is no reason to believe that he would hit upon a single induction which would subsequently be confirmed by independent evidence; no reason, that is, to believe that his inquiries would show any convergence towards the truth. When our inductive inferences tend to converge towards the truth, this is in part because our mental habits and instincts have been naturally selected for their survival value in the world in which we happen to live, subject to the regularities which here obtain:

> Nature is a far vaster and less clearly arranged repertory of facts than a census report; and if men had not come to it with a special aptitude for guessing right, it may well be doubted whether in the ten or twenty thousand years that they may have existed their greatest mind would have attained the amount of knowledge which is actually possessed by the lowest idiot. But, in point of fact, not man merely, but all animals derive by inheritance (presumably by natural selection) two classes of ideas which adapt them to their environment. In the first place, they all have from birth some notions, however crude and concrete, of force, matter, space, and time; and, in the next place, they have some notion of what sort of objects their fellow-beings are, and how they will act on given occasions. (*CP*, 2.753)

The paper concludes with the words: "Side by side, then, with the well established proposition that all knowledge is based on experience, and that science is only advanced by the experimental verification of theories, we have to place this other equally important truth, that all human knowledge, up to the highest flights of science, is but the development of our inborn animal instincts" (*CP*, 2.754).

For the sake of accuracy, it must be interjected that Peirce is wide of the mark when estimating mankind to be ten or twenty thousand years old. The human species is today thought to be more than 2 million years old.[21] On the one hand, Peirce is by no means to be blamed for his erroneous figure. It was promulgated in the early 1860s by no less an authority than Lord Kelvin, who had arrived at it by calculating the age of life on earth from the rate at which the earth's surface is cooling; Kelvin's results were not refuted until 1903, by Paul Curie.[22] On the other hand, this revision of the time scale seriously impairs, if not overturns, Peirce's improbability argument, as it did the improbability argument against natural selection. However this may be, Peirce was later to place less emphasis on instinct, which at any rate he thought insufficient to account for the evolution of mature science. Very little, therefore, depends on the age of the human species; during the two or three thousand years in which man has pursued science he has made innumerable guesses which have not been instinctive, and at least for this limited time span the improbability argument tells overwhelmingly against chance having played any considerable role.

Peirce's change of emphasis is evidenced in his "Lessons from the History of Science" from about 1896. The range of scientific knowledge, Peirce now holds, has so far been largely limited to objects which we originally came to know by means of two instincts: the instinct of feeding and the instinct of breeding (*CP*, 1.118). Peirce does not now say that the scientific mode of knowing these objects is instinctive, or even that it is a "development of instincts." Two years later, in his lectures on "Vitally Important Topics," he repeats the claim that science has so far been limited to the development of the two branches of knowledge which originated from the instincts connected with nutrition and reproduction (*CP*, 5.586). Now, however, he is even more careful in restricting the role of instinct to the origin of science, as distinct from its subsequent development:

> If you carefully consider with an unbiassed mind all the circumstances
> of the early history of science and all the other facts bearing on the
> question, which are far too various to be specifically alluded to in this
> lecture, I am quite sure that you must be brought to acknowledge that
> man's mind has a natural adaptation to imagining correct theories of
> some kinds, and in particular to correct theories about forces, without
> some glimmer of which he could not form social ties and consequently
> could not reproduce his kind. (*CP*, 5.591)

What Peirce came increasingly to realize was that the comparative exactitude of advanced science, although far from absolute, is yet vastly in excess of what has immediate survival value and hence could be expected to result from instinct (*CP*, 6.50). Moreover, hand in hand with the development towards greater exactitude, there is in the history of science a development towards ever higher abstractness, which renders scientific conclusions more fallible than the cruder and more concrete knowledge which comes from instinct (*CP*, 1.649). Consequently, although science has arisen from instinct, it cannot in its mature stage continue to rely on instinct alone. Once arisen, science does not evolve naturally; its further development is artificial and requires self-control on the part of the inquirer. This point, which has been especially well brought out by W. B. Gallie,[23] seems to be the one which Peirce is making in this comment on indubitable beliefs, from 1909:

> [The Critical Common-sensist] opines that the indubitable beliefs
> refer to a somewhat primitive mode of life, and that, while they never
> become dubitable in so far as our mode of life remains that of the
> somewhat primitive man, yet as we develop *degrees of self-control*
> unknown to that man, occasions of action arise in relation to which
> the original beliefs, if stretched to cover them, have no sufficient
> authority. In other words, we outgrow the applicability of instinct—
> not altogether, by any manner of means, but in our highest activities.
> (*CP*, 5.511)

I have elsewhere discussed the implications of this realization for Peirce's attitude towards Darwin's theory of evolution.[24] Let me here note that while Peirce in 1878 appeared quite enthusiastic about

Darwin's theory, this enthusiasm had cooled considerably by the turn of the century. His later misgivings, it is clear, stemmed from his realization that the higher reasoning powers responsible for the advance of science—and, in general, for the advance of culture—have both too great long-run utility and too small short-run utility to be attributable to the action of natural selection (*CP*, 1.657; see also *CP*, 5.366). The evolution of science, therefore, requires, in addition to natural selection, also cataclysmic and Lamarckian modes of explanation (*CP*, 1.107–9). This does not make Peirce a 'Lamarckist,' in a pejorative sense; in questioning the role of natural selection in cultural evolution, he was quite at one with Darwin's staunchest defender, T. H. Huxley, as well as with Darwin's co-discoverer of natural selection, Alfred Russell Wallace.[25] Even today it is not unusual for Neo-Darwinists to describe cultural evolution as 'Lamarckian'—meaning cumulative and goal-directed—although this remains an unresolved and highly divisive issue in evolutionary biology.[26]

These remarks are by the way. Of greater immediate interest is the question of what Peirce means by 'self-control.' Partly, of course, he is referring to the control exercised through the application of scientific method, which can be formalized in a set of methodological canons, among them the canons of induction and the three requirements for the selection of hypotheses: explanatory power, testability, and economy. But we have already seen that these requirements are not jointly sufficient to ensure convergence towards truth. Something more is needed; and this 'something more,' Peirce concluded, is the cultivation of intellectual habits to make them conform to truth-seeking as an ideal of conduct. That is to say, what is needed is intellectual virtue; but that virtue is not specifiable in terms of conformity to clearly formulated rules of action (like the canons of induction), only in terms of an ideal end to which we may endeavor to suit our habits of action. On this topic, Peirce is more than usually obscure and sketchy, but remarks such as this one from 1902 are suggestive:

> Were there nothing in reasoning more than the old traditional treatises set forth, then a rogue might be as good a reasoner as a man

of honor; although a coward could not, even under such an idea of reasoning. But in induction a habit of probity is needed for success: a trickster is sure to play the confidence game upon himself. And in addition to probity, industry is essential. In the presumptive choice of hypotheses, still higher virtues are needed—a true elevation of the soul. (*CP*, 1.576)

I take Peirce to have in mind something like the following. The formal rules of scientific inference do not and cannot include rules for how they themselves are to be applied. The canons of induction may be applied with a conscious intent of deception—or with the less conscious intent of self-deception—and if they are so applied they will not lead the inquirer towards the truth. Similarly, the requirement of explanatory power will be easily fulfilled if applied by an investigator who is satisfied with shallow or trivial explanations; the requirement of economy will be easily fulfilled to the satisfaction of a sloppy and careless mind, and so forth. The self-correctiveness of any set of rules for scientific inference will always depend on the mental and moral character of the investigator applying those rules.

This is not a book about Peirce's theory of value; readers interested in pursuing that subject are referred to the admirable account given by Vincent G. Potter.[27] Enough has been said to demonstrate that it is at best doubtful whether Peirce intended to show that either the scientific method in general or the method of induction in particular guarantees its own success. At least one predominant strand in Peirce's thinking is that the success of scientific method—that is, its tendency towards convergence through self-correction—depends on both the actual constitution of the universe and the character of scientific investigators as its existential conditions. The scientific method is justified by the convergence which actually takes place, when it takes place; this convergence cannot and need not be assumed at the outset as a postulate of science. All the same, on Peirce's view convergence is a fact of nature, a fact too obvious to be denied, but nonetheless a contingent fact, dependent on other facts which might have been otherwise than they actually are.

This interpretation of Peirce's 'justification' of induction comes close, I believe, to the one proposed by Abner Shimony in his paper "Scientific Inference." Indeed, in arriving at my interpretation I have

to a large extent been directly influenced by Shimony. In his paper
Shimony summarizes Peirce's "tempered personalism" by four
methodological ideas which he finds of great value:

> That the scientific method achieves its successes by submission to
> reality, that a hopeful attitude toward hypotheses proposed by human
> beings is indispensable to rational investigation of the unknown, that a
> usable criterion of fair sampling involves subjective and ethical
> considerations, and that it is rational to make certain weak assump-
> tions about the fairness of the data in order to permit inquiry to
> proceed.[28]

In this chapter I have been especially concerned to document the
presence in Peirce's writings of the first three of these ideas, which I
might sum up by saying that factual hypotheses concerning the
nature of the universe and the psychology and morality of investigators are required to explain the success of scientific inference. There
is, no doubt, another Peirce, who wrote as though convergence
towards truth were a necessary outcome of inquiry, capable of
mathematical demonstration. This other Peirce has been sufficiently
criticized by Lenz and Madden, among others. What I hope to have
shown in this chapter is that Peirce's central writings on induction
can be made sense of without taking account of this "other Peirce."
To the extent that I have succeeded in this, Peirce's self-corrective
thesis has been shown to be arguably consistent with the pragmatic
realism described in chapter 4.

Something is still missing from my account. What has not yet
been shown is why Peirce should have been interested in inductive
self-correction to the extent that he was. If Peirce's SCT is really an
empirical hypothesis, why does it need the questionable support of
his elaborate logico-mathematical apparatus, of which I have given
no more than a tiny glimpse? This question essentially involves the
broader question of Peirce's philosophical commitments and concerns
in general, a question which will be the subject of my next and final
chapter.

Chapter Six
Science, Belief, and Non-Scientific Knowledge

a. SCT: An answer in search of a question

IT WAS CONCEDED in the Introduction that there is a core of truth in historicism; this core found expression in Mandelbaum's insistence that in order to understand a past philosopher, we must know what his non-philosophical commitments were. This insight is not in itself novel; it was proclaimed by Collingwood forty years ago in his famous statement that in order to understand any statement from the past we must know the precise question to which the statement was an answer or, more generally, that in order to understand any historical agent we must know the question to which his actions constituted an answer.[1] In the last chapter, we saw in detail what Peirce's self-corrective thesis (SCT) says; in this chapter an attempt will be made to clarify the meaning of this thesis by ascertaining the question or questions to which Peirce intended his thesis as an answer.

Several Peirce commentators have interpreted Peirce's theory of inquiry in general as an attempt to reconcile the conflicting claims of science and of non-scientific knowledge, while preserving the integrity and autonomy of each. The clearest such interpretation that I know of is the one propounded by Gallie,[2] who does not, however, probe into the intellectual-historical reasons why Peirce should have considered this problem of such paramount importance. It is true that this is a perennial problem, not limited to the late nineteenth century but dating, in one form or another, at least as far back as the thirteenth. Still, Peirce's grapplings with this problem cannot be fully understood unless we know the exact form in which the problem presented itself to his generation of American men of science. Scholars who have gone into this question have frequently concluded by taking a dim view of Peirce's attempted reconciliation; Wiener and Murphey, for example, have concluded that in Peirce's scheme of thought natural science occupies a decidedly subordinate position to theology and metaphysics.[3] While I personally believe that Peirce succeeded to a high degree in doing justice to both science and non-science, this is not what I shall be chiefly concerned to argue. The concern of this chapter will be to show what this effort at reconciliation consists in, how it can be seen as offering an appropriate framework for interpreting Peirce's writings on induction, and in what ways this framework renders those writings much less obscure than they have hitherto been thought.

It will be useful to take our point of departure in an examination of Laurens Laudan's highly interesting criticism of Peirce in his paper "Peirce and the Trivialization of the Self-Correcting Thesis." One of the most valuable contributions of Laudan's paper is his carefully documented historical observation that the self-corrective thesis (SCT), so far from being Peirce's original invention, was in fact formulated as early as 1750, and had turned into a commonplace of scientific methodology by the middle of the nineteenth century. He also shows that the self-correction of scientific method was typically conceived of by analogy with the approximative methods employed in mathematics. Having outlined this background, Laudan proceeds to argue that what distinguishes Peirce from Hartley, Le Sage, Herschel, Comte, Whewell, and others is that rather than simply asserting SCT Peirce was the first to argue it and attempt to offer reasons in its support: "What Peirce perceived, which his predecessors had not, was that it was not at all obvious that induction, defined as the testing of an hypothesis, is, or tends to be, self-correcting."[4] Peirce's project, so the argument goes, was not to defend enumerative induction against Hume, but to defend the scientific method against cynical critics. In this project Peirce failed, by confining his actual arguments exclusively to "the 'cheapest' form of self-correction," namely to quantitative induction. Peirce offered "no cogent reasons, not even mildly convincing ones, for believing that most inductive methods are self-corrective," and in the end he had to rest his defense of the scientific enterprise on "an inarticulate faith in the ability of the mind somehow to ferret out the truth, or a reasonable facsimile thereof."[5]

This is heavy artillery; to assess its firepower and the accuracy of its aim, let us look at Laudan's formulation of SCT. He formulates the thesis in both a strong and weak version, each consisting of two claims. The strong version is stated thus:

(1) Scientific method is such that, in the long run, its use will refute a theory T, if T is false.

(2) Science possesses a method for finding an alternative T′ which is closer to the truth than the refuted T.[6]

The weak thesis repeats (1), but replaces (2) by (2′):

(2′) Science possesses a technique for determining unambiguously whether an alternative T′ is closer to the truth than a refuted T.[7]

Peirce fails, Laudan argues, to provide a plausible defense for SCT in either of these two versions. Instead, he imperceptibly shifts his problem and argues for SCT in a still weaker, or "cheaper," version.

It should be clear from all that has preceded that I take Laudan to be right in his negative conclusion that Peirce fails to give any convincing argument for SCT as that thesis is formulated above. Where I must dissent is over the question of Peirce's intentions. Laudan rests his criticism on the historical claim that Peirce's concern was to rebut cynical critics of science, and that he proposed to do this by defending SCT in one of the two versions in which it had been handed down by his predecessors. Considering Laudan's own strong language, of which we have seen several examples, I may be permitted the statement that I do not find his historical claim compelling, or even plausible. Thesis (1), as we have seen, is a thesis which Peirce indeed subscribed to, and which he defended in two versions. In (1) there appears the expression "the long run," an expression which also appears in Peirce's definition of truth as the opinion towards which inquiry will converge in the long run. Now if, in both places, "the long run" is taken to be the same long run, (1) is demonstrably and indeed trivially true; whenever Peirce defends SCT in this version he appears in the garb of the aprioristic phenomenalist who was criticized by Lenz and Madden. But they may be taken to be two different long runs. Taking truth to be the opinion to be reached in the infinite long run, and taking self-correction to occur also in any finitely long run which we are capable of encountering in the actual world, Peirce held (1) to be empirically and conditionally true; this is the line taken by the pragmatic realist Peirce.

So much for the first claim involved in SCT. As for the second claim, I have been unable to find any evidence that Peirce ever subscribed to it, whether in the strong version (2) or in the weak version (2′). There are, it is true, very few statements which I would be prepared to swear that Peirce did not somewhere make; still, I find it almost inconceivable that he could have endorsed either (2) or (2′), since they are both utterly at variance with practically everything he ever said about the short-term fallibility and long-term unpredictability of scientific inquiry. What Peirce did believe was that we have evidence of a general trend towards truth in the history of science. This is rather different from holding that we can unambiguously determine nearness to truth in the case of two rival theories. Even in his most dogmatic moments Peirce's apriorism, to the best of my knowledge, limited itself to a defense of the trivialized version of (1). It is impossible to agree, therefore, that Peirce was ever concerned to defend SCT as that thesis has been formulated by Laudan. Nor is it credible that Peirce was seriously concerned to answer cynical critics of the scientific enterprise as such. At times, it is true, we find him polemicizing against critics of science; but his typical attitude towards such people was that "a man must be downright crazy to deny that science has made many true discoveries" (*CP*, 5.172). One may attempt to persuade or dissuade people whom one takes to be crazy, but one does not seriously argue with them. This last quote, I should add, is taken from Peirce's Lowell Lectures of 1903, cited by Laudan as the *locus classicus* for Peirce's defense of SCT.[8]

On the credit side, Laudan is surely right that the clues to Peirce's intentions are to be found in the historical problem situation. All future Peirce scholars are indebted to Laudan for establishing both that SCT was already a widely accepted truism and that it was typically defended by means of an unexplored mathematical analogy. But just the fact of common acceptance suggests the unlikelihood that Peirce would be interested in providing a serious defense for SCT; why argue what is already generally accepted? Is it not more likely that Peirce's attitude towards SCT was the same as in the strongly analogous case of Herschel's definition of truth, explored in chapter 2 above? Just as Peirce gave Herschel's dictum a subtle but important new twist, so, I shall argue, his defense of SCT was really a reinterpretation of SCT for the purpose of turning a widely accepted truth into a defense of certain positions of his own which were not so widely accepted. To be quite clear about this, Peirce certainly believed in (some version of) SCT, just as he believed in Herschel's consensual theory of truth; but what he needed to argue, in both cases, were his own idiosyncratic interpretations, as well as those philosophical and extra-philosophical commitments which called for just those interpretations.

What were Peirce's commitments? I think the most important ones can be presented under five headings: (1) the autonomy of pure research; (2) the short-term fallibility of science; (3) the legitimacy of statistical explanations; (4) the rejection of Laplacian probability; and (5) the anthropocentrism of science. In the remainder of this chapter I shall discuss each of these commitments in turn, with a view to establishing both their presence in Peirce's thought and their bearing on his discussions of SCT. I have no wish to keep the reader in suspense, so I might as well announce now that the common denominator of all five will turn out to be the attempt to reconcile the integrity of science with the legitimacy and autonomy of non-scientific knowledge as we find it exemplified in common sense, religion, metaphysics, ethics, and the humanities.

b. The autonomy of pure research

To start with, Peirce was obviously concerned to endorse and defend some version of SCT. Laudan has shown—convincingly, I think—that Peirce's defense of SCT does not in fact constitute a defense of the scientific enterprise as such.[9] My suggestion is that Peirce saw no real need for such a defense; what he did see was a need to defend the autonomy of pure, basic research against those who would make science subservient either to religious dogmas or to technological or political goals. The latter half of the nineteenth century was not predominantly an era of skepticism towards science. Such people as Ruskin, Carlyle, Nietzsche, and Dostoyevsky were not representative figures but odd men out, to whom Peirce never paid any serious attention—he mentioned Carlyle only once, and then only as an example of "diseased minds" (CP, 6.484).[10] The threat to science came not from its genuine enemies but from its avowed friends, whom Peirce perceived as its would-be masters. Peirce's lifetime was an era in which the engineering spirit was an object of worship all over the world; it was an era in which various European nationalisms, armed with the slogans of Social Darwinism, increasingly claimed the loyalty of their respective scientific communities; and it was an era in which American higher education was struggling to emancipate itself from its traditional role of preparation for the pulpit. These were problems of demonstrable concern to Peirce, and they furnish sufficient motive for his wanting to show that science has its own internal path of development and so has no need of external guidance or control. Let us look at the evidence for this motivation.

Peirce spent thirty years of his life in basic experimental research, and more than that on free-lance work in logic and the foundations of mathematics. His ingenuity in inventing novel experimental techniques, especially in his pendulum experiments for measuring gravity, prove him to have been technically adept; there is evidence, however, that he was comparatively uninterested in technological applications of science where there was no experimental purpose to be served. In a report from 1882, he cites six reasons for pursuing the pendulum experiments; five are "practical," having to do with metrology, geology, and seismography; but the sixth reason is that "knowledge of the force of gravity is not a mere matter of utility alone, it is also one of the fundamental kinds of quantity which it is the business of a geodetical survey to measure" (CP, 7.20).

Among the 1,644 regular entries in Richard S. Robin's catalogue of Peirce's papers, there are eighteen catalogued under the heading "Practical Science."[11] Of these, seven are devoted to cartography (mostly brief notes) and five to engineering projects. Apparently, after his resignation from the Coast Survey in 1891, Peirce turned first to speculation in land, then tried to make a living as a consulting engineer, without notable success in either venture. In view of his undoubted technical talent, his failure as an engineer is plausibly accounted for by a lack of interest in projects which had only a practical and commercial value.

Be that as it may, Peirce's views on the relation of pure science to applied science and engineering are unequivocal and amply documented. Among his published papers, those which offer the clearest documentation are his "Lessons from the History of Science" from about 1896 (e.g. *CP*, 1.45; 1.76) and his lectures "Detached Ideas on Vitally Important Topics" from 1898. In the latter text Peirce goes so far as practically to define 'science' by its uselessness: "A useless inquiry, provided it is a systematic one, is pretty much the same as a scientific inquiry" (*CP*, 1.668). Extravagant as this may sound, Peirce's point is fundamentally the same as the one which had earlier been made by Locke, namely that a concern for utility or for anything else besides truth will inevitably divert the investigator from his search for truth and hence defeat his purpose. As Locke put it in his *Essay*: "He that would seriously set upon the search of truth ought, in the first place, to prepare his mind with a love of it. For he that loves it not, will not take much pains to get it; nor be much concerned when he misses it."[12] This Lockean sentiment is echoed by Peirce in 1898:

> It is notoriously true that into whatever you do not put your whole heart and soul in that you will not have much success. Now, the two masters, *theory* and *practice*, you cannot serve. That perfect balance of attention which is requisite for observing the system of things is utterly lost if human desires intervene, and all the more so the higher and holier those desires may be. (*CP*, 1.642)

The antagonism between science and engineering is made most explicit in various unpublished manuscripts on the ancient history of

science, dating from about 1892. In several alternate drafts of a paper
on Babylonian and Egyptian science Peirce poses the contrast
between "the worshipper of Law" and "the worshipper of force"—
namely the scientist and the engineer, respectively: "No two casts of
mind are more thoroughly antagonistic than those of the worshipper
of force and the worshipper of law" (MS, 1270, p. 2). He then goes
on to disparage the engineering temper of the ancient Egyptians in a
delightful passage which is plainly addressed to his American
contemporaries:

> As for the typical Egyptian, he was a man of great energy and of high
> intelligence. He was a wonderful engineer. In religion, too, so far as it
> concerned his own salvation, he was sincere and earnest. He might be
> called the American of high antiquity. But in ideas, philosophical,
> mathematical, or poetical, he took no stock. (*Ibid.*)

In an alternate draft, we find the opposition stated thus:

> In short, the scientific man worships ideas,—not indeed as thoughts
> necessarily, but as forms of things and of the cosmos,—while the
> engineer worships force and power. No two spirits can be more
> antagonistic. (MS, 1271, p. 2; see also MS, 1272, p. 1)

Clearly, what Peirce saw in the contemporary cult of engineering was
a resurgence of the ancient worship of force which enabled the
Egyptians to build pyramids while preventing them from competing
with the Babylonians in mathematics or astronomy.

Peirce's opposition to the subordination of science to social
goals—whether in the name of nationalism, Social Darwinism, or
whatever—is most clearly documented in his long review of Pearson's
The Grammar of Science from 1901. Karl Pearson, whose methodological and biological ideas were briefly touched on in chapter 4, was
at the time one of Britain's foremost spokesmen for eugenics, imperialism, state socialism, and Social Darwinism. *The Grammar of
Science* was prefaced, as we have seen, with the pronouncement that
the sole justification of science is its tendency to lead to more efficient
citizenship and increased social stability. Pearson makes it amply
clear that what this means, on a more concrete level, is that the
proper role of science is to cleanse people's minds of sentimental and

harmful prejudices against eugenics at home and colonialism abroad.[13] To this Peirce replied, *inter alia*:

> The only ethically sound motive is the most general one; and the motive that actually inspires the man of science, if not quite that, is very near to it—nearer, I venture to believe, than that of any other equally common type of humanity. On the other hand, Professor Pearson's aim, 'the stability of society,' which is nothing but a narrow British patriotism, prompts the *cui bono* at once. (*CP*, 8.141)

> I must confess that I belong to that class of scallawags who purpose, with God's help, to look the truth in the face, whether doing so be conducive to the interests of society or not. (*CP*, 8.143)

Finally, Peirce was notoriously dissatisfied with the state of higher education in the United States. American education, as he saw it, was dominated by the churches and the business community and dedicated to the training of respectable and successful gentlemen, rather than to the advancement of learning. For Peirce this was more than a theoretical problem, it was a tragically personal one. As described in detail by Fisch and Cope,[14] Peirce was twice the victim of short-sighted, conformist educational policies. He was denied a career at Harvard, in all probability because his personal manners and morals were not deemed to be those of a Harvard gentleman; put more bluntly, because he was quarrelsome and because he was divorced. Again, in the 1880s, after Peirce, William James, and George Sylvester Morris had held temporary lecturerships at the newly founded and rapidly expanding Johns Hopkins University, they were all bypassed for a permanent appointment by G. Stanley Hall. Hall later gained fame as an experimental psychologist, but his chief claim to superiority at that time rested on his religious orthodoxy and his good relations with the business community. After his dismissal from Johns Hopkins in 1884, Peirce never again held an academic position.

The tragedy of Peirce's checkered career was not a purely personal one. Kuklick has made the interesting observation that Johns Hopkins may equally be regarded as the loser.[15] After President Gilman had passed up the chance of securing Peirce, James, or Mor-

ris for the university, Johns Hopkins lost yet a fourth outstanding
philosopher, since Morris was followed to Michigan by his student
John Dewey. Hall left after a few years, and Johns Hopkins was
without a philosopher until Arthur O. Lovejoy was hired in 1910. By
then Harvard had established itself as the mecca of American
philosophy. Today the history of American philosophy is to a large
extent the history of Harvard philosophy; this was not written in the
stars in the early 1880s, when Johns Hopkins was the first and only
graduate school in the nation. This does not mean that Johns
Hopkins' loss was entirely Harvard's gain; the legendary President
Eliot may have been more farsighted than his colleague Gilman, but
he too failed to recognize the greatest philosopher his country has yet
brought forth. From 1884 on, Peirce was lost to the educational
establishment.

Not unsurprisingly, throughout Peirce's writings on education
we find scornful remarks about university administrators who place
the material success of their students and faculty above the one legitimate goal of a university, to wit, the advancement of knowledge.[16]
We shall note, however, that the complaint is not really that the
universities train their students to pursue low and petty goals; Peirce
is certainly not an advocate of "relevance" in the sense of service to
the community. *Any* character building, Peirce seems to hold, is inimical to the pursuit of science and hence alien to the function of a
university. Education, he suggests in 1898, should not be a function
of a university at all; an institution of learning cannot at the same
time be an institution of teaching, since these two functions are irre-
concilably opposed (*CP*, 5.583).

Peirce's argument is this. An educational institution aims at
inculcating manners and morals to prepare its pupils for life in the
community. But manners and morals are by their very nature conservative. Morality is "behaving as you were brought up to behave
. . . But to believe in thinking as you have been brought up to think
defines *conservatism*" (*CP*, 1.666). Science is, on the contrary,
essentially radical; it teaches us to reason about received opinions and
to subject them to the test of experience. Hence science cannot
flourish in institutions dedicated to the cultivation of manners and
morals. To return once more to the 1892 manuscripts, in the primi-

tive stages of science, the "whole moral weight of the community will be cast against science; because science implies a desire to learn; and a desire to learn implies a dissatisfaction with existing opinions. Thus, an early development of good morals, and still worse of good manners, is unfavorable to science" (MS, 1,289, p. 2).

If the reader thinks he has guessed why the universities preferred to do without Peirce's services, he might be well advised to guess again. In the above quotes there is intended no derogation of education, morality, or even of conservatism. From all the available evidence, Peirce was an outstanding teacher, who attached a great deal of importance to education and was rather proud of his teaching abilities.[17] He also did not hesitate to characterize himself as a conservative as far as manners and morals were concerned.[18] But in order to progress, science had to be kept safe from all practical goals, even the worthiest ones.

Peirce's argument for divorcing research from education may seem to conflict with the view explored in the last chapter, namely that scientific reasoning is itself a species of moral conduct, depending for its success upon the exercise of virtue. This may seem to conflict with the view that good morals are inimical to the development of science. But there is not necessarily any contradiction. If science requires specific virtues which are productive of scientific progress but are otherwise unproductive (or counterproductive), it stands to reason that science must come in conflict with the norms of traditional morality, norms which have been formulated in disregard of the specific ethical requirements of science. If Peirce means that all morality requires to be embodied in traditions which demand unquestioning obedience, than it would seem to follow that science tends to undermine the conditions for its own success. This is an interesting conclusion which would surely stand in need of argument; but even this conclusion is not self-contradictory.

We have seen, at any rate, that Peirce was amply motivated to defend the autonomy of basic research against the three threats stemming from engineering, political authorities, and conformist educational institutions—none of which were notable as citadels of skepticism, let alone of cynicism towards science. Their guilt lay rather in their overconfidence in science as a pliable tool for producing practical results. In defending pure research against these threats, all that Peirce needed was the weakest possible form of self-correction, a self-correction only strong enough to render external tampering with science superfluous and harmful. That is, he needed the thesis of eventual, long-run refutation of false theories. Not only did he not need a decision procedure for short-run self-correction; such a decision procedure would actually have defeated his purposes by guaranteeing immediate practical utility and thereby delivering science into the hands of his opponents.

c. The short-term fallibility of science

Peirce's attempt at making pure research safe from the demands of practice goes hand in glove with his attempt to make practical life safe from unwarranted interference on the part of science. These two attempts are strictly complementary, not contrary, and they involve deployment of the same arguments. In both cases Peirce was opposing the positivistic "scientism" of Comte, Bernard, Mach, and Pearson fashionable in his day. To the positivists the chief purpose of subordinating pure to applied science was to turn the institution of science into a reliable guide to conduct, capable of replacing religion and philosophy, tradition and common sense. Evidently, if one wishes to defend the autonomy of pure science, the price to be paid must include the renunciation of this positivistic ambition. To Peirce this was not a price but a bonus; the integrity of practical life was something which he valued on its own account. We have seen that Peirce's argument for the autonomy of pure research is based, in part, on an irreconcilable antagonism between the demands of science and the demands of practice. Any mingling of the two, so his argument goes, must inevitably imperil the integrity of both. In the last section I stressed the dire consequences for pure science; Peirce, however, equally stressed the consequences for the practical conduct of life. Thus Peirce in 1896: "When men begin to rationalize about their conduct, the first effect is to deliver them over to their passions and produce the most frightful demoralization, especially in sexual matters. Thus, among the Greeks, it brought about paederasty and a precedence of public women over private wives" (*CP*, 1.57). And again, in 1898: "If you ever happen to be thrown in with an unprofessional thief, the only very bad kind of thief, you will find that two things characterize him; first, an even more immense conceit in his own reasoning power than is common, and second, a disposition to reason about the basis of morals" (*CP*, 1.666; see also MS, 436, p. 3).

I do not know whether Peirce was acquainted with *Crime and Punishment,* but this certainly sounds like an echo of Dostoyevsky. Not that Peirce shared Dostoyevsky's aversion to science—quite the contrary, he worshipped science, understood as a pure, undiluted search for truth—but he shared Dostoyevsky's aversion to *scientism,* an aversion eloquently and recklessly expressed in the latter's *Notes from Underground.* Peirce's conclusion, which is only slightly more moderate than Dostoyevsky's, is that in practical matters, especially in matters of vital importance, we ought to distrust reason and follow the example of the lower animals who "*never* reason about vitally important topics," and who consequently "very rarely fall into error of any kind, and *never* into a vitally important one" (*CP*, 1.649).[19] In theoretical inquiry reason is sovereign, but for the purpose of making decisive practical choices, instinct is a surer guide than reason.

This sentiment may appear familiar; it recalls Hume's pronouncement that "Reason is, and ought only to be the slave of the passions."[20] But there are important differences between the two thinkers. Hume was quite prepared to trust reasoning, even inductive reasoning, as a guide to conduct; only he insisted that when we trust reasoning, we do so instinctively. Peirce's view might be said to be the opposite: when we trust instinct, we do so rationally. Peirce thinks that we should trust inductive reasoning to the extent that we have reason to do so, and distrust it where such reason is lacking. There are good reasons for proceeding inductively in science, because this is the only way to get nearer to the truth;[21] but there are no good reasons for trusting the conclusions of reasoning when they conflict with those of instinct in regard to vitally important choices. There are no such reasons because, as stressed in chapter 1 above, science progresses through the correction of erroneous hypotheses and is therefore committed to entertaining on probation, at any time, a whole host of unreliable and probably false conjectures which it would be utterly irrational to believe in (see *CP*, 1.120, 1.635).

From this vantage point Peirce's interest in self-correction can be seen to lie precisely in showing that the long-run self-correction of science does not imply the existence of any method for determining short-run self-correction. If we had such a method we should be able to rely on scientific conclusions for practical purposes, and this is just what Peirce says we are not able to do. For this purpose, he was right in opting for the most obvious type of self-correction, namely that of quantitative induction. This case, which to his scientistic predecessors would have been the easiest case, was from Peirce's point of view the hardest case. Surely we are justified in relying on predictions drawn from an inductively established ratio of, say, one to one? Not so, Peirce replies, even such a ratio refers only to the long-run relative frequency of favorable outcomes and it tells us nothing about what may or may not happen in the short run. This is emphasized in the "Notes on Scientific Philosophy" from about 1897: "Even if we could ascertain with absolute certainty and exactness that the ratio of all sinful men to all men was as 1 to 1; still among the infinite generations of men there would be room for any finite number of sinless men without violating the proportion. The case is the same with a seven-legged calf" (*CP*, 1.141; see also *CP*, 2732). In short, Peirce's concern for the integrity of instinct, faith, and morals provides him with one more motive for defending the self-corrective thesis in just the form in which he did defend it.

So far, in this section, Peirce appears deceptively like William James; some words need to be said about James's defense of faith and Peirce's reaction to it. In *The Will to Believe,* published in 1896, James proposed the following defense of religious belief against the agnosticism of T. H. Huxley and W. K. Clifford.[22] Our cognitive life is governed by two passions: the passion for knowing truth and the passion for avoiding error. These are not two different ways of saying the same thing; they are in fact conflicting passions. The former passion tempts us towards gullibility, towards believing too much; the latter passion tempts us towards skepticism, towards believing too little. In science it is necessary and proper to let oneself be dominated by the passion to avoid error. Science is not in a hurry to know the truth; its method consists in gradually approaching the truth in the long run through meticulous avoidance of error in the short run; hence science not only may, but must suspend judgment where the evidence is insufficient. In practical life, however, we are not allowed to bank on the long run; here, we are frequently confronted with options which are of momentous importance, and which are forced in the sense that a refusal to choose in itself constitutes a choice. Such an option is: "Believe in Christianity, or do not believe!" (James explicitly considers Christianity vs. agnosticism the only *live* religious option for his particular audience.) Given that the evidence for and against Christianity is insufficient to decide the choice, either hypothesis can be chosen only on insufficient evidence. The agnostic, by acting as if Christianity were not true, has not escaped the choice; he has for all practical purposes chosen atheism, and he has chosen on just as insufficient evidence as the believer. In the face of such an option, then, the attempt to avoid error by suspending judgment is doomed to fail: "Religion is a *forced* option, as far as [its] good goes. We cannot escape the issue by remaining sceptical and waiting for more light, because, although we do avoid error in that way *if religion be untrue,* we lose the good, *if it be true,* just as certainly as if we positively chose to disbelieve."[23]

This argument is similar to the one which Peirce was to set forth in his lectures two years later—possibly under direct influence from James. Yet Peirce's attitude towards *The Will To Believe* was curiously ambivalent. The book was aptly dedicated to Peirce, and in a letter to James in 1897 Peirce described the book as a "masterpiece," while at the same time registering certain reservations (*CP,* 8.249–52). Apart from some criticisms of James's use of probability, Peirce's reservations are not very illuminating. James had exemplified his thesis by saying that if a man were to postpone proposal of marriage until he had sufficient evidence that his bride-to-be was the angel she appeared to be, he might as well have decided not to propose.[24] Peirce replied that even if he were to decide to trust a man enough to take him on as his business partner, that would not stop him from collecting as much evidence about the man's honesty as possible in the time left him before a commitment was necessary. Even apart from the significant differences between marriage and a

business partnership, there is nothing in Peirce's objection which
James would have to deny. James's point was that once a commitment is necessary, further fact-finding will defeat its own purpose. At
any rate, Peirce himself does not seem to have considered his objection a very serious one.

By 1909, however, the tone had changed. Peirce now described
The Will To Believe as "a very exaggerated utterance, such as
injures a serious man very much,"[25] A possible explanation of
Peirce's change of heart may be that in the meantime, in 1898, James
had committed himself to a brand of pragmatism which Peirce did
not share; Peirce may therefore have succumbed to the temptation of
reading James's later pragmatism into the earlier book. Be that as it
may, in 1898, when Peirce gave his lectures on "Vitally Important
Topics," there were substantive differences between him and James.
Peirce was happy to use the Jamesian argument in defense of
inherited faith and instinct, traditional morality, and common sense.
But he did not consider religion entirely a matter of faith, nor did he
consider ethics (as distinct from morality) entirely a matter of tradition or instinct. Religion, metaphysics, and ethics are, he believed,
legitimate branches of human knowledge; as such, they claim to be
empirically true, and this claim cannot be defended in the Jamesian
manner. In practical choices we do well to act upon the proposition
which instinct tells us to trust; still, the truth of a religious proposition is determined in a manner no different from the truth of a scientific proposition. When they conflict, one must be false, and we cannot say *a priori* which one; only empirical inquiry can decide the
issue. Since the truth cannot be self-contradictory, religion and
science will converge in the long run, but no one can say as yet what
opinion they will converge on. This is put most clearly in "The Logic
of Events" from 1898:

> It is a damnable absurdity indeed to say that one thing is true in
> theology and another in science. But it is perfectly true that the belief
> which I shall do well to embrace in my practical affairs, such as my
> religion, may not accord with the proposition which a sound scientific
> method requires me provisionally to adopt at this stage of my investi-
> gation. Later, both the one proposition and the other may very likely

be modified; but how, or which comes nearer to the ultimate conclusion, not being a prophet or a magician, I cannot yet say. (*CP*, 6.216)

Similarly, in the unpublished portion of "The First Rule of Logic," also from 1898, Peirce defends Duns Scotus against the imputation that he held one thing to be true in philosophy and another in religion, an opinion more properly ascribed to Scotus's opponent Averroes. Still, Peirce adds, although there are not two different senses of the word 'truth,' there are two different senses of 'holding for true': "To adhere to a proposition in an absolutely definitive manner, supposing that by this is merely meant that the believer has personally wedded his fate to it, is something which in practical concerns, say for instance in matters of right and wrong, we sometimes cannot and ought not to avoid; but to do so in science amounts simply to not wishing to learn" (MS, 442, pp. 37–38).

It is clear from the latter quote that Peirce agrees with James that for purposes of practical action we cannot adopt the wait-and-see attitude required in science. But it is equally clear from the former quote that this does not constitute Peirce's entire case for the integrity of religion against scientistic trespassers. His case is almost the opposite: for purposes of truth determination both science and religion must wait and see, and there is no way of prejudging the outcome at present. Religion has been made safe only against those pseudo-scientists who would claim that science already possesses the Truth, and that religion therefore has been proved to be superstition. But science also needs to be protected from such friends. Religion has not been made safe against science, and no boundaries have been drawn to the domain of scientific inquiry. There is no religious doctrine whose truth cannot be made the subject of scientific inquiry. But so long as the conclusions of science and religion differ, and so long as there are reasonable men disagreeing over the truth of each, the conflict between them cannot be regarded as settled. In the end, the error may turn out to lie with the provisional conclusions of science, as well as with those of religion.

This last point is also made in Peirce's 1896 review of *A History of the Warfare of Science with Theology in Christendom*, by Cornell's President White. Here, Peirce objects to, among other things, the fashionable positivistic view of religion as pre-scientific myths. Equally, science may be, and at times has been, pre-religious; thus "certain Bible narratives really originated in archaic scientific speculation" (MS, 1,404, p. 2). Peirce goes on to argue that the religious mind is characterized by a "deficient love of truth" (*ibid.*, p. 12), "a want of desire to find out the truth" (*ibid.*, p. 13), but concludes by suggesting that the churches' claim to infallibility, once properly understood as a claim to *practical* infallibility, might "prove a benign influence, and a blessing to a democratic country" (*ibid.*, p. 17).

Peirce was himself a religious believer, and he did not think himself deficient in the love of truth. This deficiency, he indicates in several places, is a historical accident of religion and is inherently alien to its essence. Religion is committed in principle to objective truth, and this commitment can be honored only by bowing to experience; hence religion, like science, can be true to its own essence only by subjecting its doctrines to the test of experience and criticism. "The *raison d'être* of a church," Peirce wrote in 1895, "is to confer upon men a life broader than their narrow personalities, a life rooted in the very truth of their being. To do that it must be based upon and refer to a definite and public experience" (*CP*, 6.451). Two years earlier, in an article in *The Open Court,* he had made the same point in a passage which would deserve quoting for its poetic flair alone:

> The day has come, however, when the man whom religious experience most devoutly moves can recognize the state of the case. While adhering to the essence of religion, and so far as possible to the church, which is all but essential, say, penessential, to it, he will cast away that religious timidity that is forever prompting the church to recoil from the paths into which the Governor of history is leading the minds of men, a cowardice that has stood through the ages as the landmark and limit of her little faith, and will gladly go forward, sure that truth is not split into two warring doctrines, and that any change that knowledge can work in his faith can only affect its expression, but not the deep mystery expressed. (*CP*, 6.432)

Peirce was not engaged in clearing away knowledge to make room for faith. Eager to protect the sphere of practical action from the misapplication of scientific conjectures, he yet remained convinced that our knowledge of God, like all other knowledge, must in the end stand the test of experience and of the eventual universal agreement among all inquiring minds.

d. The legitimacy of statistical explanations

My most tentative and speculative suggestion in this chapter is that Peirce's "justification" of induction, focusing as it does almost exclusively on statistical induction, may in fact have been intended as a justification only of statistical induction. The fact is that in the mid-nineteenth century, while Newtonian mechanics was still the paradigm of scientific explanation, the role of statistics in science was controversial. Methodologists as diverse as Comte, Herschel, and Whewell agreed that a theory is explanatory only if it exactly predicts particular phenomena. Leading probability theorists, such as Laplace and Quetelet, agreed that statistical hypotheses are merely descriptions of imperfectly known phenomena and hence not truly explanatory.[26] And, as late as 1865, Bernard insisted that statistics can produce only "conjectural science," not "true" science.[27]

At the same time, statistical theories proliferated and grew increasingly important, the most notable examples being the kinetic theory of heat and Darwin's theory of natural selection. The former theory was respectable because it merely gave a statistical description of phenomena which were yet explainable in terms of deterministic mechanisms. Darwin's case was different; there was available no mechanistic explanation of mutation, so to the extent that Darwin's theory was explanatory, it relied on stochastic processes. Darwin himself, sensing this as a shortcoming, simply denied the fact: "I have hitherto spoken as if the variations . . . had been due to chance. This, of course, is a wholly incorrect expression, but it serves to acknowledge plainly our ignorance of the causes of each particular variation."[28] As has been documented in detail by Silvan Schweber, Darwin was conversant with the ideas of Comte, Herschel, Whewell, and Quetelet, and was profoundly concerned to live up to their methodological precepts.[29]

Peirce, by contrast, was an outspoken defender of the scientific legitimacy of statistical explanations. In 1878, he clearly recognized the statistical nature of Darwin's theory, praised Darwin as a successor of Clausius and Maxwell, and described the Darwinian controversy as, "in large part, a question of logic" (*CP*, 5.364). What had struck Peirce as the crux of the Darwinian revolution was the logical structure of Darwin's theory, not its theological or anthropological ramifications. And in "A Guess at the Riddle" from about 1890, Peirce says that "there remains little doubt that the Darwinian theory indicates a real cause" (*CP*, 1.395), once again endorsing the explanatory nature of Darwin's statistical hypothesis. Over the years, Peirce's admiration for Darwin cooled considerably, yet he remained an admirer of Darwin's method of explanation. In his 1893 paper "Evolutionary Love," which is chiefly an attack on the idea of natural selection, Peirce lists the advances of statistical explanations from 1847 to the publication of *The Origin of Species* in 1859 and concludes:

> The consequence was that the idea that fortuitous events may result in physical law, and further that this is the way in which those laws which appear to conflict with the principle of conservation of energy are to be explained, had taken a strong hold upon the minds of all who were abreast of the leaders of thought. By such minds, it was inevitable that the *Origin of Species,* whose teaching was simply the application of the same principle to another "non-conservative" action, that of organic development, should be hailed and welcomed. (*CP*, 6.297)

On the face of it, this is simply a historical statement; it may, however, well be taken to be autobiographical. There is little doubt that Peirce identifies himself with "those who were abreast of the leaders of thought," and that he thus explains his own favorable reception of Darwin's theory by classifying it as a particularly commendable type of theory.

Underlying Peirce's defense of the legitimacy of statistical explanations is his commitment to the metaphysical idea that the cosmos evolves through the agency of objective chance begetting physical law. And the idea of objective chance is in its turn rooted in Peirce's own laboratory experience. The reality of chance, he held, is legitimated by the advance of statistical methods of measurement, such as the method of least squares.[30] So long as physical science depends on such methods, and so long as we have no non-statistical method by which to check them, we have no empirical grounds for saying that probable errors of measurement are due to our inaccuracy rather than to the indeterminacy of nature herself. This view is suggested, rather than asserted, in "The Doctrine of Necessity Examined" from 1892:

> Try to verify any law of nature, and you will find that the more precise your observations, the more certain they will be to show irregular departures from the law. We are accustomed to ascribe these, and I do not say wrongly, to errors of observation; yet we cannot usually account for such errors in an antecedently probable way. Trace their causes back far enough and you will be forced to admit that they are always due to arbitrary determination, or chance. (*CP*, 6.46)

By 1897, Peirce was prepared to argue that statistical regularities may be explained as the result of irregularities, and that we are therefore entitled to appeal to spontaneity or chance as a real cause, a conclusion which five years earlier he had hesitated to draw: "As there is nothing to show that there is not a certain amount of spontaneity in nature, despite all laws, our metaphysical pigeon-holes should not be so limited as to exclude this general hypothesis, pro-vided any general phenomena should appear which might be explained by such spontaneity" (*CP*, 1.158).

To repeat, the bearing of this issue on Peirce's justification of induction is uncertain and conjectural. His metaphysical discussions of objective chance appear more than a decade after his chief papers on induction. Still, we do know that he favored the statistical type of explanation as early as 1878, at which time his most important work on the theory of measurement was behind him. We also know that he made a serious attempt at justifying only statistical induction. It is at least a plausible and interesting conjecture that this is the only form of induction which he was interested in justifying, because it was the only form of induction which stood in need of justification. Showing that statistical inductions are self-corrective, if any inductions are, would amount to a powerful methodological legitimation of statistical theories. Peirce's restriction of his defense of SCT to a defense of statistical induction might thus be explainable on these grounds. Such an explanation would, however, entail a more thorough examination of the earlier papers than the one I have presented.

e. The rejection of Laplacian probability

The last section was frankly conjectural and tentative; a much more cogent case may be made for seeing Peirce's justification of induction as primarily a refutation of the Laplacian conception of probability as a measure of relative ignorance and a defense of the relative-frequency view. In a number of Peirce's papers on inductive self-correction we find the same pattern repeated: Peirce starts by announcing that he is going to discuss induction, rapidly digresses into the theory of probability, produces a *reductio ad absurdum* of Laplace's Rule of Succession, and sometimes proceeds to outline a relative-frequency interpretation of the probability attaching to statistical induction— without ever getting around to discussing induction in general (e.g. *CP,* 2.669–93, 2.694–754, 5.167–70, 7.208–17). This repeated pattern strongly suggests that what is really at issue in these papers is probability, rather than induction *per se.*

The argument I want to propose is this. Inductive self-correction was, as Laudan has established, widely accepted as a truism which the leading scientists and philosophers of the day did not even bother to argue. The accepted fact of self-correction appeared to be accounted for by the Rule of Succession, according to which the probability of an inductive prediction increases with increased evidential support. This rule was originated by no less an authority than Laplace, and was defended by such leading logicians as de Morgan, and by such leading statisticians as Quetelet. This subjectivist defense of sct was later taken over by Karl Pearson, Peirce's arch-antagonist in later years.[31] In Pearson's work, by the way, the subjectivist conception of probability was exploited precisely for the purpose of presenting science as a guide to conduct and as a suitable tool for social and political goals. In rejecting the Laplacian concept of probability and advancing a relative-frequency interpretation, Peirce could not rest content with merely showing, as he did, that the Rule of Succession is inconsistent. In advancing his alternative interpretation, he was under an obligation to show that his interpretation accounted for all the undoubted facts which had been accounted for by Laplace—and one such undoubted fact was inductive self-correction. If these considerations define Peirce's problem situation, then what he was arguing was not primarily that induction is self-correcting, something which his opponents already took for granted. What he was arguing was, rather, that the relative-frequency view can fully account for this self-correction; or, to give the same point a different twist, that *there is absolutely nothing more* to inductive self-correction than what would appear from the relative-frequency interpretation. There is, on this supposition, a double purpose to Peirce's argument: both to show that the relative-frequency view does justice to all the facts accounted for by the Laplacian view, and to show that some of the 'facts' accounted for by the latter view are not facts at all.

This double purpose accounts for those numerous passages where Peirce, while insisting that the calculus of probability justifies our belief in long-run self-correction, yet strenuously denies that it gives us any justification at all for relying on particular inductive conclusions. Peirce needed long-run self-correction, not in order to defend science, but in order to defend his own interpretation of the calculus of probability, since the generation of this particular result (namely self-correction) was thought to be one of the requirements for the adequacy of any interpretation of the calculus.

Why is it plausible that his interpretation of the calculus of probability should be a matter of major concern to Peirce; of greater concern, say, than the validity of induction? As an astute logician, Peirce spotted the inconsistency in the Rule of Succession and hence found it necessary to seek an alternative interpretation of probability. This might be a sufficient explanation; if any philosopher can be credited with disinterested truth-seeking, Peirce can. Still, this does not explain why he kept insisting on this particular truth; there must have been some reason why it mattered more than a great many other truths. It mattered, I believe, for at least two reasons, one philosophical and one more broadly cultural.

For philosophical reasons, Peirce needed an interpretation of probability which would lend itself both to a verificationist semantics for probability statements and to a realist account of the pragmatics of probabilistic reasoning. The Laplacian interpretation would meet the first requirement, but not the second; to make room for a realist pragmatics Peirce needed to make probability statements refer to real facts in the external world. How the relative-frequency interpretation lends itself to such a pragmatics is brought out in "Notes on the Doctrine of Chances," Peirce's 1910 addendum to his 1878 article "The Doctrine of Chances." In the original article Peirce presented a straightforwardly verificationist account of the meaning of probability statements, perfectly in line with the general account of meaning proposed in "How To Make Our Ideas Clear," published in the same series of articles in *Popular Science Monthly.* Just as Peirce later supplemented his verificationist account of meaning in general with a realist account of reference in general, so, in 1910, he supplements his verificationist account of the meaning of probability statements with a realist account of the reference of such statements:

> I am, then, to define the meanings of the statement that the *probability,* that if a die be thrown from a dice box it will turn up a number divisible by three, is one-third. The statement means that the die has a certain "would-be"; and to say that a die has a "would-be" is to say that it has a property, quite analogous to any *habit* that a man might have . . . and just as it would be necessary, in order to define a man's habit, to describe how it would lead him to behave and upon what sort of occasion—albeit this statement would by no means imply that the habit *consists* in that action—so to define the die's "would-be"; it is necessary to say how it would lead the die to behave on an occasion that would bring out the full consequence of the "would-be"; and this statement will not of itself imply that the "would-be" of the die *consists* in such behavior. (*CP*, 2.664)

In 1910, then, Peirce supplements his relative-frequency view of the meaning of probability statements with what we today call a "propensity" theory of the nature of probability.[32] We can explain the meaning of probability statements only by citing empirically observable relative frequencies, but that does not mean that probability values refer to these frequencies. The propensity theory was already ambiguously present in the 1878 article, in Peirce's insistence that "in the long run, there is a real fact which corresponds to the idea of probability" (CP, 2.650). Peirce, after all, was a realist well before 1878. Chapters 3 and 4 were devoted to examining the extent to which Peirce's verificationism and realism are and are not mutually compatible. Here it need only be pointed out that Peirce's account of probability is simply a special case of his account of sign action in general, and is subject to the same philosophical requirements as is the general case. The relative-frequency theory fulfills these requirements, whereas no subjective theory of probability does.

Thus, the need to give a relative-frequentist account of inductive self-correction is seen to arise from Peirce's central philosophical concerns. But there are broader cultural issues at stake as well. Peirce's relative-frequentist view of probability gave him a platform from which to criticize the subjectivist "method of balancing likelihoods," a method which permitted probability considerations to be brought to bear on particular inductive conclusions, even conclusions regarding the unique and unrepeatable events studied by historians. In Peirce's time this method enjoyed a great deal of popularity among German critical historians, who were fond of applying likelihood considerations to the evaluation of ancient historical testimony as a means of debunking both the narratives of the Gospels and most of ancient history. In this, they were following in the footsteps of Hume, who had argued that whenever a miracle is reported it is always more likely that the witness is mistaken than it is that a breach of the laws of nature has actually taken place.[33] In the hands of critical historians this argument was generalized to justify the dismissal of all testimony of antecedently unlikely events. Moreover, reports of likely events were frequently dismissed by the same argument, because such events were likely to have been invented by the chronicler. Peirce himself was a sincere, if unorthodox, theist, as well as a practicing historian of enormous erudition; on both counts he found himself in opposition to the German "higher criticism."[34] So, for instance, in his "Vitally Important Topics," he prefaces his Jamesian defense of faith and instinct with a passage in which he ridicules the German historian Edouard Zeller for concluding against the likelihood that Thales once fell into a ditch while pointing out stars to an old woman (CP, 1.617). In a manuscript from 1901, and again in the Lowell Lectures of 1903, he counters Hume's attack on miracles by pointing out the unsoundness of Hume's method, that of balancing likelihoods.[35] Roughly, his criticisms are that what the historian needs to know is the veracity of the witness of one particular occasion, something which cannot be inferred from the probability that the witness is telling the truth. Similarly, the antecedent probability of the event reported is irrelevant to the question of whether it occurred on the unique occasion on which it has been reported to occur. A miracle might even be defined as an antecedently improbable event; the question of whether an improbable event has occurred cannot be answered by saying that it is improbable. Finally, even if the two probabilities (of the event and of the truthfulness of the witness) were of interest, they could not be balanced against each other, since they are not independent; we learn the veracity of a witness only from the truthfulness of his reports, that is from the occurrence of the events which he reports. In sum, probability in a mathematical sense does not enter into historical criticism, which seeks to establish what has in fact taken place.

In the long "Logic of History," also from about 1901, Peirce launches a detailed critical attack on the critical historians, proceeding from a critique of the subjective theory of probability, and concluding:

> If by "probability" be meant the degree to which a hypothesis in regard to what happened in ancient Greece recommends itself to a professor in a German university town, then there is no mathematical theory of probability which will withstand the artillery of modern mathematical criticism. A probability, in that sense, is nothing but the degree to which a hypothesis accords with one's preconceived notions; and its value depends entirely upon how those notions have been formed, and upon how much objectivity they can lay a solid claim to. (*CP*, 7.177)

Peirce holds that preconceived notions are not appropriate as yardsticks for evaluating historical testimony, but quite the reverse: agreement with historical testimony is one of the tests of the universality of our preconceived notions. "One of the main purposes of studying history ought to be to free us from the tyranny of our preconceived notion" (*CP*, 7.227).

What Peirce here opposes is the nineteenth-century positivistic thesis of the substantive unity of science, a thesis which entailed that historical testimony had to be validated by its conformity to present-day physics, psychology, etc. Peirce does affirm the methodological unity of science and characterizes the method of history, like that of physics, as the method of hypothesis, deduction, and experiment. When all the evidence we have is testimony, we test our hypotheses by performing imaginary experiments on the testimony; in such experimentation it is our hypotheses that are tested, not the testimony. In order to avoid *ad hoc* hypotheses, as well as to test the testimony itself, it is necessary to gather additional evidence; Peirce especially emphasizes the role of archaeology as the experimental testing ground for historical hypotheses—and he notes with grim satisfaction the numerous times when archaeological evidence has vindicated ancient testimony and overturned the conclusions reached by German historians on the basis of likelihood (*CP*, 2.777, 6.513, 6.536; MS, 1,404, p. 7).

To sum up: present-day science is hemmed in by the bounds of our present-day experience and preconceptions. Historical testimony is not required to justify itself at the bar of these preconceptions; on the contrary, historical knowledge ought to liberate us from the preconceptions peculiar to our own age and place. History, therefore, must aim at telling us what actually did happen, not what is likely to have happened. We see, then, that in Peirce's defense of the autonomy of historical knowledge lies a motive for divorcing the concept of mathematical probability from that of epistemic likelihood. From the point of view of this motive what is at stake in Peirce's writings on induction is not so much the progressiveness of the natural sciences—a foregone conclusion—as the autonomy of the human sciences—an issue of contention in Peirce's time as it is today.

f. The anthropocentrism of science

It was Peirce's belief that the scientific enterprise is fully intelligible only as a distinctively human activity, and that its success is explainable only on the hypothesis that man has a biological, psychological, and moral character which adapts him to the task of truth-finding. In his earlier years, for instance in his papers from 1878 and 1883, Peirce tended to emphasize the biological and psychological conditions for successful induction; in later years he came increasingly to stress virtue as an indispensable condition. In any case, throughout his writings on induction this anthropocentric conception of science looms large in his discussions of random sampling and predesignation as preconditions for successful induction. Sampling, as we have seen, is an art; as such it requires judgment and inventiveness, as well as such virtues as industry and honesty. Predesignation is simply the same thing as abduction, regarded from the point of view of the subsequent testing. It requires, besides imagination, both an instinct for guessing at the truth and a single-minded application to the search for truth. Induction does not depend for its justification upon our knowledge that these preconditions have been fulfilled; its justification lies solely in its subsequent tendency towards self-correction, a tendency which, incidentally, we can ascertain only in the long run, after all inductions have been completed and a justification is no longer required. But the actual success of induction, if such success be granted as a fact, depends on the actual fulfillment of the antecedent conditions; hence, if we are to understand the reasons for its success, we need knowledge of the human psyche and its history. This anthropocentrism is far from being an "inarticulate faith," as Laudan has it; it is an empirical hypothesis, obscurely yet unmistakably articulated in a number of places, and fully consonant with Peirce's thorough-going pragmatism and naturalism. It does, however, lead to conclusions which may appear surprising from the vantage point of more popular naturalisms.

One such conclusion is that since abduction depends on an affinity between the human mind and the universe, it follows that the anthropomorphic character of a hypothesis is actually a consideration in its favor. This conclusion is drawn, for instance, in the Lowell Lectures of 1903:

> In regard to any preference for one kind of theory over another, it is well to remember that every single truth of science is due to the affinity of the human soul to the soul of the universe, imperfect as that affinity no doubt is. To say, therefore, that a conception is one natural to man, which comes to just about the same thing as to say that it is

anthropomorphic, is as high a recommendation as one could give to it in the eyes of an Exact Logician. (*CP*, 5.47)

In the same lectures Peirce included anthropomorphism among the requirements for the construction of hypotheses under the heading of economy. Two years later, in his "Consequences of Common-Sensism," he drew the further conclusion that the hypothesis of an intelligent creator of the universe is to be recommended, precisely because it is anthropomorphic (*CP*, 5.536).

It may be well to pause and note some obvious difficulties which Peirce here runs into. On the one hand, hardly anyone would deny that all scientific conceptions have originated from anthropomorphic conceptions—'force' and 'cause' are obvious instances—or even that science can never altogether outgrow its anthropomorphic pedigree— even the most abstractly mathematical theory is formulated in the decimal system, which is natural to man because he has ten fingers. On the other hand, it is widely agreed that the scientific progress which has taken place since the Renaissance has largely consisted in rendering science gradually less anthropomorphic. According to this commonly accepted view, anthropomorphism in science is acknowledged as a fact of life, but not as a value to be striven for. Whether or not this view is correct, at least the circumstance that anthropomorphism is a fact of life does not make it a value worth striving for; on the contrary, just this circumstance makes it utterly futile to posit anthropomorphism as a value, since we are stuck with it whether we want it or not. We might as well strive to render ice cold or fire hot.

Peirce falls into a confusion, therefore, when he reasons from the fact that man cannot but view the cause of the universe in human terms to the recommendation that he ought to embrace theism as a hypothesis. This, in effect, is the way he reasons in the following passage from "Consequences of Common-Sensism":

I do not believe that man can have the idea of any cause or agency so stupendous that there is any more adequate way of conceiving it than as vaguely like a man. Therefore, whoever cannot look at the starry heaven without thinking that all this universe must have had an adequate cause, can in my opinion not otherwise think of that cause half so justly than by thinking of God. (*CP*, 5.536)

Peirce may be right that the conception of God is the best anthropomorphic conception there is for this purpose. But from the fact that man cannot think of a cause otherwise than anthropomorphically, it does not follow that he *should* think of it anthropomorphically. Such an injunction would, moreover, be perfectly idle. So Peirce's factual claim that science is inevitably anthropocentric lends no support to his methodological recommendation that we choose hypotheses which recommend themselves to the human mind. Peirce himself sensed the difficulty: while recommending the tentative acceptance of hypotheses which are natural to the human mind, he adds that "of all beliefs, none is more natural than the belief that it is natural for man to err" (*CP*, 5.592). Well and good; but exactly where does this leave us? "The logician," Peirce comments, "ought to find out what the relation is between these two tendencies" (*ibid.*), *i.e.,* the tendency to err and the tendency to guess at the truth. A tall order, but it will have to be filled if Peirce's thesis of the anthropocentrism of science is to entail any definite methodological prescriptions.

But even if Peirce's thesis does not have the methodological implications he thought it had, it does have other implications of considerable interest. One such implication is that because science is intelligible only as a human enterprise, it follows that in addition to whatever natural-scientific knowledge we may have of man there is also a legitimate branch of knowledge of man which includes natural science in its subject matter. This knowledge, which Peirce calls philosophical and which, like all knowledge, is factual and observational, is subdivided into the three branches of phenomenology, normative science, and metaphysics, a trivision set forth, e.g., in the Lowell Lectures (*CP*, 5.120–21 and ff.). I do not propose to go into the details of Peirce's classification of the branches of philosophy, or into the other, related classifications of the sciences which he sets forth in various places (*CP*, 1. Book II, passim). Those especially interested in this subject are referred, once again, to Potter's book.[36] The point which I wish to make is that when Peirce explains the success of induction by referring to natural and cultural properties of man, he thereby makes room for a conception of the humanities as autonomous vis-à-vis natural science, a conception which harmonizes well with his defense of historical knowledge considered in the last section. Peirce's anthropocentrism does not imply that the natural sciences require a justification from the human sciences—a conclusion which, for instance, Collingwood was to arrive at by a similar line of reasoning.[37] In Peirce's view no such justification is either required or forthcoming. What Peirce does imply is that our understanding of natural science is itself one of the humanities; hence, any positivistic scientism which seeks to subsume the humanities under the natural sciences will be incapable not only of understanding the phenomenon of man, but of understanding the phenomenon of natural science as well. Since this conclusion is implied, rather than stated, by Peirce, I ought at this point to declare an interest: This sort of conclusion is naturally welcome to a historian of ideas, who in everyday life finds himself ranked well below the physicist in the academic pecking order; it is especially pleasing to be able to impute such a conclusion to a mathematician, who by common consent sits at the very pinnacle of that pecking order. Be that as it may, the implication, I think, is there, and it is further corroborated by Peirce's explicit statements about the study of history quoted in the last section.

Once again, the thrust of Peirce's argument turns out to be the defense of the legitimacy and autonomy of modes of empirical knowledge other than that embodied in natural science. This defense has been made more explicitly and in greater detail by numerous other philosophers—such as Dilthey, James, and Collingwood, to mention only a few. Peirce has, I think, the perhaps unique merit of having made this defense without appreciable prejudice to the legitimate claim of natural science to *its* autonomy.

g. Conclusion

In this chapter we have looked at five different ways in which Peirce's version of the self-corrective thesis can be seen as part of an attempt to reconcile the conflicting claims of science and of non-scientific knowledge. It will not, perhaps, have escaped the reader that I am profoundly impressed with Peirce's achievement. It is only fair to Peirce's numerous rivals and critics to point out, in conclusion, that

he achieves his impressive results at a price. The problem of justifying our practical reliance on induction is not, in my reading, seriously
tackled by Peirce; at the very least, it is not solved. One consequence
is that what suffers in Peirce's account is the institution of engineering or, in general, of applied science. Peirce's pragmatic realism, as it
has here been presented, is an attempt to explain the contribution
which scientific theorizing and experimentation make to the success
of our total conduct. Now, to the extent that science does make such a
contribution, this is explained by Peirce's realism. As we saw in
chapter 4, our ability to rely on inductive predictions is explained by
the hypothesis that the regularities exhibited by our experimental
results testify to the reality of universal laws of nature. But such laws
are known to be real only through an infinitely long run of inquiry,
and so only our eventual success in the long run is explained by this
hypothesis. In the short run, however, until all the possible evidence
is in, we do not know which regularities are lawlike and which are
spurious, and so presumably we do not know which inductive predictions to trust. There may be a Peircean way out of this dilemma. If
stability of belief in the infinite long run constitutes truth, then
stability over a few centuries, generations, or even decades of critical
inquiry would presumably count as evidence from which we may
tentatively infer the truth of a belief. Indeed, unless we are entitled to
use such evidence, the history of science would no longer be able to
lend empirical support to realism. Peirce in fact held that the rational
attitude to take for the man of action is to treat as "established
truths" those propositions which are no longer questioned by the
scientific community (CP, 5.589). It does not appear, however, that
this signifies anything more than a cautious conservatism in the realm
of action: it is rational to act on that which has been tried and tested.
The fact that we sometimes and for certain practical purposes find it
rational to discard ancient and entrenched prejudices in favor of quite
recent scientific findings does not seem to have been accounted for.

Peirce himself was not greatly worried by this omission. As we
have seen, the cause of applied science was not a matter close to his
heart; in fact, he appears at times as the very embodiment of the pure
scientist's contempt for the world of applied science. So, for instance,
he was quite content to declare that "the practising physician whose

only object is to cure one patient after another, pursues an art, not a science" (MS, 1,293, p. 1) and that the applied scientist's belief in scientific results is "extra-scientific" and "no concern of science" (*CP*, 5.589). While Peirce offers cogent arguments why such beliefs can be no concern of pure science, he hardly ever considers the claim of applied science to constitute a rational activity in its own right. Peirce's failure to provide a rationale for applied science may be viewed either as a strength or as a shortcoming of his philosophy. For instance, in an unpublished work, Gary Jacobsohn has persuasively argued that precisely this aspect of Peirce's philosophy may be seen as a healthy antidote to the legal scientism practiced by Justice Holmes, which culminated in the case of *Buck v. Bell* in 1926.[38] In that case the United States Supreme Court upheld the State of Virginia's involuntary sterilization of mental defectives; the opinion of the Court was based on recent statistical findings on the hereditary transmission of feeble-mindedness, findings which have later been invalidated. Jacobsohn goes on to point out that Holmes was a Deweyan pragmatist, as well as an admirer of Karl Pearson, whose injunction to employ statistical results in the making of public policy may be seen as a rationale for the Court's decision. From the perspective of this case, then, Peirce's reluctance to offer a philosophical rationale for applied science compares favorably with the contrary outlook of Holmes and Pearson. On the other hand (as Jacobsohn does not deny), there clearly are situations in which it is rational to base our actions on the most advanced, i.e. most recent, scientific knowledge; and it might be held to be one of the tasks of the philosophy of science to explain when and why this is rational. I, for one, would like reasons for my intuition that Semmelweis was right in advising his medical colleagues to wash their hands before delivering babies and that the conservatism of his colleagues in this respect was irrational. Peirce, presumably, would agree; yet it is far from clear that his philosophy allows for making such claims. This shortcoming is not peculiar to Peirce; in fact, I would be hard put to name any philosopher who succeeds in doing justice both to the autonomy of pure science and to the rationality of applied science. Moreover, it would probably be anachronistic to criticize Peirce on this score. Today the defense of applied science against populism and irrationalism is a real problem; in Peirce's day the problem was rather to stem the overconfidence of the ideologists of engineering. Still, the defense of applied science as a rational activity is worth mentioning as a current problem the solution to which we cannot hope to find in Peirce's philosophy.[39]

The problem for which I think Peirce has offered a not implausible solution is that of reconciling the autonomy of basic natural science with the equal autonomy of the human sciences, as well as of religion, morality, and common sense. Himself a spokesman for the experimentalist movement of the nineteenth century, Peirce was not an adherent of the scientistic orthodoxy characteristic of most spokesmen for that movement; rather, he was a profound and original dissenter from that orthodoxy. In these pages I have attempted to spell out exactly wherein his dissent consists. The implications of that dissent for our present-day understanding of the role of science in our contemporary culture and society remain to be explored and assimilated. As a student of the history of ideas, I am happy to leave that arduous task to those more at home in the world of contemporary science than I am.

Notes

Introduction

1. The term "hermeneutical circle" stems from Wilhelm Dilthey (1833–1911), although the concept can be traced back at least to Schleiermacher (1768–1834). For a clear, concise, and general account of the nature and history of hermeneutics, see Flöistad (1973).

2. Murphey (1961). For the other interpretations listed, see Ayer (1968), Boler (1963), Buchler (1939), Feibleman (1946), Gallie (1966), and Goudge (1950).

3. Putnam (1978), pp. 4–5. Both Putnam's qualifying adjective "empirical" and Peirce's "pragmatic" are explicitly intended to convey a Kantian ancestry.

4. Murphey (1979), p. 4.

5. Rescher (1978), p. ix.

6. Mandelbaum (1977), p. 565.

7. Murphey (1979), p. 4.

8. *Ibid.*, p. 16; Mandelbaum, p. 570.

9. Collingwood (1939), pp. 63–64.

10. Mandelbaum, p. 571.

1. Outline of Peirce's Theory of Inquiry

1. On Peirce's scientific career, see Victor F. Lenzen (1964).

2. See Ralph Barton Perry (1948), p. 288.

3. These include Hardwick (1977), and Ketner and Cook (1975). At the present time, a new and more comprehensive edition of the *Collected Papers* is being prepared by the Peirce Edition Project at Indiana University, under the supervision of Max H. Fisch. The Project has also issued a microfiche edition of Peirce's published writings.

4. Scheffler (1974), pp. 42–57.

5. *Ibid.*, pp. 56–57.

6. Neurath (1932), p. 206.

7. Wittgenstein (1953), Part I, par. 107.

8. See Quine (1969), esp. pp. 16, 82–85, 127.

9. This has become a widely used rebuttal of skepticism. We find it echoed, e.g., in

Strawson (1959), p. 35: "The sceptic pretends to accept a conceptual scheme, but at the same time quietly rejects one of the conditions for its employment. Thus his doubts are unreal, not simply because they are logically irresoluble doubts, but because they amount to a rejection of the whole conceptual scheme within which alone such doubts make sense." A similar argument is deployed against Berkeley in particular by Bush (1977).

10. Aristotle, *Posterior Analytics,* Bk. I, chs. 2, 9, 19–22.

11. Wittgenstein (1953), Part I, pars. 269–75, and *passim.* There may have been an indirect influence from Peirce by way of Wittgenstein's friend P. F. Ramsey, who was an admirer of Peirce. See Gallie (1966), pp. 42–43.

12. See Popper (1972), esp. pp. 106–52.

13. *Ibid.,* pp. 242–44, esp. p. 244: "Our schema allows for the development of error-eliminating controls (warning organs like the eye; feed-back mechanisms); that is, controls which can eliminate errors without killing the organism; and it makes it possible, ultimately, for our hypotheses to die in our stead."

14. Murphey (1968).

15. Fisch (1954), p. 442.

16. Wiener (1949), pp. 71–76, and *passim.*

17. Perry, p. 292.

18. Bruce Altshuler (1977), ch. 1.

19. Bruce Kuklick (1977), p. 118. Kuklick also notes Peirce's ambivalent attitude towards Darwin, of which more below, p. 00.

20. See especially David Hume (1734), Bk. III, Part 2, Sect. VII: "Of the origin of government," and Adam Smith (1776), Bk. I, ch. 2: "Of the Principle which gives occasion to the Division of Labour."

21. See Popper (1945), 2:216–17, and Campbell (1974), *passim.*

22. This general conclusion was brilliantly argued by Alasdair MacIntyre in 1962, before Soviet dissidence had attracted international attention. MacIntyre illustrated his argument with the example of the Moscow purge trials in the 1930s: "To make a *1984* you need agents; and these agents at least are unimpressed by the confessions, for they extorted them. So they are the next danger. On this view it is no accident that Bukharin and Rakovsky were accompanied in the dock by the police-chief Yagoda and followed by the police-chief Yezhov." MacIntyre (1962), p. 69.

23. Scheffler, p. 70.

24. *Ibid.,* p. 71.

25. Murphey, p. 13. See also Ayer (1968), pp. 33–34.

26. I have elsewhere speculated that Peirce's solution is that the scientific method is selected by the exercise of reason, and that the original acquisition of reason is immediately useful; see Skagestad (1979). The weakness of this solution, it seems to me now, is that it would gratuitously bridge an evolutionary chasm by postulating a character (reason) which comes as an indivisible unit and which is both immediately useful and has effects beyond immediate usefulness. This would be purely *ad hoc* unless it were shown that reason is indeed an indivisible character; unfortunately, the findings of animal psychology indicate that reason comes in innumerable gradations. See Sagan (1977), esp. pp. 105–24.

Moreover, in Peirce's own view, once reason elects to go for long-run utility, it loses its short-run utility and, hence, will be selected against at that stage. This consideration, among others, led Peirce to become increasingly skeptical about natural selection as the sole evolutionary force. See *CP,* 1.649, 657, 5.366 and footnote.

27. For a clear and thorough exposition of hypothetico-deductive method, see Popper (1959), *passim*.

28. Madden (1960), esp. p. 255. Madden's criticisms are further discussed in chapter 5, below.

29. Pearson (1892), pp. 10–11.

2. Peirce's Early Realism

1. The *OED* also gives 1840 as the first occurrence of 'physicist' in the sense of a student of physics; as late as 1871 this word is used in the sense of an opponent of vitalism in biology. Both 'scientist' and 'physicist' were coined by William Whewell, that great neologist, who was much admired by that other great neologist Charles Peirce.

2. For a clear statement and discussion of Fechner's psycho-physical law, see William James (1890), 1:534–39.

3. Peirce (1878), p. 5.

4. Dewey (1929, 1960), p. 103.

5. *Ibid.*, p. 136.

6. Dewey (1916), pp. 305–6.

7. Moore (1964), pp. 403–4.

8. To review all the interpretations that have been offered might be a worthwhile and interesting undertaking—interesting at least to professional Peirce scholars. This, however, is not my present undertaking; I am interested in interpreting Peirce, not in interpreting his interpreters. At the same time, only a philosopher of A. J. Ayer's prestige and reputation can permit himself the luxury of ignoring the scholarly contributions made by his predecessors; see in this regard his (1968), p. 10, as well as the criticism by White (1973), p. 113. In this book, the contributions of other scholars will be taken into account wherever appropriate, to the extent that I am familiar with them. Suffice it to note at this point that I have learned a great deal about Peirce's realism from the works of John F. Boler and Murray G. Murphey, while I find myself unable to accept either Boler's somewhat too charitable view, that Peirce's pragmatism is not nearly as destructive as it seems, or Murphey's too uncharitable view, that pragmatism and realism are inherently incompatible with each other. See Boler (1963), esp. pp. 106–7, and Murphey (1968), pp. 13–14.

9. Goudge (1950), esp. pp. 5–7.

10. This is a simplified statement; scientific realism, so formulated, is open to a variety of interpretations. Is it a metaphysical doctrine about science as it ideally should be, or an empirical statement about science as it actually is? If the latter, to what does 'science' refer? The science of today, science as it has developed to date, science at its best (verging on the metaphysical interpretation), or science as a "natural kind" which can be expected to go on developing in the future as it has in the past? These questions must be postponed for now; they will be discussed in chapter 4, below.

11. This point has recently been conceded even by the ardent anti-essentialist Karl Popper. See Popper (1976), pp. 20–21.

12. Except for occasional slips of the pen, Peirce never says that universals *exist*. Like the scholastics, he is careful to distinguish between 'existence,' which denotes the mode of actual

being of individual things, and 'reality,' which denotes a mode of virtual being, belonging to universals.

13. See Boler (1963) and Moore (1964).

14. Kuklick (1977), esp. pp. 116–17. For further background, see Schneider (1946), esp. chs. 4 and 6.

15. Gallie (1966), p. 127.

16. Peirce (1878), p. 2.

17. Altshuler (1977), pp. 75–77.

18. Immanuel Kant (1781, 1787), A 255; B 310–11. English trans. Kemp Smith (1929), p. 272.

19. Kant, A 259–60; B 315; Kemp Smith, p. 275.

20. Thayer (1973), p. 60, n. 154.

21. Russell (1939), p. 144; quoted by Thayer, p. 69.

22. Lenz (1964), pp. 153–54.

23. Herschel (1851), p. 10.

24. *Ibid.,* p. 69.

25. Bernard (1927), p. 220.

26. Pearson (1892), p. 30.

27. Altshuler (1977), pp. 73–74, and Altshuler (1979). On the "veil of ignorance" see Rawls (1971), pp. 136–42.

28. MacIntyre (1966), p. 100.

29. This statement foreshadows what is today often called the "assertive redundancy" theory of truth; for a modern formulation, see Quine (1970), p. 12.

30. There is an interesting parallel between Peirce's notion of an ideal community as the locus of truth and Karl Mannheim's idea of the "free-floating intelligence" as the locus of class-transcendent rationality; the free-floating intelligence is partially and imperfectly *represented* by the free-floating (that is, relatively classless) intelligentsia, without being *identical* with the latter. See Mannheim (1936), pp. 136–46.

31. See esp. Quine (1960), p. 4, and (1969), p. 25.

32. Quine (1969), p. 26.

3. Pragmatism as a Criterion of Meaning

1. Murphey (1979), p. 16.

2. For details, see Fisch (1954).

3. This, at least, is the judgment of the hostile critic Brand Blanshard, whose reaction to the pragmatic maxim is summed up thus: "What is depressing is to consider that it was offered by a logician of distinction with the specific purpose of furthering clarity; what is cheering is to think that in the course of seventy-five years philosophy has gone so far in self-criticism that a logician of equal distinction would hardly be capable of writing so loosely today." Blanshard (1962), p. 194.

4. See James (1907), pp. 103–23, esp. p. 122.

5. E.g., by Lovejoy (1963), pp. 6–10; Morris (1970), pp. 29–32; and Scheffler (1974), pp. 100–4.

6. See e.g., Ayer (1952), esp. pp. 5–26.

7. Hacking (1975b), p. 95: "The success of the verification principle is amazing, for, as we shall see, no one has succeeded in stating it!"

8. See Ayer (1952), p. 16, and Hempel (1950), pp. 125–26. Both Ayer and Hempel deny that the verifiability criterion is an empirical hypothesis; Ayer calls it a definition, while Hempel says that it is a proposal and, as such, neither true nor false. They both further deny that the criterion is either arbitrary or unrevisable. In this, they seem to be right; the criterion was from the start understood to carry definite boundary conditions; as it became clear that it did not meet these conditions, the criterion was first revised, and later abandoned. But this in no way conflicts with my description of the criterion as *a priori*. The criterion did not itself specify the conditions which it was meant to meet; when it became clear that the criterion did not give a meaning to dispositional terms, the logical empiricists could consistently have dismissed such terms as meaningless and upheld their criterion. The fact that they did not do so testifies only to the good sense of the logical empiricists; it says nothing about the logical status of the verifiability criterion.

9. Morris (1937), p. 33.

10. *Ibid.*, pp. 23–25.

11. So, for instance, Burks (1951), p. 52: "Peirce . . . is faced with the paradox that pragmatism assumes a theory to be true (and hence meaningful) which by its own criterion of meaning is meaningless!" Similarly Nagel (1954), p. 43: "Peirce's own formulation of the pragmatic maxim leaves much to be desired in the way of explicitness and clarity; and more recent formulations, such as those by Professor Carnap and others, have the same general intent but superior precision." And Ayer (1968), p. 55: "Peirce's pragmatic maxim is indeed identical, for all practical purposes, with the physicalist interpretation of the verification principle."

12. This was pointed out by Burks; see the preceding note.

13. On the history of logical empiricism, see Joergensen (1951), which was, in fact, published as part of the *Encyclopedia*. It might be added that the more immediate influences on logical empiricism were Mach, Frege, Russell, and Wittgenstein. With the significant exception of Hans Reichenbach (the leader of the Berlin group and not really a member of the Vienna Circle), the logical empiricists were not influenced by Peirce.

14. Goodman (1965), esp. pp. 3–9.

15. See Hempel (1965), p. 109, and Scheffler (1974), pp. 76–82.

16. Carnap (1953), pp. 53–58.

17. For a statement of "weak verifiability," see Ayer (1952), pp. 36–39. For a statement of the most serious objections to this doctrine, see his new Introduction to the second edition, pp. 5–26.

18. Hempel (1965), pp. 101–33.

19. One of Peirce's rare utterances on politics is found in a 1908 letter to Victoria Lady Welby: "Being a convinced Pragmaticist in Semeiotic, naturally and necessarily nothing can appear to me sillier than rationalism; and folly in politics cannot go further than English liberalism. The people ought to be enslaved; only the slaveholders ought to practise the virtues that alone can maintain their rule. England will discover too late that it has sapped the foundations of culture." Hardwick (1977), p. 78.

20. See esp. *CP*, 1.109–15, and Wiener (1958), pp. 137–41.

21. Goodman (1965, p. 3) acknowledges a general indebtedness to C. I. Lewis, who was in turn a profound student of Peirce, and who was greatly occupied with counterfactuals. This link was pointed out to me by Israel Scheffler.

22. Carroll (1939).

23. Boler (1963), p. 106.

24. Wennerberg (1962), p. 144.

25. The same point is made with a slightly different example in "Prolegomena to an Apology for Pragmaticism," reprinted in *CP*, 4.546. Peirce here considers the two intuitively very different statements (p) "There is some married woman who will commit suicide in case her husband fails in business," and (q) "Some married woman will commit suicide if all married men fail in business." The formalization of these statements is too complex to be worth carrying out here; it would involve binary predicates, such as "is the wife of" and "is the husband of," along with added assumptions, such as "if x is the husband of y, then y is the wife of x," etc. However, the equivalence of the two statements may be exhibited informally. Let us take "p" to be true; then either some married woman commits suicide or someone's husband (i.e. some married man) does not fail in business; in either case, "q" is true as well. Now let us take "p" to be false; this is the case only if all husbands fail in business while no married woman commits suicide; in that case, "q" is also false. So "p" implies "q." Does "q" imply "p"? We use the same procedure in reverse. If "q" is true, either some married woman commits suicide, or some married man does not fail in business; in either case, "p" is true. If "q" is false, all married men fail in business while no married woman commits suicide; in that case, "p" is false. Hence "q" implies "p." The two statements mutually imply each other, which means they are logically equivalent.

26. The inconsistency in this argument was pointed out to me by Professor Morton White. Although White has saved me from some earlier misconceptions, I do not know whether he would agree with my final formulation.

27. Aristotle, *Metaphysics*, Bk. A, ch. 9; 990b, 15–17.

28. Plato, *Parmenides*, 132, a and b.

4. Peirce's Pragmatic Realism

1. After James' death in 1910, Peirce began signing his own name Charles Santiago Sanders Peirce, thereby canonizing his old friend "Santiago," i.e., St. James.

2. Some interesting sidelights on the early history of semiotic are found in Hacking (1975a). The acknowledged modern classics in the field are Ogden and Richards (1923) and Morris (1946), both of which reflect Peirce's influence.

3. Of course, opinions will vary as to how much is necessary, and I apologize to readers who feel that I have short-changed this centrally important area of Peirce's thought. My excuse is that, theoretically, a book on Peirce might branch off into an infinity of directions, and that consequently one has to draw some arbitrary boundaries simply in order to complete one's work. For a fuller survey of Peirce's semiotic, the reader is referred to Goudge (1950), ch. 5, B.

4. The terms 'dimension' and 'level' are introduced in Morris (1938), which is recommended as a brief and readable introduction to semiotic.

5. See, e.g., Skinner (1957).

6. For definitions of these terms, see Morris (1938), pp. 6–7.

7. Hardwick (1977), p. 11.

8. See Altshuler (1977), (1978).

9. Wiener (1949), p. 90: "Ideas are the meanings of events, and evolve in time with the growth of knowledge."

10. Gallie (1966), p. 137: "Like the activity of Inquiry, of which it is the most obvious

and important expression, sign-activity is essentially directed towards a goal which, in any particular case, it cannot be said ever to have fully and finally achieved."

11. Wennerberg (1962), p. 147.

12. *Ibid.*

13. Kuhn's book was, however, preceded eleven years earlier by *Science and Common Sense*, by Kuhn's teacher James Bryant Conant. Many of the central ideas of Kuhn's book are found in Conant's book. It is of some interest to note that Conant's book, which eschewed pretentious jargon and which can be both understood and enjoyed by the layman, made little or no impact on the philosophical community which was later to hail Kuhn's book as a major turning point in the philosophy of science.

14. Hardwick (1977), p. 83.

15. See "On Sense and Reference" in Gottlob Frege (1952), pp. 56–78, esp. p. 57.

16. See "On Denoting" in Bertrand Russell (1956), pp. 41–56, esp. p. 49.

17. E.g. "Is Semantics Possible?" and "Meaning and Reference," both reprinted in Schwartz (1977), pp. 102–18 and 119–32. Schwartz's anthology also includes relevant papers by Donnellan and Kripke.

18. *Ibid.*, p. 125.

19. Putnam (1978), p. 100.

20. Hardwick (1977), pp. 68–69.

21. Manley Thompson, "Peirce's Experimental Proof of Scholastic Realism," in Moore and Robin (1964), esp. pp. 418–22. For a more sympathetic view of Peirce's realism see Thompson (1978). For my own reservations to some of Thompson's more general conclusions, see Skagestad (1980).

22. For formulations of the falsifiability criterion, see Karl Popper (1959), esp. pp. 41 and 86. Essentially Popper's idea is that for a statement to count as falsifiable and hence as empirical, it must be contradicted by a set of spatio-temporal singular statements. As Popper has later conceded, this requirement is not fulfilled by the theory of natural selection, a theory which he himself greatly admires; see Popper (1972), p. 242. And it has been pointed out by Imre Lakatos that the requirement is not met even by Newton's mechanics, Popper's prototype of an empirical theory; see Lakatos and Musgrave (1970), p. 133.

23. See the editorial summary of Putnam's "Scientific Explanation" in Suppe (1977), pp. 424–33.

24. Putnam (1978), p. 25.

25. Collingwood (1933), pp. 130–31. Collingwood, I should add, made his argument excessively unpalatable by citing Anselm's Ontological Argument as a paradigm case of an inference whereby an existential proposition is established as a presupposition of science. On Collingwood's use of pragmatic arguments, see Ketner (1973).

26. Ryle (1935). For discussions of the Ryle-Collingwood exchange, see Rubinoff (1970), pp. 200–4, and Skagestad (1973), ch. 2.

27. Although the fictional illustrations which follow are my own, the problem which they are meant to illustrate was urged upon me by Israel Scheffler.

28. See Weber (1958), pp. 47–48.

29. See Kuhn (1970), p. 10 ff.

30. Ayer (1968), pp. 85–86.

31. Popper (1962), pp. 217, 385, 391.

32. William Whewell (1858); selections reprinted in Butts (1968), see esp. p. 160.

33. Quine (1960), pp. 271–72.

34. See also *CP*, 1.83, 5.162, 5.534.

35. Boler (1963), p. 88.

36. Collingwood (1940), p. 148. Our nominalist objector, by the way, is not entirely imaginary. I do not know whether Ayer ever played the game of "Heads I win, tails you lose," but Ernst Mach certainly did, in his dispute with Max Planck over the reality of atoms. See Mach (1919), pp. 10–11; English translation in Toulmin (1970), pp. 36–37. Mach's argument illustrates how one may always defend nominalism by turning the realist–nominalist issue into a question of what existential commitments are involved in an adequate linguistic formulation of *present* scientific knowledge. On those terms, nominalism is irrefutable, and the issue is a pseudo-problem.

37. This point, which is emphasized in *CP*, 1.121, seems to have been missed by Nicholas Rescher, who charges Peirce with putting instinct and insight in the place of scientific method; see Rescher (1978), p. 61.

38. Goodman (1965), p. 74.

39. Claude Bernard (1872), p. 17: "Toutefois il ne faut point oublier qu'une maladie n'est jamais caractérisée par un seul symptôme; elle consiste au contraire dans une série de symptômes qui sont unis entre eux par un rapport de cause à effet." Also, p. 21: "Non seulement nous parvenons à produire chez les animaux des symptômes morbides par des moyens artificiels, mais encore nous développons chez eux des séries de symptômes, c'est-à-dire de vraies maladies avec tout l'ensemble de leurs conséquences." I do not think either quote would bear Peirce's uncharitable construction.

40. *Ibid.,* p. 16.

41. Bernard (1927), pp. 53–55, 67–68, 69, 172, 175, and *passim.*

42. *Ibid.,* p. 201.

43. Roll-Hansen (1976), p. 80.

44. *Ibid.,* p. 89.

45. E.g. *CP*, 2.71, 5.468, 5.597, 6.517, 8.155–56. See also Peirce's review of the first edition of Pearson's book, in Ketner and Cook (1975), pp. 160–61.

46. Karl Pearson (1892), p. 11.

47. *Ibid.,* pp. 109, 144–45, 136.

48. In *CP*, 8.155, Peirce says: "Prof. Pearson declares that the sole business of science is to describe past experience and not at all to predict the future." But on p. 163, Pearson says clearly enough that the business of science *is* precisely to predict the future. I think what Peirce had in mind was the following passage from p. 136, to the effect that scientific predictions cannot be proven but must be taken on faith, a view reasonably close to Peirce's own: "Science in no case can demonstrate any inherent necessity in a sequence, nor prove with absolute certainty that it must be repeated. Science for the past is a description, for the future a belief; it is not, and has never been, an explanation, if by this word is meant that science shows the *necessity* of any sequence of perceptions." Pearson (1892), p. 136.

49. B. Norton (1975), esp. pp. 544–49.

50. *Ibid.,* pp. 549–50.

51. *Ibid.,* p. 552.

52. Helen M. Walker (1968).

5. Convergence and Its Conditions

1. Laudan (1974); von Wright (1965), p. 226, n. 3.

2. Lenz (1964); Madden (1960).

3. Lenz (1964), pp. 156–57.

4. *Ibid.*, p. 155.

5. *Ibid.*, p. 153.

6. Goudge (1950), pp. 180–83.

7. Venn (1866).

8. Von Mises (1939); Reichenbach (1938). For good summaries and popularizations of the conflicting views, see Nagel (1939) and Skyrms (1975).

9. Locke (1690), Bk. 4, ch. 15.

10. Goudge (1950), p. 167.

11. Pinkham (1967), p. 103.

12. Though they foreshadow the modern conception of mathematical likelihood, expounded e.g. in Hacking (1965), ch. 5.

13. *Ibid.*, pp. 122–23.

14. Madden, pp. 254–55.

15. *Ibid.*, p. 255.

16. Duhem (1954), pp. 183–90; Quine (1953), esp. p. 41.

17. Aristotle, *Prior Analytics*, Bk. II, ch. 25, 69, 20–38.

18. See especially Hanson (1961).

19. James (1896), p. 249; Jevons (1892), p. 577.

20. As Hanson noted, p. 20, this view is found in Popper (1959), p. 31; Reichenbach (1938), p. 382; and Braithwaite (1953), pp. 20–21. Reichenbach introduced the now famous distinction between "context of discovery" and "context of justification," limiting logical analysis to the latter context. For the origin, development, and recent fate of this view, the Introduction to Suppe (1977) is especially recommended.

21. See Mayr (1970), p. 380.

22. A clear and engaging account of the history of this issue is found in Eiseley (1958), ch. 9.

23. Gallie (1966), p. 89.

24. Skagestad (1979).

25. T. H. Huxley (1898); Wallace (1870). Darwin himself, it should be added, never advocated the all-sufficiency of natural selection, and in later years increasingly came to rely on Lamarckian modes of explanation. See esp. his (1874).

26. For modern concessions to 'cultural Lamarckism,' see J. Huxley (1953), p. 14, and Medawar (1977), p. 14. For the present-day debate over the nature of human evolution, see Caplan (1978).

27. Potter (1967).

28. Shimony (1970), pp. 129–30.

6. Science, Belief, and Non-Scientific Knowledge

1. Collingwood (1939), ch. 5.

2. Gallie (1966), esp. p. 89.

3. Wiener (1949), (1952); Murphey (1968).

4. Laudan (1974), pp. 288–89.

5. *Ibid.*, pp. 295, 293, 294.

6. *Ibid.*, p. 273.

7. *Ibid.*, p. 300.

8. *Ibid.*, p. 289.

9. This has recently been controverted by Nicholas Rescher, who has undertaken to defend Peirce on this score against von Wright, Shimony, Laudan, Lenz, and Cheng. See Rescher (1978), pp. 1–17. All that Rescher actually argues, however, is that science is "self-monitoring," something which none of these critics has denied. What they have denied is that Peirce has *proved* this, a question which Rescher does not address.

10. To complete the record, Peirce also once (in the *Collected Papers*) refers to Ruskin, but only to the extent of noting his "polished style." See *CP,* 7.233.

11. Robin (1967), pp. 153–54.

12. Locke (1690), Bk. 4, ch. 19.

13. Pearson (1892), pp. 32–33, 438, and footnote.

14. Fisch and Cope (1952).

15. Kuklick (1977), p. 124.

16. Wiener (1958), pp. 331, 333. See also *CP,* 1.650, 5.585.

17. On Peirce's teaching abilities and educational ideas, see Eisele (1964), and Jastrow (1916).

18. See Hardwick (1977), pp. 19, 78.

19. Peirce's repetition of the phrase "vitally important" is a thinly veiled swipe at James, who had arranged for these lectures to be given. Peirce had originally submitted a prospectus for a course of lectures on logic, to which James replied, *inter alia*: "Now be a good boy and think a more popular plan out. . . . Separate topics of a vitally important character would do perfectly well" (Perry, 1948, p. 285). Peirce's lectures, entitled "Detached Ideas on Vitally Important Topics," are chiefly a biting attack on the idea that philosophy should concern itself with topics of vital importance.

20. Hume (1734), Bk. II, Part 3, Sec. 3: "Of the Influencing Motives of the Will."

21. Scientific reasoning, to be sure, depends on the *existence* of an instinct for truth; but we have reasons for believing that there is such an instinct, and it is thanks to the existence of this instinct that we may hope to succeed in science by proceeding rationally.

22. The parallel between Peirce's and James' respective arguments is strengthened by the interesting circumstance that Peirce's arch-opponent was Karl Pearson, Clifford's heir apparent as the leader of the British Free-Thought movement, as well as the editor of Clifford's posthumous publications.

23. James (1896), p. 26.

24. *Ibid.*

25. Perry (1948), p. 291.

26. See Schweber (1977).

27. Bernard (1927), pp. 138–39.

28. Darwin (1968), p. 173.

29. Schweber (1977).

30. Both this method and Peirce's applications of it are presented in an illuminating way in Thayer (1973), pp. 48–49. For Peirce's experimental use of the method of least squares, see esp. Peirce (1878).

31. Pearson (1892), pp. 171–80.

32. This name and the most influential recent formulation of the theory are Karl Popper's; see his (1957), *passim.*

33. Hume (1748), Sec. 10: "Of Miracles."

34. Peirce's actual criticisms of the "higher criticism" are confined to the history of

ancient science and philosophy, while he pleads ignorant of Biblical criticism and the history of religion; see *CP*, 6.513 and MS, 1,404, p. 1.

35. Wiener (1958), pp. 289–321; *CP*, 6.522–47; MS, 472.

36. Potter (1967), Part 1.

37. Collingwood (1924), pp. 185–87.

38. Jacobsohn (1979), esp. p. 27.

39. Some might think that this problem was solved by John Dewey. My opinion, which happens to have been shared by Peirce (*CP*, 8.239–44), is that Dewey paid the price of sacrificing pure science; to argue this would, however, require another book.

Bibliography

Altshuler, Bruce. 1977. "The Pragmatic Maxim of C. S. Peirce: A Study of its Origin and Development," Ph.D. dissertation, Harvard University, Cambridge, Mass.

—— 1978. "The Nature of Peirce's Pragmatism," *Transactions of the Charles S. Peirce Society* (Summer 1978), 14(3):147–75.

—— 1979. "Peirce's Theory of Truth and his Early Idealism," forthcoming in *Transactions of the Charles S. Peirce Society.*

Ayer, Alfred Jules. 1952. *Language, Truth, and Logic.* 2d ed. New York: Dover Publications.

—— 1968. *The Origins of Pragmatism.* London: Macmillan.

Bernard, Claude, 1872. *Leçons de pathologie expérimentale.* Paris: J. B. Ballière.

—— 1927. *Introduction to the Study of Experimental Medicine.* London: Macmillan. (French original, 1865.)

Blanshard, Brand. 1962. *Reason and Analysis.* La Salle, Ill.: Open Court.

Boler, John F. 1963. *Charles Peirce and Scholastic Realism: A Study of Peirce's Relation to John Duns Scotus.* Seattle: University of Washington Press.

Braithwaite, Richard B. 1953. *Scientific Explanation.* Cambridge: Cambridge University Press.

Buchler, Justus. 1939. *Charles Peirce's Empiricism.* New York: Harcourt, Brace.

Burks, Arthur W. 1951. "Introduction to C. S. Peirce." In Max H. Fisch, ed., *Classic American Philosophers.* New York: Appleton-Century-Crofts.

Bush, Eric. 1977. "Berkeley, Truth, and the World," *Inquiry,* (Summer 1977), 20(2–3):205–25.

Butts, Robert E., ed. 1968. *William Whewell's Theory of Scientific Method.* Pittsburgh: University of Pittsburgh Press.

Campbell, Donald T. 1974. "Evolutionary Epistemology." In P. A. Schilpp, ed., *The Philosophy of Karl Popper.* Library of Living Philosophers. La Salle, Ill.: Open Court. Pp. 413–63.

Caplan, A., ed. 1978. *The Sociobiology Debate.* New York: Harper & Row.

Carnap, Rudolf. 1953. "Testability and Meaning." In H. Feigl and M. Brodbeck, eds., *Readings in the Philosophy of Science.* New York: Appleton-Century-Crofts. Pp. 47–92.

Carroll, Lewis. 1939. "What the Tortoise said to Achilles." In *The Complete Works of Lewis Carroll,* London: Nonesuch Press. Pp. 1104–8.

Collingwood, Robin George. 1942. *Speculum Mentis.* Oxford: Clarendon Press.

—— 1933. *An Essay on Philosophical Method.* Oxford: Clarendon Press.

—— 1939. *An Autobiography.* Oxford: Clarendon Press.

—— 1940. *An Essay on Metaphysics.* Oxford: Clarendon Press.

Darwin Charles R. 1874. *The Descent of Man.* New York: Rand, McNally.

—— 1968. *The Origin of Species.* Rpt. of 1st ed. (1859), Harmondsworth: Penguin Books.

Dewey, John. 1916. *Essays in Experimental Logic.* 1916; reissued, New York: Dover Publications, n.d.

—— 1929, 1960. *The Quest for Certainty.* Gifford lectures, 1929; reissued New York: Capricorn Books, 1960.

Duhem, Pierre. 1954. *The Aim and Structure of Physical Theory.* Princeton: Princeton University Press.

Eisele, Carolyn. 1964. "Peirce's Philosophy of Education in his Unpublished Mathematics Textbooks." In Moore and Robin (1964), pp. 51–75.

Eiseley, Loren. 1958. *Darwin's Century: Evolution and the Men Who Discovered It.* New York: Doubleday.

Feibleman, James K. 1946. *An Introduction to the Philosophy of Charles S. Peirce.* New York: Harper.

Fisch, Max H. 1954. "Alexander Bain and the Genealogy of Pragmatism," *Journal of the History of Ideas,* 15:413–44.

Fisch, Max H. and Jackson L. Cope, 1952. "Peirce at the Johns Hopkins University." In Wiener and Young (1952), pp. 277–311.

Flöistad, Guttorm. 1973. "Understanding Hermeneutics," *Inquiry* (1973), 16:445–65.

Freeman, Eugene. 1934. *The Categories of Charles Peirce.* La Salle, Ill.: Open Court.

Frege, Gottlob. 1952. *Translations from the Philosophical Writings of Gottlob Frege.* P. T. Geach and M. Black, eds. Oxford: Basil Blackwell.

Gallie, W. B. 1965. *Peirce and Pragmatism,* New York: Dover Publications.

Goodman, Nelson. 1965. *Fact, Fiction, and Forecast.* 2d ed., New York: Bobbs-Merrill.

Goudge, Thomas A. 1950. *The Thought of C. S. Peirce,* Toronto: University of Toronto Press.

Hacking, Ian. 1965. *Logic of Statistical Inference.* Cambridge: Cambridge University Press.

—— 1975a. *The Emergence of Probability.* Cambridge: Cambridge University Press.

—— 1975b. *Why Does Language Matter to Philosophy?* Cambridge: Cambridge University Press.

Hanson, Norwood Russell. 1961. "Is There a Logic of Scientific Discovery?" In H. Feigl and G. Maxwell, eds., *Current Issues in the Philosophy of Science.* New York: Holt, Rinehart, and Winston. Pp. 20–42.

Hardwick, Charles S. 1977. *Semiotic and Significs: The Correspondence Between Charles S. Peirce and Victoria Lady Welby.* Bloomington: Indiana University Press.

Hempel, Carl G. 1950. "The Empiricist Criterion of Meaning," *Révue Internationale de Philosophie,* vol. 4; rpt. in A. J. Ayer, ed., *Logical Positivism.* New York: Free Press, 1959. Pp. 108–29.

—— 1965. *Aspects of Scientific Explanation.* New York: Free Press.

Herschel, John. 1851. *Preliminary Discourse on the Study of Natural Philosophy.* 2d ed. London: Longman, Brown, Green & Longmans.

Hume, David. 1734. *A Treatise of Human Nature.* London: John Noon; new ed. by L. A. Selby-Bigge. Oxford: Clarendon Press, 1888, 1968.

—— 1748. *An Enquiry Concerning Human Understanding,* London: Millar; posthumous ed. with additional material. London: Cadell, 1777.

Huxley, Julian. 1953. *Evolution in Action.* New York: New American Library.

Huxley, Thomas H. 1898. *Evolution and Ethics and Other Essays.* New York: Appleton.

Jacobsohn, Gary. 1979. "Science and Constitutional Jurisprudence: Implications of Conceptual Evolution." MS.

James, William. 1890. *The Principles of Psychology.* 2 vols. New York: Henry Holt; reissued Dover Publications, 1950.

—— 1896. *The Will To Believe and Other Essays in Popular Philosophy.* New York: Longmans, Green.

—— 1907. *Pragmatism: A New Name for Some Old Ways of Thinking.* New York: Longmans, Green.

Jastrow, Joseph. 1916. "Charles S. Peirce as a Teacher," *Journal of Philosophy,* 13:723–26.

Jevons, Stanley. 1892. *The Principles of Science.* 2d ed., London: Macmillan.

Joergensen, Joergen. 1951. *The Development of Logical Empiricism.* International Encyclopedia of Unified Science, 2(9). Chicago: University of Chicago Press.

Kant, Immanuel. 1781, 1787. *Kritik der reinen Vernunft.* Edition A, Riga, 1781; edition B, Riga, 1787. See Kemp Smith (1929).

Kemp Smith, Norman. 1929. *Critique of Pure Reason.* Trans. of Kant (1781, 1787). London: Macmillan.

Ketner, Kenneth L. 1973. *An Emendation of R. G. Collingwood's Doctrine of Absolute Presuppositions.* Graduate Studies Texas Tech University, No. 4, July 1973, Lubbock.

Ketner, Kenneth Y. and James E. Cook, eds. 1975, *Charles Sanders Peirce: Contributions to the Nation. Part One: 1869-1893,* Graduate Studies Texas Tech University, No. 10, December 1975, Lubbock.

Kuhn, Thomas S. 1970. *The Structure of Scientific Revolutions.* 2d ed. International Encyclopedia of Unified Science, 2(2). Chicago: University of Chicago Press.

Kuklick, Bruce. 1977, *The Rise of American Philosophy.* New Haven, Conn.: Yale University Press.

Lakatos, Imre. 1971. "History of Science and its Rational Reconstructions," *Boston Studies in the Philosophy of Science,* R. Buck and R. Cohen, eds. Dordrecht: Reidel. 8:91-135.

Lakatos, Imre and Alan Musgrave. 1970. *Criticism and the Growth of Knowledge.* Cambridge: Cambridge University Press.

Laudan, Laurens. 1974. "Peirce and the Trivialization of the Self-Correcting Thesis." In R. Giere and R. Westfall, eds., *Foundations of Scientific Method: The Nineteenth Century.* Bloomington: Indiana University Press. pp. 275-306.

Lenz, John W. 1964. "Induction as Self-Corrective." In Moore and Robin (1964), pp. 151-62.

Lenzen, Victor F. 1964. "Charles Sanders Peirce as Astronomer." In Moore and Robin (1964), pp. 33-50.

Locke, John. 1690. *An Essay Concerning Human Understanding.* London; new, abridged ed. by A. S. Pringle-Pattison, Oxford: Clarendon Press, 1924.

Lovejoy, Arthur O. 1963. *The Thirteen Pragmatisms.* Baltimore: Johns Hopkins University Press.

Mach, Ernst. 1906. *The Analysis of Sensations.* 5th ed.; reissued, New York: Dover Publications, 1959.

—— 1919. *Die Leitgedanken meiner naturwissenschaftlichen Erkenntnislehre und ihre Aufnahme durch die Zeitgenossen,* Leipzig: Johann Ambrosius Barth.

MacIntyre, Alasdair. 1962. "A Mistake About Causality in Social Science." In P. Laslett and W. G. Runciman, eds., *Philosophy, Politics, and Society.* 2d series. Oxford: Basil Blackwell. Pp. 48-70.

—— 1966. *A Short History of Ethics.* New York: Macmillan.

Madden, Edward H. 1960. "Charles Sanders Peirce's Search For a Method." In R. M. Blake, C. J. Ducasse, and E. H. Madden, *Theories of Scientific Method: The Renaissance through the Nineteenth Century.* Seattle: University of Washington Press. Pp. 248-62.

Mandelbaum, Maurice. 1977. "The History of Philosophy: Some Methodological Issues," *The Journal of Philosophy,* (October 1977), 74(10):561-72.

Mannheim, Karl. 1936. *Ideology and Utopia: An Introduction to the Sociology of Knowledge.* New York: Harcourt, Brace.

Mayr, Ernst, 1970. *Populations, Species, and Evolution.* Cambridge, Mass.: Harvard University Press.

Medawar, Peter Brian. 1977. "Unnatural Science," *New York Review of Books,* 24(1).

Mises, Richard von. 1939. *Probability, Statistics, and Truth.* London: W. Hodge.

Moore, Edward C. 1964. "The Influence of Duns Scotus on Peirce." In Moore and Robin (1964), pp. 401–13.

Moore, Edward C. and Richard S. Robin, eds. 1964. *Studies in the Philosophy of Charles Sanders Peirce.* 2d series. Amherst: University of Massachusetts Press.

Morris, Charles W. 1937. *Logical Positivism, Pragmatism, and Scientific Empiricism.* Actualités Scientifiques et Industrielles, no. 449. Paris: Hermann.

—— 1938. *Foundations of the Theory of Signs.* International Encyclopedia of Unified Science. 1(2). Chicago: University of Chicago Press.

—— 1946. *Signs, Language, and Behavior.* New York: Prentice-Hall.

—— 1970. *The Pragmatic Movement in American Philosophy.* New York: George Braziller.

Murphey, Murray G. 1961. *The Development of Peirce's Philosophy,* Cambridge, Mass.: Belknap Press of Harvard University Press.

—— 1968. "Kant's Children: The Cambridge Pragmatists," *Transactions of the Charles S. Peirce Society,* 4:3–33.

—— 1979. "Toward an Historicist History of American Philosophy," *Transactions of the Charles S. Peirce Society,* 15(1):3–18.

Nagel, Ernest. 1939. *Principles of the Theory of Probability.* International Encyclopedia of Unified Science, 1(6): Chicago: University of Chicago Press.

—— 1954. *Sovereign Reason.* Glencoe, Ill.: Free Press.

Neurath, Otto von. 1932. "Protokollsätze," *Erkenntnis,* no. 3:204–14.

Norton, Bernard. 1975. "Metaphysics and Population Genetics: Karl Pearson and the Background to Fisher's Multi-factorial Theory of Inheritance," *Annals of Science,* 32:537–53.

Ogden, C. K. and I. A. Richards. 1923. *The Meaning of Meaning.* New York: Harcourt, Brace.

Pearson, Karl. 1892. *The Grammar of Science.* London: Walter Scott.

Peirce, Charles Sanders. (*CP*). *Collected Papers of Charles Sanders Peirce.* Vols. 1–6, C. Hartshorne and P. Weiss, ed. Vols. 7–8, A. Burks, ed. Cambridge, Mass.: Belknap Press of Harvard University Press, 1931, 1936, 1958.

—— (MS). Manuscripts in Houghton Library, Harvard University, Cambridge, Mass.

—— 1878. *Photometric Researches.* Annals of the Astronomical Observatory of Harvard College. Vol. 9. Leipzig: Wilhelm Engelmann.

Perry, Ralph Barton. 1948. *The Thought and Character of William James.* Briefer version, Cambridge, Mass.: Harvard University Press.

Pinkham, Gordon. 1967. "Reply to Chung-Ying Cheng," *Transactions of the Charles S. Peirce Society,* 3(2).

Popper, Karl R. 1945. *The Open Society and its Enemies.* London: Routledge & Kegan Paul.

—— 1957. "The Propensity Interpretation of the Calculus of Probability, and the

Quantum Theory." In S. Körner, ed., *Observation and Interpretation*. London: Butterworths Scientific Publications. Pp. 65–70.

—— 1959. *The Logic of Scientific Discovery*. London: Hutchinson.

—— 1962. *Conjectures and Refutations*. London: Routledge & Kegan Paul.

—— 1972. *Objective Knowledge: An Evolutionary Approach*. Oxford: Clarendon Press.

—— 1976. *Unended Quest: An Intellectual Autobiography*. Glasgow: Fontana/ Collins.

Potter, Vincent G., S. J. 1967. *Charles S. Peirce on Norms and Ideals*. Amherst: University of Massachusetts Press.

Putnam, Hilary. 1978. *Meaning and the Moral Sciences*. London: Routledge & Kegan Paul.

Quine, Willard V. O. 1953. *From A Logical Point Of View*. Cambridge, Mass.: Harvard University Press.

—— 1960. *Word and Object*. Cambridge, Mass.: M.I.T. Press.

——1969. *Ontological Relativity and Other Essays*. New York: Columbia University Press.

—— 1970. *Philosophy of Logic*. Englewood Cliffs, N.J.: Prentice-Hall.

Rawls, John. 1971. *A Theory of Justice*. Cambridge, Mass.: Belknap Press of Harvard University Press.

Reichenbach, Hans. 1938. *Experience and Prediction*. Chicago: University of Chicago Press.

Rescher, Nicholas. 1978. *Peirce's Philosophy of Science*. Notre Dame, Ind.: University of Notre Dame Press.

Robin, Richard S. 1967. *Annotated Catalogue of the Papers of Charles S. Peirce*. Amherst: University of Massachusetts Press.

Roll-Hansen, Nils. 1976. "Critical Teleology: Immanuel Kant and Claude Bernard on the Limitations of Experimental Biology," *Journal of the History of Biology* (Spring 1976), 9(1):59–91.

Rubinoff, Lionel. 1970. *Collingwood and the Reform of Metaphysics*. Toronto: University of Toronto Press.

Russell, Bertrand. 1939. "Dewey's New *Logic*." In P. A. Schilpp, ed., *The Philosophy of John Dewey*. Library of Living Philosophers. Evanston, Ill.: Northwestern University. 1:135–56.

—— 1956. *Logic and Knowledge*. R. E. Marsh, ed. London: Allen & Unwin.

Ryle, Gilbert. 1935. "Mr. Collingwood and the Ontological Argument," *Mind* (April 1935), 44(174):137–51.

Sagan, Carl. 1977. *The Dragons of Eden: Speculations on the Evolution of Human Intelligence*. New York: Random House.

Scheffler, Israel. 1974. *Four Pragmatists: A Critical Introduction to Peirce, James, Mead, and Dewey*. New York: Humanities Press.

Schneider, Herbert W. 1946. *A History of American Philosophy*. New York: Columbia University Press.

Schwartz, Stephen P., eds., 1977. *Naming, Necessity, and Natural Kinds.* Ithaca, N.Y.: Cornell University Press.

Schweber, Silvan. 1977. "The Origin of the *Origin* Revisited," *Journal of the History of Biology* (Fall 1977), 10(2):229–316.

Shimony, Abner. 1970. "Scientific Inference." In R. G. Colodny, ed., *The Nature and Function of Scientific Theories.* Pittsburgh: University of Pittsburgh Press.

Skagestad, Peter. 1973. "R. G. Collingwood's Theory of Presuppositions: Its Origin and Development and Contemporary Philosophical Significance." Ph.D. dissertation, Brandeis University, Waltham, Mass.

—— 1979. "C. S. Peirce on Biological Evolution and Scientific Progress," *Synthese,* 41(1):85–114.

—— 1980. "Pragmatic Realism: The Peircean Argument Re-Examined," *The Review of Metaphysics* (March 1980), pp. 527–40.

Skinner, B. F. 1957. *Verbal Behavior.* New York: Appleton-Century-Crofts.

Skyrms, Brian. 1975. *Choice and Chance: An Introduction to Inductive Logic.* 2d ed. Encino, Calif.: Dickenson.

Smith, Adam. 1776. *The Wealth of Nations.* London: W. Strahan; abridged ed. Harmondsworth: Penguin Books. 1970.

Strawson, P. F. 1959. *Individuals: An Essay in Descriptive Metaphysics.* London Methuen.

Suppe, Frederick, ed. 1977. *The Structure of Scientific Theories.* 2d ed. Urbana: University of Illinois Press.

Thayer, H. S. 1973. *Meaning and Action: A Study of American Pragmatism.* New York: Bobbs-Merrill.

Thompson, Manley. 1964. "Peirce's Experimental Proof of Scholastic Realism." In Moore and Robin (1964), pp. 414–29.

—— 1978. "Peirce's Verificationist Realism," *The Review of Metaphysics* (September 1978), 32(1):74–98.

Toulmin, Stephen, ed. 1970. *Physical Reality.* New York: Harper & Row.

Venn, John. 1866. *The Logic of Chance.* London: Macmillan.

Wallace, Alfred Russell. 1870. *Contributions to the Theory of Natural Selection.* London.

Walker, Helen. 1968. "Pearson, Karl," *International Encyclopedia of the Social Sciences.* David L. Sills, ed. New York: Macmillan. 11:496–503.

Weber, Max. 1958. *The Protestant Ethic and the Spirit of Capitalism.* New York: Scribner.

Wennerberg, Hjalmar. 1962. *The Pragmatism of C. S. Peirce.* Lund: C. W. K. Gleerup.

Whewell, William. 1858. *Novum Organon Renovatum.* London: J. W. Parker.

White, Morton G. 1973. *Pragmatism and the American Mind.* Oxford: Oxford University Press.

Wiener, Philip P. 1949. *Evolution and the Founders of Pragmatism.* Cambridge, Mass.: Harvard University Press.

—— 1952. "Peirce's Evolutionary Interpretation of the History of Science." In Wiener and Young (1952), pp. 143–52.

Wiener, Philip, ed. 1958. *Values in a Universe of Chance: Selected Writings of Charles S. Peirce.* New York: Doubleday.

Wiener, Philip P. and Frederick H. Young, eds. 1952. *Studies in the Philosophy of Charles Sanders Peirce.* Cambridge, Mass.: Harvard University Press.

Wittgenstein, Ludwig. 1953. *Philosophical Investigations.* Oxford: Basil Blackwell.

Wright, Georg Henrik von. 1965. *The Logical Problem of Induction,* 2d ed. Oxford: Basil Blackwell.

Index of Names

Index of Subjects

Index